Racism, sexism, power and ideology

Racism, sexism, power and ideology argues that there is nothing 'obvious' or 'natural' about our ideas of sex and race; and their historical evolution is one of the key concerns of this collection of essays.

Colette Guillaumin contends that the slow crystallization of ideas on human 'races' over the last few centuries can be traced and understood through the study of signs and their systems.

But clearly, race and sex are more than just symbolic phenomena. They are the hard facts of society: to be a man or woman, black or white are matters of social reality. To be a member of a particular race or sex brings with it different opportunities, rights and constraints. The study of semiotic systems must therefore be complemented by an examination of such material constraints, of how they operate and shape our life experience.

Guillaumin tackles the links between the daily materiality of social relationships and mental conventions. Materiality and ideology (in the sense of 'perception of *things*') are two sides of the same coin: those who are objects in social relations are so in both thought and reality.

Written with verve and insight, this book is a significant contribution to our understanding of the complex links between sexism, racism and power.

Colette Guillaumin is Head of Research at the National Centre for Scientific Research, Paris.

Critical Studies in Racism and Migration
Edited by Robert Miles
University of Glasgow

Racism, sexism, power and ideology

Colette Guillaumin

London and New York

First published 1995
by Routledge
11 New Fetter Lane, London EC4P 4EE

Simultaneously published in the USA and Canada
by Routledge
29 West 35th Street, New York, NY 10001

Typeset in Times by LaserScript, Mitcham, Surrey
Printed and bound in Great Britain by
Mackays of Chatham PLC, Chatham, Kent

British Library Cataloguing in Publication Data
A catalogue record for this book is available from the British Library.

Library of Congress Cataloging in Publication Data
Guillaumin, Colette.
    Racism, sexism, power, and ideology/Colette Guillaumin.
    p. cm. – (Critical studies in racism and migration)
    Includes bibliographical references and index.
    1. Racism. 2. Sexism. 3. Power (Social sciences) I. Title.
    II. Series.
HT1521.G86
305.8 – dc20   94–12149
                                              CIP

ISBN 0–415–09384–8 (hbk)
ISBN 0–415–09385–6 (pbk)

Contents

Part III

Preface

The reader of this book should know a little of its origin and rationale. It constitutes the first complete publication in English of the most important essays on racism and sexism written by Colette Guillaumin since the late 1960s. Up until now, access to these papers has been restricted to those who read French or to those who found those papers previously translated into English in the restricted circulation of specialist journals.

Yet, for a long time, there has been a vague awareness of Guillaumin's work in the English-speaking world, partly because of the wide readership of a UNESCO publication which included in English translation the important paper 'The Idea of Race and its Elevation to Autonomous Scientific and Legal Status' and partly because of the translation and publication by the US journal *Feminist Issues* of several of Guillaumin's key papers on the oppression of women. Indeed, there have also been passing references in the English literature on racism to her major book, *L'Idéologie raciste*, first published in 1972 and now out of print and still (sadly) untranslated.

The publication of these papers is intended to bring her most important ideas and arguments to the attention of those interested and engaged in those multifaceted debates (in English) about the nature and origin of racism and sexism, and about their articulation. When evaluating Guillaumin's contribution to these debates, it is essential to recall that most of her important ideas were first published in French before or at the same time as similar or parallel ideas were first articulated and debated by other writers in English. Her previously mentioned book, *L'Idéologie raciste*, was written during the period 1967–68! It is therefore a product of the period and events that shaped, for example, Carmichael and Hamilton's *Black Power* and Rex's *Race Relations in Sociological Theory*, to cite two titles which have had considerable impact on the English-language debate about racism.

Yet, the papers here (in their totality) do not constitute a faint, or even loud, echo of a position or positions that we know so well in the English-language debates. They constitute a highly original and power-ful theoretical and political position which deserves close examination. Guillaumin's writing represents, in English, another new voice. The significance of the novelty is heightened when one reflects on when the papers included here were first written and published.

Chapters 1, 3, 4, 5 and 13 are translated and published in English here for the first time. They were translated by Andrew Rothwell with Max Silverman as a result of financial assistance provided by the *Service Culturel* of the *Ambassade de France* in London. I am especially grateful to Maryse Fauré for her advice and help when I was seeking the necessary funding and, indeed, for her comments, work on and close involvement in many other aspects of the production and publication of this volume. There is no doubt that the project would not have reached completion without her effort, insight and encouragement, for which I thank her.

The original dates and sources of these papers are as follows:

'Caractères spécifiques de l'idéologie raciste', *Cahiers internationaux de sociologie*, 1972, vol. LIII: 247–74.
'"Je sais bien mais quand même" ou les avatars de la notion "race"', *Le Genre humain*, 1981, 1: 55–65.
'IMMIGRATIONSAUVAGE', *Mots*, 1984, 8: 43–51.
'Les mains rapaces de la destinée', *Lectures*, 1984, 15: 97–114.
'Nature et histoire: à propos d'un "matérialisme"', in M. Olender (ed.) *Le racisme, mythes et sciences*, Bruxelles: Editions Complexe, 1981.

The remaining chapters have appeared previously in English translation in the following places. The original translator is also recorded, along with bibliographic information concerning the original publication in French where appropriate:

'The Idea of Race and its Elevation to Autonomous Scientific and Legal Status' in UNESCO (ed.) *Sociological Theories: Race and Colonial-ism*, Paris: UNESCO, 1980.
'Race and Nature: the System of Marks', *Feminist Issues*, 1988, 8(2): 25–43. Translated from French by Mary Jo Lakeland. Originally published in *Pluriel-Débats*, 1977, 11.
'Women and Theories about Society: the Effects on Theory of the Anger of the Oppressed', *Feminist Issues*, 1984, 4(1): 23–39. Translated from French by Mary Jo Lakeland. Originally published in *Sociologie et sociétés*, 1981, 13(2).

'Sexism, a Right-wing Constant of any Discourse: a Theoretical Note', in G. Seidel (ed.) *The Nature of the Right: A Feminist Analysis of Order Patterns*, Amsterdam: John Benjamins Publishing Company, 1988. Translated from French by Caroline Kunstenaar.

'The Practice of Power and Belief in Nature: Part I The Appropriation of Women', *Feminist Issues*, 1981, 1(2): 3–28. Translated from French by Linda Murgatroyd. Originally published in *Questions féministes*, 1978, 2.

'The Practice of Power and Belief in Nature: Part II The Naturalist Discourse', *Feminist Issues*, 1981, 1(3): 87–109. Translated from French by Linda Murgatroyd. Originally published in *Questions féministes*, 1978, 3.

'The Question of Difference', *Feminist Issues*, 1982, 2(1): 33–52. Translated from French by Hélène Vivienne Wenzel. Originally published in *Questions féministes*, 1979, 6.

'Herrings and Tigers: Animal Behaviour and Human Society', *Feminist Issues*, 1983, 3(1): 45–59. Translated from French by Mary Jo Lakeland. Originally published in *Critique*, 1978, 34(375/6).

In order to assist the reader to understand and contextualize Guillaumin's work, I commissioned Danielle Juteau to write an Introduction. Danielle Juteau is an ardent advocate of many of Guillaumin's central propositions and she has used them as a foundation for her own original contributions to the debates about racism, sexism, nationalism and ethnicity. Guillaumin's work has provided a point of common reference for our ongoing, if (too) infrequent contact, and I use this moment to thank Danielle Juteau not only for her contribution to this volume (a contribution that extended beyond the writing of the Introduction) but also for teaching me so much about the issues discussed in this book (not to mention about Québec).

The order and presentation of the papers have been determined by Colette Guillaumin. She has also commented on the translation of those papers that appear in English for the first time. I have assembled the book, therefore, in accordance with her desires and instructions. After much thought and with her agreement, I decided to present the papers individually as they were originally written rather than to edit and cross-reference them to try to ensure that they constitute a seamless 'totality'. Inevitably, perhaps, there is some repetition, and no single bibliography. The book may seem to lack a certain formal tidiness as a result, but this is more than counter-balanced by the authenticity of the presentation of the arguments as they were originally formulated, developed and published. I thank her for her help and encouragement, and for her patience and understanding with my still limited facility in the French language.

Robert Miles (Series Editor)
Glasgow

Introduction

(Re)constructing the categories of 'race' and 'sex': the work of a precursor

Danielle Juteau-Lee[1]

The texts gathered in this anthology almost span a twenty-year period; twenty years during which Guillaumin has become one of the leading figures among French-speaking social scientists analysing and combating racism and sexism, or, to be more exact, among those deconstructing the notion of 'race' and the notion of 'sex'. Anglophones will finally have the opportunity, thanks to this publication, to join her other readers. Until recently, the latter fell into two groups, one primarily interested in understanding 'race'[2] relations and the other, 'sex'-gender relations, each one seemingly unaware of her other publications.[3] This dichotomization of her work is further reinforced since both groups continue to classify it into two distinct and discrete categories.

Such interpretations of Guillaumin's work remain, as we shall see, superficial and misleading. For they emphasize the categories, 'sex' and 'race', under scrutiny and ignore the common thread running through the author's theoretical endeavour: a relentless pursuit to uncover the social relations of domination which structure social inequality and (dis)organize our mental categories. Her *démarche* identifies the processes constructing 'race' and 'sex' as given and self-evident categories and more importantly the social relations within which they are embedded.

There exist many ways of making sense of a corpus; the light shed on it depends on the value orientations, on the questions deemed relevant and asked by the researcher. No account can, nor will, totally exhaust 'reality'; such is the essence of knowledge.[4] Furthermore, it is now well established that one's own reading is subjected both to constant fluctuation and internal contradictions (Fuss 1989: 35).

My own concerns in the late 1970s resided in the development of a theoretical perspective capable of escaping economic and cultural forms of reductionism in the analysis of 'sex'-gender and ethnico-national relations. This involved articulating an approach which did not reduce ethnicity and femininity to cultural content and differentiae (Juteau-Lee and Roberts 1981), and which did not equate the whole of ethnic and gender relations to ethnicity and femininity. This new approach would include the economic dimension of ethnic and gender relations without reducing it and them to class analysis; it would not relegate ethnic and gender relations to an ideological instance determined in the last analysis by the relations constitutive of the capitalist class and the proletariat. It would focus on analytically distinguishable systems of social relations, and would encompass all levels of the social structure, economic, political, cultural and ideological, without reducing the structure of social formations to a single line of determination (Juteau-Lee 1979; 1983a). It seemed crucial to transcend what is now called horizontal and vertical types of reductionism (Hall 1986: 11).[5]

I was groping with these issues when I was introduced to Guillaumin's work and read, first of all, the two articles on 'Pratique du pouvoir' [Chapters 9 and 10 in this book]. I entered the corpus from that specific angle and discovered a social scientist who saw things differently, a social scientist who put what seemed to be the cart before what seemed to be the horses. The approach she articulates emphasizes knowledge of the subject on the basis of labour as a central category, thus exhibiting a perspective rooted in social relations.[6] Her materialist approach combats essentialism and naturalism, thus destabilizing and transforming the dominant way of thinking about things. She reversed the relation between racism and 'race'; she demonstrated that choice of a signifier (colour or anatomical sex) follows and does not precede a social relation of appropriation; she constructed as *indissociable*, as two faces of the same coin, the social appropriation of social agents and the discourse on (their) Nature.

I will first examine some of the key themes identified by Guillaumin; in doing so, I will reconstruct her chain of reasoning and indicate how her analyses of 'race' and 'sex' interrelate. We will then see how this pioneering work illuminates and elucidates some of the issues which presently traverse most debates in the social sciences, namely the opposition between essentialism and constructionism, the relation between identity politics and *différence*, and the articulation between class, 'race' and 'sex' within the framework of a complex unity.

RACISM AS AN IDEOLOGY PRODUCING THE NOTION OF 'RACE'

Les recherches reprennent comme concept de base une notion qui est le produit spécifique de l'idéologie raciste elle-même.

(1972: 250)

Guillaumin's reflection on racism begins in the 1960s, at a time when the topic is almost absent from the French intellectual scene. It has been pointed out (Simon 1970) that the centrality of the social question in French sociological discourse and the dominance of the Jacobinist ideology have led to the non-existence, until very recently, that is, of areas of inquiry dealing with the study of immigration, racism, ethnic and national relations.[7]

She starts by expressing her dissatisfaction with the definitions and explanations of racism in vogue at the end of the 1960s in other parts of the world. The exclusive focus on racist practices misses the point, she argues. Racism cannot be equated with aggressivity and violence; not all aggressivity is racist, and racism is not necessarily aggressive. Furthermore, racism can be laudatory; don't we hear people say that Blacks dance well, Italians sing well, Jews are good at business?

To define racism exclusively as a theory establishing a hierarchy between the 'races' is also problematical. For racism as a theory is built upon the acceptance of 'races' as givens, as categories exhibiting a *caractère d'évidence*. But what is this category, 'race', whose existence we accept without question and which seemingly gives birth to racism? The unquestioned acceptance of 'race' as a given biological or social category, Guillaumin writes in 1972, is based upon a mode of apprehension of reality shared by a whole culture. This way of apprehending the world, where 'race' constitutes a category of perception, is precisely what constitutes racism as an ideology. This *système perceptif et significatif* engenders the idea of 'race', leading to the categorization of human beings into discrete, endogenous, and empirically based categories; it is more diffuse than the theory which it precedes and makes possible. As we will see, the distinction between racism as an ideology and racism as a theory constitutes a central aspect of Guillaumin's contribution to the analysis of racism.

What becomes essential for Guillaumin is understanding the construction of the idea of 'race', that is of the racist ideology which will eventually serve as a support of racism as a practice. It is, she affirms, racism as an ideology which produces the notion of 'race' and not 'races' which produce racism. This inversion, recently accepted in some social science milieux (Gilroy 1987; Miles 1982, 1989; Omi and Winant 1986), was quite spectacular at the time, and put the body back on its feet. New paths of inquiry were opened, as Guillaumin went on to examine the emergence, at a specific time in history, of the notion of 'race' and of the idea of nature.

THE IDEA OF NATURE IS A SOCIAL FACT ... WHICH HIDES SOCIAL FACTS

> . . . un rapport social, ici un rapport de domination, de force, d'exploitation, celui qui sécrète l'idée de nature . . .
>
> (1977: 185)

Guillaumin had set a direction to her work, a theoretical, political and epistemological agenda, and continued her pursuit. If racism is the ideology which constructs 'races', what constitutes its own basis? What factors engender this mode of apprehension of reality? Answering this question led her to uncover the socio-historical processes producing the naturalist ideology and to explore the mechanisms through which it operates. But first, a closer look at the idea of nature.

Behind and beneath the idea of nature

Guillaumin situates the ideology of 'race', that is racism, within the broader framework of naturalism and, more specifically, in terms of the modern idea of nature. The latter includes, in addition to the status of thing and the intended purpose of the thing under consideration, the idea of a determinism internal to the thing itself. Those who talk about the natural specificity of the 'races', of the sexes and of other social groups are in fact saying that a specific nature produces social practices. This amounts, as she reminds us, to a substantialism, a pseudo-materialism, a material and not a materialist position; the properties attributed to matter 'arise *not* as *consequences* of the relations which the material form maintains with its universe and its history . . . but actually as *characteristics intrinsically symbolic of matter itself*' (1981: 107).[8] The 'natural' is seen as internally programmed, be it by blood, instinct, genes, chemistry, etc. To the old idea of finality was superimposed the idea of endogenous determinism; furthermore, and this is crucial, the internally programmed 'natural' applies not to single individuals but to a class in its totality, each member representing only a fragment of the whole.

But when is a given nature assigned to a whole category of individuals? Guillaumin identifies a specific constellation of historical factors, including modern science and its conception of internal programmation as well as a particular type of social relation, appropriation. The ideology of nature is secreted in the context of social relations involving dependency, exploitation and, more specifically, appropriation, be it of land, of humans, of their bodies and of their labour, as well as of the products of their bodies and of their labour. The unlimited appropriation of labour power, that is, of the physical material individuality of persons constitutes the object of the relationship.

These social relations of appropriation produce the construction of specific categories made up of interchangeable individuals: slaves, indentured labourers, and women.[9] Slaves are objects as their physical material individuality is appropriated. And because they are things in reality, they are also thought of as things in the mind, they are naturalized; here, the concrete and ideological dimension of a social relation are inextricably tied and represent two sides of a coin.

Guillaumin once again saw things differently: it is not because individuals possess a specific nature that they are appropriated, it is because they belong to an appropriated category that they are attributed a specific nature. Her analysis makes visible the material foundations which precede and make possible racialization, that is, 'the representational process whereby social significance is attached to certain biological (usually phenotypical) human features, on the basis of which those people possessing those characteristics are designated as a distinct social collectivity' (Miles 1989: 74).

Guillaumin emphasizes that the allocation of individuals into racial [and sexual] categories can only occur once they have been socially constituted and naturalized. Once constituted, these categories must be identified; marks, arbitrary marks, will then be chosen. The choice of a signifier follows the establishment of social categories; and, as we will see, *it is precisely because there exists a social category that the signifier is operative.*

Choosing an (arbitrary) mark

Once constituted, 'racial' categories are characterized by a symbolic sign that is an arbitrary mark assigning each individual his or her position as a class member. No one denies the existence of somatic, biological (in the case of the sexes) and phenotypical differences between human beings. Nor does anyone deny that skin colour exists and cannot be removed. But choice of a signifier does not happen haphazardly. The fact that skin colour [and sexual anatomy] and not eye colour, shape of ears or length of feet are usually used as signifiers in our society is explainable; it results from the conjunctural association between an economic relationship and physical attributes.

Another reversal is effected here by Guillaumin, between the signifier and the position occupied in a given system; it is not because your skin is black that you were enslaved, that you became a slave, but because you were a slave that you became black or more precisely that colour becomes significant. In this case, the sign is permanent and not removable, in opposition to hairstyle and clothes, for example. Although the disappearance of the social category would not bring about the disappearance of the sign, its social significance would dissolve.

She reminds us that the process of enslavement was underway for close to a century before taxonomies based on somatic characters were elaborated. Colour became discriminant when a social group was in fact constituted. In other words, slavery as a system was not built on the appearance of its agents but on the appropriation of their labour.

The chronological order is now clearly re-articulated; first slavery and the constitution of a social category whose physical material individuality is appropriated, then the invention of the ideology of 'race' (racist ideology); this makes possible and leads to the construction of taxonomies, the emergence of racialization as a representational process (more on this later) and the elaboration of racist theories.

Guillaumin then pursues her analysis of signifiers and indicates how they now fulfil a new function. Signifiers have become the signs of a specific nature. The use of signifiers to identify existing groups in a society is not recent, she affirms, but signifiers are historically variable; sometimes they are removable, such as uniforms and hairstyles, and at other times, they are permanent, such as tattoos inscribed on the bodies of slaves and prisoners in concentration camps. What is new, argues Guillaumin, is the use of somato-morphological criteria as a basis of classification. First considered as an emblem, as a *signifier*, skin colour is now transformed into the expression of a specific nature. From that point on, the signifier is considered as preceding the classification, as causing the classification and eventually, as determining one's position in society.

As Guillaumin reminds us, this naturalist ideology hides the relations which constitute 'racial' [and 'sexual'] categories; consequently, groups which are interconnected in such a way that each one is a function of the other are deemed to be distinct and discrete entities characterized by closure. The processes through which these categories are constructed and through which social agents are allocated to certain positions are rendered invisible; more importantly, the appropriation of their labour is occluded. As a result, 'race' and 'sex' are treated as biologically and/or socially constituted independent variables, causing the observed social positions and inequalities. Naturalism thus makes history invisible and hides the fact that the association between the social category and the signifier is born in the context of specific social relations. As such, it replaces materialism by substantialism and postulates that the properties of objects emerge spontaneously from matter.

Many, but not all, social scientists analysing racism have finally caught up with the ideas presented by Guillaumin twenty years ago. But, as we will now see, the incapacity to uncover the social relationship which constructs other naturalized categories still remains, even among those claiming to have left the naturalist discourse far behind.

THE SOCIAL APPROPRIATION OF WOMEN OR 'SEXAGE'

> ... The social relationship of appropriation ... entails the belief that a corporeal substratum motivates, and in some way 'causes', this relationship, which is itself a material-corporeal relationship.
>
> (1981: 88)

New modes of conceptualization and theorization do not appear haphazardly and they do not emerge from nothingness, like a rabbit from a magician's hat. They usually result from the meeting and combination of different factors which coalesce to produce new questions and interpretations, to uncover new facts and to shed new light on old ones. Guillaumin's analysis of the sex-gender system benefits from the conceptual and theoretical advances developed in her work on the ideological construction of 'races'. It allows her to articulate, in conjunction with other French feminists,[10] a new theoretical project; materialist feminism examines the social relations constituting the sexes and moves beyond the impasses faced by radical and Marxist feminism. When it has not been ignored, this approach has encountered tremendous resistance;[11] this brings me to reposition at length her argumentation.

The social relationship of appropriation[12]

Many issues were raised during the debate opposing radical and Marxist feminists in the 1970s. Radical feminism emphasizes the fundamental opposition between men and women, the central oppression of women *qua* women. All men, irrespective of class or 'race', benefit, though in different ways, from a system of domination where women are economically, politically, legally and culturally subordinated to men. Radical feminists recognize the existence of 'sex'-gender relations that are socially constructed mainly within the family, and suggest different interpretations as to their basis. Firestone (1970), faithful to de Beauvoir, ascribes the inequality of the sexes to the process of biological reproduction, while Millett (1970) presents a theory of patriarchy as a power system formed by the fundamental relationship between men and women, namely sexual relations. This strand of radical feminism was unable to identify adequately the material basis of the oppression and exploitation of women by men. In France, however, radical feminism offered a different twist. Delphy (1970) examines the relationship which constitutes men as the main enemy. She argues that women's position in society can be understood in terms of their position in the domestic mode of production, which exists alongside the capitalist mode of production. In this distinct system of social relations, men, all men, have free access to their wives and to their labour power. As such, it is women's position within the domestic mode of production that explains why their work is excluded from the realm of value. By arguing that it is not the nature of their work that accounts for their position in the relations of production, she inverted the analyses provided by early Marxist feminists.

Walby (1990: 3–4) points out that, for Marxists, gender inequality derives from capitalism and is not to be constituted as an independent system of patriarchy, since men's domination over women is a by-product of capital's domination over labour (Benston 1972; Dalla Costa 1972). Marxist feminism usually limited its materialism to the economic and the economic to relations constitutive of capitalist social classes, i.e. the bourgeoisie and the proletariat; consequently it usually located gender in the ideological instance and affirmed that gender inequality derived from capitalism and benefited capitalists (Barrett and McIntosh 1979; Eisenstein 1979; Molyneux 1979).

The long-standing opposition between radical feminist and Marxist approaches dates as far back as the beginning of the movement. In 1971, Juliet Mitchell was already contrasting the positions of Marxist and radical feminists on the oppression of women. Recognizing the pertinence of analyses accounting for the opposition between the sexes, she asserted that it was necessary to ask feminist questions and to give them Marxist answers. Further exchanges and confrontations between these two approaches led to the transformation of their initial positions (Hartmann 1981; Kuhn and Wolpe 1978; Sokoloff 1980; Walby 1986) and to the emergence of new perspectives ranging from an integrated system of capitalist patriarchy to approaches favouring an autonomy model and dual systems theory.[13]

The debate opposing Delphy to Barrett and McIntosh in the 1970s none the less indicates that materialist feminism and Marxist feminism could not be reconciled. In my opinion, Marxist feminists could not accept the centrality accorded to sex class by the autonomy model of 'sex'-gender relations. By focusing on class relations between the sexes, or more precisely on the specific relations constitutive of sex class, materialist feminism provided radical feminism with the non-biological, non-essentialist basis it lacked while not reducing the relations between the sexes to capitalist social relations.

Both radical feminism and Marxist feminism combated the naturalist ideology and emphasized the social construction of women: 'You are not born a woman, you become one'. Gender became a central concept. Biology is not destiny and femininity is constructed, it is added on to females; to put it differently, females become women and males become men. This rejection of biological determinism constitutes a significant improvement; but a crucial problem remains since the categorization of humans into two sexes is considered to be self-evident, not requiring an explanation. This, you will notice, is similar to the logic according to which differences in skin colour naturally engender the construction of racial categories . . . and, as we shall see, just as unsatisfactory. Guillaumin argues that sexual categories are constructed, and not on the basis of biological differences; the latter become significant because they correspond to 'real' groups, which are constituted in the context of a relation involving the appropriation of their labour power. It is in the context of this relation that markers are chosen and used to assign people to a specific group or class.

How does Guillaumin develop this perspective and reach such conclusions? Rather than asking herself how domestic labour was related to paid labour, their own and that of their spouses, rather than asking herself how the domestic mode of production was related to capitalism, Guillaumin focuses on the fact that in our society some labour, including mainly the physical, material and emotional upkeep of human beings, young, old, sick, as well as that of able-bodied men, is still performed without pay. Now unpaid labour, she points out, is an indicator and an expression of a specific type of social relations usually associated with a certain form of slavery and distinct from capitalist social relations, where labour is paid, badly paid sometimes but nevertheless paid. As Guillaumin points out, in this day and age, the simultaneous occurrence of subjection, material servitude and oppression is principally embodied in the class of women. When the agents are men on the one hand and women on the other, this specific mode of appropriation is called *sexage*.

Guillaumin also argues, and this aspect of her work is crucial, that the appropriation of one's body and labour is not restricted to wives or companions in the 'domestic' sphere but to women as a category. Private appropriation, which puts some women into relationships with some men through marriage, is a particular and restrictive form of collective appropriation. The latter, according to Guillaumin, is a generalized relationship involving two classes which exist before private appropriation and outside of it.

The construction of sexual categories

The social appropriation of women comprises two aspects: the concrete, which corresponds to the appropriation of their physical material individuality, their bodies and labour power, and the ideological-discursive as exemplified in the discourse on their specific Nature. As appropriated physical entities women are turned into things within the realm of thought itself. The naturalist ideology operates in different manners; in some cases, physical characteristics such as sexual anatomy are seen as causing domination; but nowadays, social scientists usually dissassociate gender from 'sex' and recognize that women's subordination[14] does not rest upon a biological basis. None the less, the strength of the idea of nature is such that sexual categories still seem evident and self-explanatory; real biological differences are thought to bring about the construction of sexual categories as well as the allocation of human beings to these categories when, in fact, Guillaumin argues, it is because certain humans are appropriated that they are constructed as females and as women. It is not because you are female that you are appropriated but because you are appropriated that you are female; and thus designated by the female genitals, females become women.

Once again we are confronted here by one of Guillaumin's famous reversals, which obliges us to reorient our thinking. Clearly, our analyses must go beyond the process of gendering, beyond the construction of gender on the basis of a given biological category whose existence is treated as unproblematic. What we must understand is why social significance is attached to anatomical differences which serve to assign people to distinct social collectivities. I call this representational process 'sexualization'.[15]

This crucial foray allows us to examine, not the relations established between the two 'sexes' or sexual categories, not the gendering of these biological beings, but the categorization of humans into two distinct sexual categories; this leads to the uncovering of the social relations of appropriation producing sexualization and naturalization. It is because we are appropriated that we are 'sexualized' and 'genderized', not because we are sexually different that we are appropriated.

RETHINKING THE UNTHINKABLE

Guillaumin's contribution to our understanding of women's positions, widely diffused and highly influential in Francophone Canada, went largely unnoticed in the Anglophone world.[16] As mentioned previously, recent reactions are mixed but most often negative. Women, it is argued, cannot constitute a sex class since they belong to social classes and are divided in terms of racial categories (Barrett and McIntosh 1979). Furthermore, how can one pretend that women constitute one category when the lives of white women and of women of colour, of bourgeois and working-class women, are so different (Spelman 1988)? Is Guillaumin hopelessly trapped in essentialism, reductionism, binarism and victimization? Let us examine some of these issues.

Social class and sex class

Interestingly, when it was pointed out that the proletariat was not homogeneous, that there existed an international division of labour also differentiated by gender, when it was recognized that the proletariat does not only comprise white males from advanced capitalist nations but also includes male and female Blacks and female Whites, and when it was discovered that Blacks (women and men) and Whites (women and men) and women (black and white) and men (black and white) – all of these categories also involving the relation between the 'centre' and the 'periphery' do not occupy the same positions in the social division of labour – Marx's analysis of social classes and the social relations of production was not labelled as essentialist. Economistic? Yes. Reductionist? Yes. But essentialist? Never! Social scientists, Marxist feminists for example, tried to articulate the divisions internal to the working class, but they never questioned the existence of the proletariat. It is accepted that the working class is internally divided, not that it is non-existent.

It can also be shown that ethnic groups are usually divided along class and 'sex' lines, yet the usefulness of theorizing their dynamic *qua* ethnic groups is not rejected. The same can be affirmed for other social categories such as immigrants, people of colour and visible minorities although they belong to distinct social classes and sex classes.

Why, then, question the existence of women as a distinct social category? Why negate the existence of a sex class even if women belong to the bourgeoisie (which, by the way, is unusual) or to the working class, as well as to subordinate and dominant ethnic groups? Why do we treat social class and sex class so differently? Belonging to a sex class, Guillaumin would argue, does not entail sameness, identity of situation, of interests and of life-styles; it means being part of an appropriated category constituted as females. *Sexage* articulates with other social relations to produce a multiplicity of positions and overlapping categories of women, as we shall see in our final section.

'Race' and 'sex'

Let us now go on and examine the construction of 'sex' as a social category and compare its trajectory to that of 'race'. First, 'race' is considered to be evidence and behaviour is imputed to morphological characteristics. Second, there is an attempt to separate the biological fact from social and psychological characteristics; biological 'race' does not determine behaviour and social position as there exists no necessary relation between these two components. Third, some scientists will affirm that 'races' do not exist as biological entities; at that stage, remarks Guillaumin, the notion of 'race' is thrown back as a hot potato to the social sciences. Fourth, some social scientists discover the relations producing social groups and fostering the construction of the ideology of 'race'. Signifiers, in this case skin colour, are finally seen as chosen after the establishment of social categories.

Why not pursue the same reasoning with the notion of 'sex'? First, sex is seen as evidence, there are two biological sexes and, therefore, two sexual categories. 'Sex' is an independent variable, it determines the place occupied in the sexual division of labour and in society in general. Second, biological sex is separated from gender: 'you are not born a woman, you become one'. Efforts are made so as to understand gender relations and gendering. At this point, the categorization of human beings into two distinct biological categories is not questioned; biological differences between men and women are seen as self-evident and as leading to sexualization as a process of signification. Femininity and masculinity are considered to be added on to femaleness and maleness. Third, some social scientists, mainly materialist feminists, argue that the bipartition of gender is foreign to the existence of sex as a biological reality. Using Guillaumin's theory of *sexage*, Mathieu (1989) suggests that societies employ the ideology of the biological definition of sex to legitimize and support a hierarchy of gender based on the oppression of one sex by the other.

Therefore, 'race' and 'sex' are first conceptualized as being constructed on the basis of biological differences; in both cases, Guillaumin argues, this mode of reasoning must be reversed. 'Race' and 'sex' are real but only as ideological constructs used to identify groups socially constituted in the context of a relation of appropriation. Why is the resistance to this perspective greater when it is applied to 'sex'? Actually, and frankly speaking, many reasons come to mind.

First of all, it is said that men do not treat women like slaves; they 'love and cherish' them, they care for them and support them. But this truth is a partial truth; one must also take into account the concrete dimension of the relationship, namely the appropriation of women's labour power and bodies; appropriation because much of the work performed by women is done so without pay, without contracts specifying time limits and working conditions. This labour, involving the physical, material, emotional and intellectual upkeep of the young, the old, the sick, the handicapped, as well as of able-bodied men, benefits men because it frees them to pursue other occupations and tasks, including paid labour. Furthermore, violence is often employed to reproduce this system of domination; women, like members of other minorities, are harassed, beaten, raped, maimed and murdered because they are women.

Second, the appropriation of women also differs from that of slaves because it no longer precludes paid labour. Nowadays, in many societies, women, at some point in their life, sell their labour power. But this phenomenon is relatively recent; not so long ago they were barred from the labour force or were not allowed to keep their salaries. The implications of women's entrance into the labour force will be examined in the following section.

Third, there are real biological differences between the sexes. Sex is indeed an empirically valid category; does it follow that sexual differences cause appropriation and sexualization? But women do have the babies, people affirm. Quite true, but then why do we not differentiate between mothers and non-mothers? And they do lactate. Quite true again, but let us take a new look at having babies . . . The humanization[17] of new-borns has engendered a wide variety of social arrangements as indicated by the broad range of solutions found across time, countries and social classes in spite of a common biological fact. Some women, as Badinter (1981) points out, did not look after their children and entrusted them to nursemaids. In addition, it has been convincingly argued that it is not because of their position in production and reproduction that women are dominated, but that women, as a subordinate group, are socially assigned specific locations in the systems of production and reproduction (Mathieu 1989; Tabet 1987). Tabet, for example, presents the amazing number of constraints, such as heterosexuality and monogamy, exerted on women in order to ensure that they keep their place; the presence of such constraints indicate, in true Durkheimian fashion, that we are confronted here by a social fact and not by a biological fact.

Fourth, the continuing existence of *sexage* makes it difficult even to begin to think of deconstructing the ideology of the biological definition of 'sex'. Let me explain. The discourse on Nature is inextricably tied to the concrete dimension of appropriation and renders invisible the socio-historical processes that produce it. The relatively recent transformation of the situation of minorities who are still exploited, oppressed and racialized, but no longer subjected to appropriation, allows for the possibility of questioning and deconstructing the dominant discourse on 'race'. It is now easier to put a wedge in the crack, and to show that 'race' is a construct.

Fifth, and this represents a major problem, one cannot pinpoint the historical period when the ideology of the biological definition of sex was constructed, and consequently, one cannot empirically reconstruct its occurrence. And, it would seem, what cannot be seen cannot exist! How can one make a convincing argument in a situation where the empirical demonstration can only be partial? Many answers come to mind.

One can describe appropriation, its expressions and its modalities as well as the means used to enforce it, as Guillaumin does in the first 'Pratique du pouvoir' article (Chapter 9 of this book). One can also evaluate the usefulness of the theory, of its capacity to generate new questions and to explain previously unexplainable data. Her emphasis on *sexage* and collective appropriation sheds light on most contemporary problems left unsolved by other feminists' approaches. These are, for example: the existence of patriarchy outside the home, the continuing oppression of women even when they evolve outside marriage, as unmarried and/or divorced women, as nuns or as lesbians, the specific forms of violence exerted against them in different sites and in different historical periods, the continuing poverty and pauperization of women, the fact that in the last instance, poor or rich, black or white, from the 'centre' or the 'periphery', they are still responsible for the unpaid upkeep of human beings.[18]

Finally, when analysing 'sex' as an ideological construct, one must adhere to a mode of argumentation and demonstration different from the one used when dealing with the notion of 'race'. How can this be done?[19] Guillaumin interrogates the dominant perspective, the so-called 'truth'. 'Quel est le lieu de la Vérité?' is what she would ask. She displaces the dominant discourse into the past, and opposes it to a viewpoint that she reconstructs, thus revealing the 'truth' as a fiction. It is precisely because there has been construction that the dominant discourse is so well hidden and so difficult to question. Guillaumin focuses on the moment that is not mythology, or genesis. She is interested in what we can re/trace, she can show, by the present situation, that there has been a constructed link between naturalization and appropriation, but she cannot identify, as it has been done for 'race', the moments at which this occurred. This historical process sits between imagination and the present relations of appropriation.

Thus, she destabilizes once again current practices and modes of reasoning; it requires indeed a great effort of understanding to establish, as she has, the link between a logic relying on empirical facts and one relying on an a priori.

The final test of the usefulness of an approach is to assess its contribution to the solution of existing impasses. We will now turn to this object.

DIFFERENCE AND COMPLEX UNITY: MATERIALIZING THE CONSTRUCT

Il serait bien temps que nous nous connaissions pour ce que nous sommes: idéologiquement morcelées parce que utilisées à des usages concrets dispersés. Mais uniques et homogènes en tant que classe appropriée.

(1992: 106)

We have seen that Guillaumin's anti-essentialism is rooted in a materialist perspective focusing on the concrete and ideological dimensions of social relations, which she considers to be inextricable. Appropriation of the physical individuality of human beings comprises their naturalization and engenders a discourse which reverses the chain of reasoning and the real sequence of events. The nature of the appropriated and/or their physical characteristics are seen as causing their behaviour, or at least their subordinate position. As I have pointed out throughout this Introduction, Guillaumin's work consists of questioning dominant discourses, of decentring and destabilizing them, and in some cases, of reversing them.

She develops, as I have previously shown, an epistemology based on the ontological structure of labour; labour is seen as constituting humans, subjects and their knowledge (Haraway 1990: 200). This epistemological position allows her to cast a new light on the production of racial and sexual categories. As the following examples will demonstrate, it also helps us, amongst other things, to move beyond the debate opposing essentialism to constructionism, to examine critically the politics of difference, and to rethink the complex articulation between difference and unity.

Beyond the essentialism of (some) constructionists

Essentialism, 'a belief in the real, true essence of things, in the invariable and fixed properties which define the 'whatness' of a given identity' (Fuss 1989: ix) is often associated with feminisms that emphasize a commonality uniting women, while constructionism is associated with those emphasizing differences and diversity.

But in fact the situation is not so clear-cut since many constructionists fail to escape essentialism (Fuss 1989: 20). For they take diversity into account by fragmenting the subject into multiple identities: women of colour, white women, bourgeois women, proletarian women, black proletarian women, and so on. But this operation, as Fuss convincingly argues, specifies, and does not counteract essentialism, as each sub-category is seen as possessing its own self-referential essence.

Spelman's work offers a good illustration of such an attempt. She begins with the now widely accepted idea that one becomes a woman. Being a woman is defined culturally, as gender identity, in conjunction with other forms of identity, is added on to females, a category which could only be defined in biological terms. The only thing women possess in common, femaleness, is irrelevant, since biology is not destiny as she reminds us that they belong to many categories. Her analysis thus begins with the construction of gender and this is what poses many problems. She assumes that sex [and 'race'] are givens thus concealing the central question of the production of these categories. Diversity is examined in terms of sub-categories of women, black women, white women, bourgeois women, and so on, as she ends up specifying essentialism and not escaping it.

If even constructionists can be essentialist, do we have to accept, as Fuss sometimes seems to suggest, that essentialism is inescapable? Not necessarily so.[20] Guillaumin articulates a strong anti-essentialism while she argues that females share a point of commonality. As a matter of fact, it is precisely in her materialist position that she roots the point of commonality of females and women. Their homogeneity is not common biology but sex class. A class which is not based on biological sex but where 'sex' operates as a signifier; the latter serving to identify a group constituted in the context of a social relation of appropriation. In addition, her materialist analysis of the production of the categories of 'race' and 'sex' leads up to a scathing critique of *différence* combined, and this may seem surprising, to the argument that these categories should not be eliminated from our critical vocabularies.[21]

A critique of *différence*

As far back as *L'Idéologie raciste*, Guillaumin's work can be interpreted as a long and unified quest to criticize approaches that centre on difference. What minorities have in common, she wrote in 1972, is not to be different but to be subordinate, to be constructed as different from the majority which is seen as universal and incarnating the norm. Difference for Guillaumin has always been tied to domination, therefore she has always remained suspicious of exhortations to claim the right to be different, be it ethnically, racially or sexually. Very early in her studies, she pointed out that racism is not necessarily aggressive, that it can be celebratory; that dominant groups can also appreciate the differences of 'their' subordinates and fight for the maintenance of such differences, which are treated as givens. Fighting for your right to be different can mean fighting for your subordination, cautions Guillaumin. Thus her relentless critique of *le féminisme de la différence*[22] does not come as a surprise; as she indicates, the political usefulness of *différence* can easily be superseded by its numerous disadvantages. It renders invisible the social construction of the naturalist discourse and perpetuates it. It occludes that women, blacks and other dominated social groups are not categories existing of and by themselves; that they are constructed in the context of a social relation of domination and dependence.

Her position was not readily accepted in post-1968 France as many movements, Basque, Occitan and Breton, for example, used the argument of the right to difference in order to fight political and cultural domination. But the current situation in France and elsewhere in the world[23] does attest to the dangers inherent in accepting without question *la différence*. The extreme right in France has taken over slogans of difference and uses them to justify returning foreigners to their countries of origin where they will experience the joy of finding more fertile ground to express fully their wonderful *différence*. Furthermore, this approach fosters the development of an essentialist theory of identity and of identity politics by making invisible the processes constituting groups as a social category. It also allows for and strengthens the attacks on the supposed essentialism of those advocating that women are constituted in a relation of appropriation.

On the other hand, affirming that women constitute a sex class does not preclude the analysis of diversity. But instead of specifying subcategories of women on the basis of attributes such as skin colour and income, Guillaumin's approach explores differences in terms of the different usages women are put to: for example, some perform domestic chores for their family while others contribute to their husband's career by offering intellectual and psychological services as well as supervising the cleaning woman. In some societies, such as French Canada at the beginning of the century, the labour power required for the material, physical, intellectual, spiritual and emotional upkeep of human beings was provided without pay by two main categories of women: the first category produced children, many children, and looked after them and the husband in the home; the second category of women, comprised of nuns, looked after all those humans that the family could not cope with, such as the sick, the old, the orphans, the priests, the mentally ill, the 'delinquents'. There is no doubt that the lives and the work of these women differed; nuns were not expected to provide sexual services and to re/produce children. But in both cases, women provide without pay labour which then serves to re/produce human beings. Thus, the multiplicity of their positions can be examined in terms of the modalities of their appropriation as well as in terms of their articulation with other forms of subordination (see Juteau-Lee and Laurin 1988, translated 1989). Understanding the multiplicity of forms that appropriation takes around the world allows us to account for what Carby calls the development of specific forms of sex/gender systems (1982: 224).

The differences between us

Guillaumin's materialist position leads to a profound critique of *différence*: 'race' and 'sex' as categories are produced in the context of social relations of domination. But, as we will now see, her anti-essentialism moves beyond strict constructionism and helps us understand the differentiated 'us'.

'Race' and 'sex' as constructed and empirically valid

The categories of 'race' and 'sex' are constructed in the context of specific social relations which produce distinct groups as one furnishes labour and the other benefits from it. Arbitrary signs are then used to identify these socially constituted groups, in this case, colour of skin and sexual anatomy. The processes of sexualization and racialization then function so as to allocate humans within specific social categories and positions. Thus, these categories are constructs; but, as we will now see, they are also, in a certain way, real.

Guillaumin argues that, paradoxically, 'race' exists and does not exist; although an imaginary formation and an ideological construct, it is real, a brutal and tangible reality. Both 'race' and 'sex' are empirically effective categories; they are political realities which also enter into legislation. Since they are operative, since they function to exploit and to kill, she suggests that they be kept and not be eradicated from our critical vocabulary. To ban these terms can unfortunately serve to hide the relationship which gives birth to them, and it will certainly not bring about the eradication of racism and sexism. In other words, if one could eliminate the notions, it would only serve to mask the presence of the social relations of domination which produced them. On the other hand, changes in social relations themselves do bring about changes in the ideological-discursive level, which leads to the greater rigidity found in the discourse about sexual categories. The latter have not undergone the same transformation, deconstruction and displacement as have racial categories, *entre autres*, because they are still seen as inevitable.

To argue that 'race' and 'sex' constitute empirically valid categories and should be maintained in our critical vocabulary does not mean that they are rooted in Nature. Nor does it imply that they represent categories which are trans-culturally or transcendentally fixed (Hall 1990). For class belongingness has nothing to do with sameness and fixity, as we will see in the next and final section.

Understanding the differentiated 'us'

As pointed out by Hall (1985: 94–96), our positioning within the structures of social relations does not automatically lead to specific political practices and ideological formations. In other words, ideologies, identities and politics are not inscribed in sociological genes; this absence of necessary correspondence between the different instances of the social formation obliges us to account for their articulation. Although Guillaumin's work does not focus on the political instance and on political practices, it does help us to think our way out of horizontal forms of reductionism and essentialist-type identity politics.

First, her analysis of the relations producing 'race' and 'sex' figures the existence of distinct systems of social relations, each one related to a distinct form of subordination. Her approach is akin to those espousing the autonomy model of 'race' and 'sex'-gender relations and can be compared to what Miles calls the radical model of 'race' relations (1984: 218). While radical feminists theorize the relations between the sexes, which are taken as biological givens, materialist feminists seek to understand the relations which constitute and construct the social categories of sex.

Each system of social relation must be understood in terms of all levels of the social formation. Racial and sexual categories should not be relegated to the ideological instance of capitalist social relations and the sex-gender system just as the racial social formation cannot be reduced to class analysis. This is not to say that these analytically distinguishable systems of social relations systems are not empirically interwoven; they must be articulated, but not in a reductionist fashion nor in terms of fixed categories. The articulation of these systems is what allows us to construct the differences between women as diverse modalities of their appropriation, both at one time and through time. Understanding the articulation of *sexage* and *esclavage*, for example, allows us to see the very real differences between the lives of women who are appropriated as women and as slaves and those who are appropriated 'only' as women. It also shows that men who are not slaves possess women who are slaves and those who are not.

Guillaumin's unusual mode of articulating social class and sex class also opens up many avenues for understanding changes in women's positions. Rather than focusing on sexual categories and class positions, i.e. bourgeois women versus proletarian women, rather than linking two systems of domination, patriarchy and capitalism, she examines the evolving relationship between two types of contradictions: the first one lies in the contradiction between the private and the collective forms of appropriation while the second involves the contradiction between the social appropriation of women and the fact that they can sell their labour power. This contradiction, i.e. appropriated individualities who can none the less sell their labour power is the key to understanding changing modalities of the appropriation of women in contemporary societies. In other words, the growing participation of women in paid employment has brought about, certainly in the western world, a transformation of the modalities of the appropriation of women and thus a major restructuring of the relations between the sexes.

Class consciousness as distinct from species consciousness and identity politics

Guillaumin helps us discover that 'sex' is not a given, it is not *un fait de nature*; her analysis makes visible the processes leading to the naturalization of sex. Although she exposes the fundamental unnaturalness of sex (Butler 1990: 149), she does not treat it as a phantasmatic construction (1990: 142). And she also refuses to consider identity categories as transcendental, foundational, fixed and trans-cultural. Actually, Guillaumin is quite silent on the topic of identity; she focuses instead on 'the building of the consciousness of our class, *our class consciousness*, against spontaneous belief in ourselves as a natural species' (1981: 107).

'We women' involves the construction of a unity resting not on a common substance but on the realization that we are formed in very concrete and daily social relationships. Given both the multiplicity of systems of *sexage* and the diversity of forms and modalities of women's oppression, an effective practice of struggle remains difficult to achieve.

In my opinion, attempts to provide a sex-gender account of ethnically structured economic and patriarchal relations and to stitch together the fragments of the multiple forms of women's oppression remain crucial. They can help generate those political practices seeking to abolish the systems which produce, in addition to their appropriation, exploitation and domination, the categorization of females as a biological category.

NOTES

1 I would like to thank Natasha Lee, Robert Miles and Elizabeth Probyn for their most useful comments, which improved the content and the form of this presentation.
2 Throughout this presentation, the inverted commas 'race' and 'sex' are used so as to remind the reader that we are dealing here with categories that are constructed; the analysis of the processes at work represent the heart of Guillaumin's work.
3 Many Francophone feminists are unaware of her work on racism, while social scientists focusing on racism often express misgivings and sometimes

hostility about her work on the sex-gender system, finding it irrelevant or provocative. A third and more recent category of interlocutors composed mainly of Anglophone (British, Canadian and Australian) feminists (those who hear her presentations at various international colloquia) express the opinion that the concept of sex class is misguided and that Guillaumin is not sufficiently preoccupied by the articulation of gender, 'race' and class. Sex class, it is argued, negates the differences between women and comes dangerously close to essentialism.

4 Value orientations and questions deemed important and significant by researchers are highly variable; thus, the data and explanations contributed by social scientists will always remain partial.

5 The former type of reductionism fails to conceptualize the various systems of social relations as analytically distinct while the latter flattens the mediations between the economic, political and ideological levels of the social formation.

6 Although this materialist approach may appear close to Marxist feminism (Haraway 1990: 200–202), we shall see that many differences separate them.

7 Michel (1956), Memmi (1972) and Simon (1970, 1973a, 1973b, 1974) constitute the main exceptions. Only in the late 1970s will a group working on these issues emerge, setting up and publishing a journal, *Pluriel-Débats*, which (it is interesting to note) stopped publication around the time that the field became fashionable in France.

8 Italic here corresponds to that in Guillaumin's text.

9 More about women in the next section.

10 I am referring here to the women around *Questions féministes* (*Feminist Issues* in the United States) who published in this journal, such as N. Bisseret, C. Capitan, E. de Lesseps, C. Delphy, C. Guillaumin, N. C. Matthieu, M. Plaza and M. Wittig.

11 This perspective is very rarely mentioned in presentations on the evolution and articulation of diverse strands of feminisms; see, for example, *Signs* (1981) and, more recently, Spivak (1992). Duchen (1986) represents a noteworthy exception.

12 I have examined elsewhere the specific position held by materialist feminism in the constellation of feminisms as well as its distinctive contribution (Juteau-Lee and Laurin 1988, translated in *Feminist Issues* 1989).

13 'In the first, we find the assumption of a unified capitalist patriarchal system, capitalism being necessary to patriarchy and vice versa (Eisenstein 1979); gender relations are inseparable from class. Some authors relegate patriarchy to the ideological sphere, with capitalism alone occupying the economic one (Mitchell 1971). Other theorists emphasize women's work in reproduction (Dandurand 1981; O'Brien 1981) and articulate that sphere with production. Edholm, Harris and Young (1977) point out that several studies along this line contain a major defect, since they have a tendency to reduce reproduction to biological reproduction and to place the work of biological reproduction at the centre of the sexual division of labour, of women's place in both production (Armstrong and Armstrong 1983) and in history (O'Brien 1981). But the work of Mathieu on social maternity (1979) and that of Tabet on imposed reproduction (1987) clearly show that women's

place in reproduction and production is dependent on the relations of domination between the sexes, not the reverse. Hartmann's (1981) analysis shows that the control exercised by men over women's labour, domestic and unwaged, is central to the relations of domination between the sexes as well as to their understanding' (Juteau-Lee and Laurin 1989: 20–1).

14 Usually, but not always; the return of sociobiology, the importance accorded to the biological differences between the sexes, the use of reproductive organs to explain the position of women in our societies, the refusal to consider as appropriated women who do not encounter class or racial forms of discrimination, all this indicates that we are still a far cry from a generalized acceptance of the existence of women's subordination.

15 Sexualization is to be differentiated from genderization as it implies the construction of social categories differentiated in terms of biological attributes. We shall see that these categories are not givens.

16 A perusal of articles and theses written in Canadian Francophone universities indicates the determining influence of materialist feminism in these circles. In spite of *Feminist Issues*, a journal founded in 1980 in order to translate and diffuse the work of materialist feminists, American books and articles on French feminist thought, such as those published in *Signs* (1981) focus on the psychoanalytical perspectives of Cixous and Irigaray and completely ignore the work of materialist feminists. This seems to be changing as very recent books (Butler 1990; Fuss 1989) take into account Wittig's work, but they none the less understate the importance of the materialist dimension of her work. In Great Britain, the work of Delphy has been translated and publicized in the context of the debate opposing her to Barrett and McIntosh. But the work of Guillaumin, which differs from that of Delphy, remains unknown.

17 New-borns must be transformed into human beings, into social and socialized beings; for a longer analysis of this process, see Juteau-Lee (1983b).

18 For an analysis of the relevance of *sexage* to understanding the contemporary situation of women, see Juteau-Lee and Laurin (1988, translated 1989).

19 I would like to thank Natasha Lee, graduate student at the Université de Montréal, for the crucial insights contained in this paragraph.

20 Furthermore, as Mouffe (1992) and Smith (1991) point out, the repetition of a sign does not imply essentialism.

21 This position is also defended by Anthias and Yuval-Davis in their introduction to *Racialized Boundaries* (1992).

22 Cixous, Irigaray, Leclerc, to mention a few names.

23 The importance of the extreme right and its naturalist discourse.

BIBLIOGRAPHY

Anthias, Floya and Nira Yuval-Davis. 1992. *Racialized Boundaries, Race, Nation, Gender, Colour and the Anti-racist Struggle*. London and New York: Routledge.

Armstrong, Pat and Hugh Armstrong. 1983. 'Beyond Sexless Class and Classless Sex: Towards Feminist Marxism', *Studies in Political Economy*, 10 (Winter): 7–43.

Badinter, Elizabeth. 1981. *L'Amour en plus: histoire de l'amour maternel (XVIIe–XXe siècle)*. Paris: Flammarion.

Barrett, Michele and Mary McIntosh. 1979. 'Christine Delphy: Towards a Materialist Feminism?' *Feminist Review*, 1: 95–101.

Benston, Margaret. 1972. 'The Political Economy of Women's Liberation'. In *Women in a Man-Made World*. Edited by Glazer-Malbin, Nona and Helen Waehrer. Chicago: Rand McNally.

Butler, Judith. 1990. *Gender Trouble: Feminism and the Subversion of Identity*. New York and London: Routledge.

Carby, Hazel. 1982. 'White Woman Listen! Black Feminism and the Boundaries of Sisterhood'. In *The Empire Strikes Back: Race and Racism in 70's Britain*. Edited by the Centre for Contemporary Cultural Studies at the University of Birmingham. London: Hutchinson.

Dalla Costa, Mariarosa. 1972. 'Women and the Subversion of the Community'. In *The Power of Women and the Subversion of the Community*. Edited by Dalla Costa, Mariarosa and Selma James. Bristol: Falling Wall Press.

Dandurand, Renée. 1981. 'Famille du capitalisme et production des êtres humains'. *Sociologie et sociétés* 13(2): 95–113.

Delphy, Christine. 1970. 'L'Ennemi principal'. *Partisans* 54–55: 157–172.

Duchen, Claire. 1986. *Feminism in France. From May '68 to Mitterand*. London, Boston and Henley: Routledge and Kegan Paul.

Edholm, Harris and Young. 1977. 'Conceptualizing Women'. *Critique of Anthropology* 3: 101–130.

Eisenstein, Zillah R. 1979. 'Developing a Theory of Capitalist Patriarchy and Socialist Feminism'. In *Capitalist Patriarchy and the Case for Socialist Feminism*. Edited by Zillah R. Eisenstein. New York: Monthly Review Press.

Firestone, Shulamith. 1970. *The Dialectic of Sex: The Case for Feminist Revolution*. New York: William Morrow.

Fuss, Diana. 1989. *Essentially Speaking. Feminism, Nature and Difference*. New York and London: Routledge.

Gilroy, Paul. 1987. *There Ain't no Black in the Union Jack: The Cultural Politics of Race and Nation*. London: Hutchinson.

Guillaumin, Colette. 1972. *L'Idéologie raciste*. Paris: Mouton.

Guillaumin, Colette. 1977. 'Race et nature: système des marques, idée de groupe naturel et rapports sociaux'. *Pluriel-Débats* 11: 39–55.

Guillaumin, Colette. 1981. 'The Practice of Power and Belief in Nature. Part II. The Naturalist Discourse'. *Feminist Issues* 1(3): 87–109.

Guillaumin, Colette. 1992. 'Question de différence'. A chapter in *Sexe, race et pratique du pouvoir. L'idée de Nature*. Paris: Côté femmes.

Hall, Stuart. 1985. 'Signification, Representation, Ideology: Althusser and the Post-Structuralist Debates'. *Critical Studies in Mass Communication* 2(2): 91–114.

Hall, Stuart. 1986. 'Gramsci's Relevance for the Study of Race and Ethnicity'. *Journal of Communication Inquiry* 10(2).

Hall, Stuart. 1990. 'Cultural Identity and Diaspora'. In *Identity, Community, Culture, Difference*. Edited by Jonathan Rutherford. London: Lawrence & Wishart.

Haraway, Donna. 1990. 'A Manifesto for Cyborgs: Science, Technology, and Socialist Feminism in the 1980s'. In *Feminism/Postmodernism*. Edited by Linda J. Nicholson. New York and London: Routledge.

Hartmann, Heidi. 1981. 'The Unhappy Marriage of Marxism and Feminism: Towards a More Progressive Union'. In *Women and Revolution: A Discussion of the Unhappy Marriage of Marxism and Feminism*. Edited by Lydia Sargent. Montreal: Black Rose Books.

Juteau-Lee, Danielle. 1979. 'La Sociologie des frontières ethniques en devenir'. In *Frontières ethniques en devenir/Emerging Ethnic Boundaries*. Edited by Danielle Juteau. Ottawa: Editions de l'Université d'Ottawa.

Juteau-Lee, Danielle. 1983a. 'Enjeux ethniques. Production de nouveaux rapports sociaux'. *Sociologie et sociétés* 15(2).

Juteau-Lee, Danielle. 1983b. 'La Production de l'ethnicité ou la part réelle de l'idéel'. *Sociologie et sociétés* 15(2): 39–54.

Juteau-Lee, Danielle and Barbara Roberts. 1981. 'Ethnicity and femininity: (d')après nos expériences'. *Canadian Ethnic Studies/Etudes ethniques au Canada* 13(1): 1–23.

Juteau-Lee, Danielle and Nicole Laurin. 1988. 'L'Evolution des formes de l'appropriation des femmes: des religieuses aux "mères porteuses"'. *The Canadian Review of Sociology and Anthropology* 25(2): 183–207.

Juteau-Lee, Danielle and Nicole Laurin. 1989. 'From Nuns to Surrogate Mothers: Evolution of the Forms of the Appropriation of Women'. *Feminist Issues* 9(1): 13–40.

Kuhn, Annette and Ann-Marie Wolpe (eds). 1978. *Feminism and Materialism: Women and Modes of Production*. Boston: Routledge and Kegan Paul.

Laurin, Nicole, Juteau, Danielle and Duchesne, Lorraine. 1991. *A la recherche d'un monde oublié: les communautés religieuses de femmes au Québec de 1900 à 1970*. Montreal: Le Jour.

Mathieu, Nicole-Claude. 1979. 'Biological Paternity and Social Maternity'. In *The Sociology of the Family*. Edited by C. C. Harris *et al.* London: Sociological Review Monograph, Keele.

Mathieu, Nicole-Claude. 1989. 'Identité sexuelle/sexuée/de sexe?' In *Catégorization de sexe et constructions scientifiques*. Edited by Anne-Marie Daune, Marie-Claude Hurtig and Marie-France Pichevin. Paris: ADAGP.

Memmi, Albert. 1972. *Portrait du colonisé, suivi de Les Canadiens-français sont-ils des colonisés?* Montreal: L'Etincelle.

Michel, Andrée. 1956. *Les Travailleurs algériens en France*. Paris: Centre national de la recherche scientifique (CNRS).

Miles, Robert. 1982. *Racism and Migrant Labour*. London: Routledge and Kegan Paul.

Miles, Robert. 1984. 'Marxism Versus the Sociology of "Race Relations"?' *Ethnic and Racial Studies* 7(2): 217–237.

Miles, Robert. 1989. *Racism*. New York: Routledge.

Millett, Kate. 1970. *Sexual Politics*. New York: Doubleday.

Mitchell, Juliet. 1971. *Women's Estate*. New York: Vintage Books.

Molyneux, Maxine. 1979. 'Beyond the Housework Debate'. *New Left Review* 116: 3–27.

Mouffe, Chantal. 1992. 'Feminism, Citizenship, and Radical Democratic Politics'. In *Feminists Theorize the Political*. Edited by Judith Butler and Joan W. Scott. New York and London: Routledge.

O'Brien, Mary. 1981. *The Politics of Reproduction*. London: Routledge and Kegan Paul.

Omi, Michael and Howard Winant. 1986. *Racial Formation in the United States: From the 1960s to the 1980s.* New York: Routledge and Kegan Paul.

Signs. 1981. 7(1): entire issue on French feminist theory.

Simon, Pierre-Jean. 1970. 'Ethnisme et racisme ou "l'école de 1492"'. *Cahiers internationaux de sociologie* vol. XLVIII: 119–152.

Simon, Pierre-Jean. 1973a. 'Relations inter-ethniques et relations inter-raciales: perspectives de recherche'. *ASEMI* 4(2): 3–31.

Simon, Pierre-Jean. 1973b. 'Propositions pour un lexique des mots-clefs'. *ASEMI* 4(2): 33–46.

Simon, Pierre-Jean. 1974. 'Propositions pour un lexique des mots-clef'. *ASEMI* 5(3): 53–62.

Smith, Anna Marie. 1991. '(Review of) Essentially Speaking. Feminism, Nature and Difference'. *Feminist Review* 38 (Summer): 109–111.

Sokoloff, Nathalie. 1980. *Between Money and Love: The Dialectics of Women's Home and Market Work.* New York: Praeger.

Spelman, Elizabeth. 1988. *Inessential Woman: Problems of Exclusion in Feminist Thought.* Boston: Beacon Press.

Spivak, Gayatri. 1992. 'Woman in Difference: Mahasweta Devi's Doulouti the Bountiful'. In *Nationalisms and Sexualities.* Edited by Andrew Parker, Mary Russo, Doris Sommer and Patricia Yaeger. New York and London: Routledge.

Tabet, Paola, 1987. 'Imposed Reproduction: Maimed Sexuality'. *Feminist Issues* 7(2): 3–31.

Walby, Sylvia. 1986. *Patriarchy at Work: Patriarchal and Capitalist Relations in Employment.* Minnesota: University of Minnesota Press/Cambridge: Polity Press.

Walby, Sylvia. 1990. *Theorizing Patriarchy.* Oxford: Basil Blackwell.

Wittig, Monique. 1992. *The Straight Mind and Other Essays.* Boston: Beacon Press.

Part I

Chapter 1

The specific characteristics of racist ideology

INTRODUCTION

Racism can be reduced neither to racist theory, nor to racist practice. Theory and practice do not cover the whole field of racism, which extends beyond conscious thought. As an ideology racism is opaque, unconscious of its own meaning.

The aim of this essay is to cast light on the specific characteristics of contemporary racist ideology. After first showing that it cannot be defined simply in terms of aggressivity, stereotyping or 'doctrine', we shall set out to delimit the four characteristics which give it its particular form. These characteristics are defined in relation to those which guided perceptions of race in the past, and can only be understood by comparison with them. They are as follows:

(a) Race today is a 'geneticist' category, whereas in the past it was a legal one.

(b) It is altero-referential in nature rather than auto-referential, as it used to be in the old system. In other words, racist thinking is now centred on 'others', instead of on the 'self'.

The social groups which bear the mark of race are no longer the same as formerly. In the distant past the term 'race' was applicable only to 'noble families', whereas now it is wider social groups, in a minority or marginal situation in relation to the holders of power, who find themselves so designated.

(c) Finally, the concept of race has become spatial in character, and so radically different from earlier temporal perceptions. We are now faced with a synchronic organization instead of a diachronic one.

The hypothesis that the emergence of racism can be traced to a precise point in history is hotly debated. Even if agreement were to be reached on the possibility of such a dating, the actual date chosen would remain controversial. This is primarily because the phenomenon itself has been inadequately defined. Some see it as a form of practical social behaviour, others as a doctrine, and these different views lead to divergent datings.

If we adhere to the notion of a racist 'practice', then the hypothesis of a possible dating is undermined by arguments so strong as to appear irrefutable: its existence from time immemorial would seem to be proven by well-known and unquestionable historical facts. The constant presence (or frequent re-appearance) of such facts throughout history does indeed tend to suggest that racism is an omnipresent and constant factor. The long history of slavery, the Greek concept of the 'barbarian' peoples, the status of foreigners in ancient societies, the ghettos and the status of Jews in Europe and the Arab world, the widespread tendency to reserve the attribution of human status to one's own group (national, religious or social), are all facts. So is the feeling, from which few cultures seem exempt, that the customs of foreigners are always strange. Finally, and above all, hatred, exclusion, hostility, aggression and genocide are anything but modern phenomena. All of which contributes to a picture which seems to prove that racism has always existed.

Racism and aggressivity

That is indeed correct, as long as racism is defined solely in terms of aggressivity. But while aggressivity is often associated with racism, in our view that only happens at a secondary stage. Moreover, aggressivity is a form of behaviour which is in no way limited to situations of social alienation. Aggressivity often connotes racism, but does not denote it. It is neither a sufficient condition (aggressivity is not always racist), nor a necessary one (racism exists before overt hostility, in a certain type of relation to the other in society). To confuse racism with aggressivity is to leave out of account both the specificity which it introduces into relations between human groups, and the particular form which it gives to the use of force. Racism is a specific symbolic system operating inside the system of power relations of a particular type of society. It is a signifying system whose key characteristic is the irreversibility which it confers on such a society's reading of reality, the crystallization of social actors and their practices into essences.[1] Aggressivity as such does not depend on the essentialization of signs which is the specific mark of racism. In the present situation (the one in which we have been living since the first half of the nineteenth century), aggressivity and racism tend increasingly often to coincide, which no doubt explains the widespread confusion between the two. Yet the link is by no means an obligatory one; racism can be, and sometimes is, benevolent and even laudatory. In the absence of any immediately explosive situation (either because power relations are so overwhelmingly unbalanced that there is no possibility of revolt on the horizon, or on the contrary because they are approximately balanced), racism remains 'pure', restricted to establishing the other as essentially different. Do we need reminding of the political Far Right's fascination with the 'Other', be it Tibet or Nepal, Judaism, the Eternal Feminine, Islam . . .?[2] Fanatics of the esoteric and the 'vital impulse', browsers in the flea market of archetypes and essences, all rivet their blind gaze on such fantasy-emblems. This is a cultural phenomenon, which may or may not be accompanied by physical violence, depending on the circumstances: history may have the power to reveal what is latent, to transform ambivalence into aggressivity, but the signifying system of racism, with its notions of 'essential nature' and 'biological specificity', remains the single necessary ingredient.

Racism and stereotyping

The same is true of stereotyping, which as far as anyone can tell is as old as aggressivity and is often regarded as a specific characteristic of racism. However, we also see it being used both towards those of our own group and within other professional groups, and in general within any activity where over-simplification takes the place of knowledge. Unlike aggressivity, stereotyping is undoubtedly always associated with racism, but not with racism alone, so to that extent it cannot be regarded as an explanation of racism in its specificity.

Racism and racist doctrine

If, in line with the other current approach, racism is regarded as a doctrine and defined as the theory of the inequality of races, then there will be a large measure of agreement about its historical dating. Historians, sociologists, anthropologists and psycho-sociologists concur in situating its origin at a precise moment in the history of the West.[3] That the complete theory of the inequality of races coalesced between the end of the eighteenth century and the opening decades of the nineteenth is a hypothesis as difficult to challenge as that which sees aggressivity as an ancient form of behaviour. Bringing together these two conceptions of racism, it is easy to conclude that it is a tendency which has existed since time immemorial, but was theorized in the West during the nineteenth century; that is certainly the position of the human sciences today.

However, that would be to leave out the ideological character of racism. Taking this into account raises the possibility of a third definition which allows its specific features to be more accurately delimited. It involves taking the analysis into a realm where behaviour patterns have not yet evolved beyond being simple mental schemata, the realm in which, well before any explicit theory (which is only the final stage in the process), the specific organization of perceptions within a given culture comes about. This ideological level covers the complete set of meanings, whether empirical or doctrinal, which direct social behaviour. At this level there is much disagreement among experts. Some set the origin of race ideology back in the twelfth century, at the end of medieval feudalism, while for others it began at the time of the first European journeys to the 'New World', or again in the sixteenth century with the birth of capitalism; finally, a considerable number of scholars locate its origin in the way other peoples were perceived by the ancient inhabitants of the Mediterranean region.[4] To differing degrees these datings still rely on an identification of racism with aggressivity; while such approaches do privilege a certain type of relation to others, they do not distinguish it clearly from aggressivity, which remains a necessary component. Hence the privileging of conflictual periods of active aggression or doctrinal formulation. These divergent interpretations are largely due to the fact that the ideological character of racism has not been clearly defined theoretically.

The search for understanding in which we are now engaged is in fact already heavily mortgaged to the ideology of racism. Research has adopted as one of its basic concepts a notion, that of race, which itself is a specific product of racist ideology, and taken as its field of investigation the very topic in which racist theory situates the problem: aggressivity. In creating and hypostasizing race, racist ideology set up a metaphysics of relations of social heterogeneity which was adopted as it stood by everyone. However, the human sciences have now reached the point where we are starting to realize that if race is indeed real, it is so as a symbolic rather than as a concrete object. It will be granted that this is an important difference, though one which is far from having passed into scientific practice.[5] Yet this difference opens up the possibility of analysing the meaning of the notion of race, and thereby of gaining access to the ideological core of both racist behaviour and race theory. We shall thus concentrate on the notion of race as the medium of racist ideology, attempting to describe its specificity and discover its origin in time.

HISTORICAL CIRCUMSTANCES OF THE BIRTH OF RACE IDEOLOGY

The ideological notion of race was formed in the course of the nineteenth century in Europe. The process by which this came about was part of a wider movement, many aspects of which were then new, and cannot be seen separately from the other mental and social productions of the time; to treat race as a phenomenon closed in on itself, set apart both from other ideological developments and from its own social substrate, would be to reduce it to the status of a 'psychological trait' and so mask its singularity and diminish its importance.

History

These new developments took place in a society undergoing radical political and economic change. The socio-economic organization and practice of power were evolving with a rapidity accentuated by the brutal alternation of monarchic and revolutionary regimes (in France: 1789, 1792, 1798, 1815, 1830, 1848, 1852 . . .). By 1789, the traditional governing class had been dispossessed, practically and symbolically, of political power, in favour of a class vastly more numerous than itself. The nobility, which accounted for only 2–3 per cent of the population, was supplanted by a section of the third estate – the bourgeoisie – who, after acquiring a substantial share, if not the entirety, of the economic power, would now take over political power too. Unlike the group that it replaced, which was highly conscious of being a coherent caste, it did not regard itself as an institutional group. In its own eyes, 'the bourgeoisie [was] so far from being a class that its doors [were] open to anyone wishing either to enter, or to leave';[6] it saw itself not as a class, but as a sum of individuals who made up an 'élite' and had gained power through their own abilities.[7] With the growth of industrialization, the third estate also produced the industrial proletariat. The urban and rural poor became the 'industrial men' whose consciousness of constituting a working class crystallized in the course of the nineteenth century. A large portion of the population moved in this way from a peasant existence into industry, from a subsistence to a wage economy, from a low- to a high-density living environment. Over a hundred-year period these changes affected more than a third of the population, of whom more than half were peasants; at the turn of the nineteenth century 80 per cent of the population was rural, while a century later the figure had fallen to 41 per cent.[8] This gives a measure of the scale of the changes, economic, ecological and in type of work. In addition to these changes affecting the socio-economic conditions of the members of each class, the global economy became transformed by the growth of colonization, which from about 1830 led to the world's being divided up among the western nations, and turned a hitherto indigenous production system into a colonial economy of the type we still have today.[9]

Associated cultural traits

The seizure of political, by way of economic, power by a class which had taken several hundred years to emerge from political non-existence, the birth of the working class, the subjugation of foreign peoples, all bore the hallmarks of individualism, the claim to equality, and nationalism, which formed the background against which the ideology of race made its appearance. These ideological characteristics have remained largely unchanged to the present day. The European nationalisms were born in the revolutionary period and served to cement the desire for popular unity;[10] they embodied a new group consciousness radically different from the organization into 'orders' which preceded them. This period was also marked by the spread of an individualistic morality and sensibility,[11] which led to the definitive fragmentation of the earlier 'societal' identity: the social group lost its referential priority to the individual. Finally, revolutionary aspirations to equality had a profound effect.[12] The striking novelty of this ideological picture is obvious when it is compared to what went before.

These ideological changes were tied term by term to politico-economic developments. The bourgeoisie took over power, and its legitimacy was proclaimed in the doctrine of equality, from the *Encyclopédie* to the society of the first Revolution. At the same time, among the ruins of those theologically based bastions of community organization that were the orders, individualism was breaking out everywhere in support of an intoxicated but unsure bourgeoisie which regarded itself as a collection of individuals. Initially the fruit of economic success, individualism became an alibi for political domination once power had been acquired; from Protestant free will to the free market (liberal) economy, or the success of those best equipped to succeed, it moved from being a means of laying claim to power, to one of asserting the legitimacy of power. 'All political power, all privileges, all prerogatives, the whole of government became enclosed and as if heaped up within the boundaries of that one class', wrote de Tocqueville. Finally, there came into being the 'nation', the name given to itself by the 'people' as it formed itself into the quasi-caste which it had never been in the past. In a world governed by aristocrats and constrained within jealously guarded boundaries,[13] the people, from being nothing, entirely without definition, utterly relative (X's serf, Y's subject, Z's Jew . . .), suddenly started to invent itself, fixing its territory, its language,[14] its constitution, its laws, and affirming its opposition to the hierarchs. (The same phenomenon can be seen today in the opposition of Third World nationalisms to the hierarchs of the West.) Territory, language, laws came in to fill the void left by the people's earlier status, maintained by subjection, as subjects (a word which, by a striking linguistic paradox, actually means the state of being an object).

Finally, the theory of the inequality of races itself crystallized in the middle of the nineteenth century, at the moment of the bourgeoisie's triumph and the birth of class consciousness among workers.[15] Gobineau's *Essai sur l'inégalité des races humaines* was published just as the Second Republic, born in 1848, was collapsing to make way for the Bonapartist socio-political order.[16] A few decades later the theory would enter into social practice and become a systematic part of the country's institutions, a process of application which in no way suggests any causal link between theory and institutionalization.[17]

Race (or racist) ideology

But the theory, a mode of perception rationalized into a doctrine, attracts all the attention at the expense of the ideology that engendered it, and people tend all too readily to confuse two things, one of which feeds on the other but without exhausting its potential. Ideology, more diffuse but also more widespread, is the mode of apprehension of reality shared by a whole culture, to the point where it becomes omnipresent and, for that very reason, goes unrecognized. The ideology of race (racism) is a universe of signs: it is what mediated the specific social practice of western society as it became industrialized, and as political activity was taken over by a class which had formerly been excluded from it. It is a universe of signs far more extensive than simply the 'theory' into which it crystallized in the course of the nineteenth century.

Indeed, the theory stresses human 'differences' and inequalities, and affirms the superiority and inferiority of groups of people in line with criteria more or less explicitly defined, according to author, but that is all. The theory takes race as something irrefutably given, practically as an 'immediate datum of the senses'; as a self-evident truth, rather than a scientific tool or concept. Thus the *Essai sur l'inégalité* gives no definition of race; worse still, it makes no attempt to establish any causal link whatsoever between physical phenomena and mental or social ones. When Gobineau compares the brain weights of Blacks and Whites, the meaning he attributes to the comparison is syncretic: brain weight equates to degree of intelligence. A causal link between mental and physical facts was subsequently deduced a posteriori, in an over-zealous attempt to rationalize the idea, with the result that the assertion of a causal link is now presented as the distinguishing characteristic of racist doctrine.[18] Nothing could be further from the conscious intentions of the theory, whose only explicit postulate is one of hierarchy,[19] but the effect is to hypostasize the existence of races. As for a theory of biophysical causality, there is none; in terms of the biophysical argument, syncretism rules the day.

These two things, the hypostasis of race and biophysical syncretism, are the key characteristics of racist ideology in that they are unconscious, experienced as natural, spontaneous and self-evident.[20] In other words, the theory grows in ground ready prepared to receive it, which it would not dream of trying to define or of questioning. It presupposes that ideology, the inventor of the perceptive term 'race', is there in the background to support it. In treating (and perceiving) race and culture from the start as if they were identical, theoretical racism shows that both its premises and its methodology are motivated by a racist ideology. Even today, anti-racism campaigners only bolster this system when they try to prove propositions such as 'race and culture must be separated', 'culture is not dependent on race', 'race is not properly defined biologically', etc., negations which all implicitly accept the original syncretic position.[21]

Inequality, superiority, inferiority, differences in ability, are in fact no more than secondary aspects of an overall belief, never expressed because it is obvious and imperative, that human activity is a biophysical phenomenon. And this proposition is a new invention of the industrial era. We have come a long way from aggressivity, and further still from the simple theory of a hierarchy of 'races'.

We shall therefore leave to one side the subject of aggressivity, and racist theory itself, because they not only contain nothing more than the ideology, but do not even contain all of that. If we understand the ideology we will understand its theoretical rationalization, whereas understanding just the theory would give us only a partial view of the ideology. What we shall therefore attempt to illuminate is the perceptive and signifying system, the ideology, which unlike the theory is shared by all the members of a given culture.[22] If we examine the birth of the ideology of race, we will see that it does indeed turn out to be a historically datable phenomenon.

JURIDICAL AND GENETICIST VIEWS

There is a subtle trap laid for us by words whose forms do not alter over time, for we tend to ascribe to them with no hesitation the identity of a fixed meaning. At best, we may note semantic changes as they are presented in the manuals of linguistic history, while still hypostasizing the current sense, and only mentioning the recognized variants around a supposedly stable denotation. This is clearly what happens with the term 'race', of which the human sciences, from anthropology to social psychology, have made such widespread use. It has become the backbone of racist ideology, and we saw a clue to its importance in the fact that it seemed so self-evident that the theory itself did not even bother to define it.

At the end of the last century Freud, looking back over his own life, remarked: 'my origins, or, *as people were beginning to say, my race*',[23] thereby noting a new usage of a term which was far from new. So the meaning of the word could not be taken for granted at the very period when it was coming into widespread use. This meaning is actually quite recent, for as with the all-conquering families of the nineteenth-century bourgeoisie, its pedigree is a modern invention; in the words of one of Lampedusa's characters: 'Yours is an ancient family, or at least, it soon will be'.[24] Like these families, the word 'race' became venerable very quickly. From its attested use in France from the early sixteenth century, but long restricted to a particular social group,[25] the existence of a permanent signified underlying the signifier was extrapolated. This was helped by the fact that the old sense, used in and by a class steeped in the prejudices of 'inheritance' and very touchy on the subject of purity of 'blood', seemed closely related to the sense we give it today. But this is, of course, an illusion, which can blind us to what is specific about the modern use of the term.

In the successive uses of a word we often observe a phenomenon comparable to homonymy, whereby signifieds diverge beneath a common signifier. But the comparison is only valid up to a point, because in the process of historical drift, a term's identity is not wholly reducible to its use in individual utterances; there is a 'remainder', a minimal core sense which stays constant from one period to another. It is this minimal core sense that leads to confusion because it can too easily be regarded as a guarantee of the whole of the meaning, and so of its permanence. That is the case with the notion of race. If the word designates a restricted, well-defined object specific to the period of its use, that object nevertheless has a real relationship with its predecessors, an abstract relationship that shrinks down into the skeleton of a meaning. In this way, race comes to have as its permanent semantic core the meaning 'coherent group of people', and nothing else.[26] Each period then adds a certain number of connotations, giving the term a more specific meaning. Each period also tends to charge recurrent old meanings with the new connotations, thus masking the profound changes undergone by people's perception and grasp of social realities. In the current meaning, the core sense of 'coherent group of people' has added to it a biological or somatic content. This other sense is dominant and dictates our whole understanding of the term. The biological idea is the current hypostasis of the notion of race, and it tends to be taken, whether spontaneously or on reflection, as a constant component of the word's usage and meaning, thus unifying over time a notion which closer examination shows in fact to be extremely heterogeneous. For this feeling of permanence is an illusion, the biological colouring is new and was not part of the old term 'race'. Such a shift in meaning is highly significant for our understanding of human groups in industrial societies, for what seems like an age-old reality is actually quite the reverse.

In order to detect shifts in meaning behind the façade of permanence, we have at our disposal that most commonplace of tools, the dictionary. It needs to be consulted in accordance with certain rules.

– The first rule is that we must use dictionaries of different periods, rather than being satisfied with the datings given in a single work. A single dictionary of whatever period will provide only the contemporary sense of a given term, and the date suggested for its origin will apply to the word, rather than the notion, so that the signifier will be dated but not the signified (except where there is a sharp break in meaning). The current signified will be taken as the primary sense, and older signifieds which seem significantly out of tune with the modern sense will often be relegated to the role of minor or specialized senses, without any mention being made of the central role they occupied in the past. Even when (in the best possible case) senses are arranged in chronological order, connotations will become transferred and overflow from the modern meaning to those of earlier periods. At least, that is what happens with the semantic cluster which has built up around the term 'race'.

- The second rule is to compare definitions from different periods. Isolated definitions, however significant may be their 'period' flavour, lose much of their meaning if studied on their own, for they become totalizing and trap us with their appearance of a 'full sense', whereas comparing them with their counterparts from other periods reveals the variations and gaps in meaning characteristic of a particular moment, the novel elements and particularities which trace the evolution and successive content of ideologies.
- The third rule is to compare one with another the elements of the same semantic field, at the same period, in order to check the conclusions drawn from the historical comparison.
- The fourth and most important rule is to treat a definition not as a thing, completely contained in and delimited by the explicit meaning of the term, but as a set of connotations. A definition can actually work on two different levels, one explicit, the other implicit.[27] The first, visible, level is a definition in the usual sense of the term, clear and well-articulated, both logically and syntactically. The other, rendered invisible by its very self-evidence, is created by juxtaposition of terms: logic and syntax are completely evacuated, as is negation, whose status of logical production is well known, whether in a Russellian or a psychoanalytic perspective.[28] The terms used to lay down the definition all come together to form a connotative portrait of the notion. It is this connotative portrait, rather than the clear exposition which actually conceals it, that creates the meaning, closely following the line of the ideology and pointing up its variations. The type of semantic analysis employed here will therefore deliberately turn its back on anything consciously elaborated, whether in terms of social discourses (ignoring theory in favour of ideology), or articulated definitions (preferring sets of connotations to explicit definitions). However, this decision results in the adoption of a particular attitude, rather than a different field of investigation: the same texts are examined whichever approach is used.

Our analysis will therefore be synchronic in so far as it takes account of the whole semantic field of the notion under investigation: the term 'race' will be examined not in isolation, but in the company of those other words which, according to a common-sense view, would be grouped together with it. It will be diachronic in the comparisons made between successive usages.

The semantic field of the notion of race is that of racist ideology in general, with the word 'race' itself at its epicentre. Around it stand its present-day associates, the designators of racialized groups (Arabs, Israelites, Asiatics, Jews, Negroes, Blacks), as well as certain of its much older corollaries (blood, nobility). The term 'inheritance', for its part, is characteristic of both the older and the modern period; like the word 'race', it is a constant, and can therefore be used as a measure of the changes of meaning which have occurred since the eighteenth century.

The hypothesis advanced above,[29] that racist ideology was born in the revolutionary period and developed through the nineteenth century, will now be tested by reference to two dictionaries of French: the first, the *Wailly*, a popular dictionary published in Year IX of the Revolution (1802), and the second, the *Robert* (first edition), which came out in 1953.

Each definition will be quoted exactly, but the connotative discourse will also be highlighted, so combining denotation and connotation in the same assessment. The eighteenth-century text will always be given first; the quotations are complete, despite their brevity.[30] This method of presentation will bring out the great burden of biology which the modern definitions carry, in comparison with the much 'lighter' older text.

Let us look first at the term 'race', which prior to the Revolution (honour to whom honour is due) was applied solely to noble families.

Race. *18th c.*: *Lignée*: (line of) descent, all those who come from the same family.
[Conversely, under *lignée* we find race]

So the term refers strictly to family continuity. NB: continuity of the family, not genetic continuity, which is not mentioned here, in contrast to later definitions.

20th c. [we are told that the word goes back to the 16th]: **1)** Family considered in its successive generations. **2)** Subdivision of species, itself divided into sub-races and varieties, constituted by individuals with common hereditary characteristics which represent variations within the species.[31] **3)** With reference to human groups: subdivision of the human race, equivalent to the division of an animal species into 'races' (breeds).
1749. (Buffon). In the strict sense, each ethnic group which is differentiated from others by a set of hereditary physical characteristics representing variations within the species. *19th c.* (By ext., or improperly). Natural group of people with similar characteristics

deriving from a common past . . . This broad meaning, quite close to that of '(line of) descent', is often used and understood as in *2)*, in disregard of the scientific facts.

These meanings all seem self-evident to us today, and are completely integrated into our perception of the term. The word *generation* marks a shift, for in becoming the corollary of the 'family' definition, it introduces a biophysical schema ('generation' comes from 'engender') in place of a legal concept, that of 'line of descent'. Thus a biological continuity replaces a juridical continuity.

Hereditary species, animal species, hereditary physical characteristics, species, natural group, scientific facts . . . are among the terms which order the current definition; they take us to the heart of the geneticist assumptions underlying the modern meaning of the term. By the nineteenth century, the whole field had become highly coloured by physiology and nature, evidence of a faith in the physical solidarity of humans and animals. Moreover, this somatic density of race was consecrated by the prestige of science, the new metaphysics; in an age when people believed only in tangible things, skeleton, brain, skull, height, weight, skin-colour were the new realities of the day. They were now felt to be the entire truth behind human phenomena, and seemed to drag along in their wake their anaemic elders, language, religion, law, economics, which were no more than their pale and wavering reflection.

Moreover, we see the use here of the word *hereditary*, whose properly biological meaning dates from the end of the first half of the nineteenth century. It casts its shadow over the earlier usage of notions which have only come to imply it in more recent times: can we now think of 'race' without reference to 'inheritance' in the physical sense? Yet such a reference was unthinkable before the nineteenth century, so much so, as Goblot notes, that:

A remarkable characteristic of the modern French bourgeoisie is . . . the importance it attaches to the purity of the family. In this, it is infinitely superior to the *ancien régime* aristocracy. It is a matter of some astonishment that a hereditary caste, so obsessed with its ancestors and attributing such importance to blood and race, should have been so little concerned with authenticity of filiation. In this aristocratic society of the 17th and 18th centuries adultery, by both husband and wife, is commonplace, and meets with no reprobation at all. The writings of the period, and in particular the memoirs, leave us in no doubt about that. Natural, physiological filiation is of no importance; all that counts is conventional, legal filiation: *is pater quem nuptiae demonstrant*, the father is, by legal definition, the mother's husband. In fact, it is neither blood nor race that carry value, it is name.[32]

Neither blood nor race carry value? On the contrary. How can we avoid being convinced of their importance when it is ceaselessly proclaimed by the caste that defines itself by reference to them? It is just that blood and race are synonymous with 'name', and 'name' lacks the biophysical content grafted onto the other two terms in the nineteenth century, a content which Goblot assumes in his use of them. This blood and race are not the same as ours, and that is what Goblot fails to recognize at the very moment when he succeeds so well in grasping their deeper meaning. Meaning simply a legal line of descent, race had not yet picked up the genetic overtones we know today; name was what mattered, not genes. It is now scarcely possible for us to identify imaginatively with such a meaning, so strong has been the recurrent contamination by the modern meaning. Let us then look at the changes affecting the terms 'blood' and 'noble', which filled the semantic field of 'race' before the nineteenth century.[33]

> **Blood.** *18th c.*: Red liquor flowing through the veins and arteries of animals. *Fig.* Race, descendance. *20th c.*: **1)** Physiology: red, viscous liquid of insipid flavour, etc. **2)** Particularly from 1170: in speaking of blood spilled . . . etc. **3)** Blood traditionally considered as the carrier of racial and hereditary characteristics. *See* Inheritance, race . . . *See* Blood, mixed . . . *See* Consanguineous, related. *See* Relationship. *See* Half-blood . . .

The appearance of 'race' in both definitions should not be allowed to mislead us. The first sense, which we know means household or family, has been transformed in the modern version into 'racial and hereditary characteristics', expressing the utterly metaphysical idea of a physical path of transmission.

> **Noble.** *18th c.*: One who, by birth or royal patent, is superior in rank to the third estate. *20th c.*: Superior to other beings or objects of the same type. **1)** In the domain of intellectual or moral qualities, and human values in general. **2)** In the domain of behaviour or physical appearance, that which commands respect and admiration by its distinction and natural authority. Specially, 'one who is elevated above the common people by birth, appointment to high office, or royal favour' (Furetière), and therefore belongs to a privileged social class within the State.

The current 'special' definition in fact repeats word for word the old sociological definition given in Furetière's *Dictionary*,[34] which is, as can be seen, virtually identical to that in *Wailly*. Moreover, it shows very well how, in contrast to modern races, an aristocrat could be made (by royal patent or appointment to high office). There is no appeal here to some *sui generis* virtue, whereas nowadays notions like being, species, physical, natural . . . introduce just such a biological colouring. Not, incidentally, without a certain reticence that we shall find in no other definition, reflecting perhaps the daring required to draw such a vulgar association between a prestigious left-over social distinction and today's resolutely proletarian notion of race. To see the concept of nobility and other ideas of the same epoch through modern eyes as aspects of a racist system of thought, to read the religion of 'blood', line of descent and 'race' in this racialist light, is adventurous in the extreme, given the historical absence of any reference to a biophysical basis for human social and mental activity, on which the whole of our current use of such terms is predicated. Without that, there is no point of comparison, and the old aristocracy's touchiness on the subject of its own continuation must be seen as purely legal in origin. Saint-Simon's snobbism and his enthusiasm for the legitimate Bourbons are well known, as is the zeal with which he attacked the social status of the royal bastards. But on the subject of the legitimate filiation of the Condé branch, he writes in tones that will surprise a modern reader:

Mlle. de Condé died in Paris on 24 October after a long chest illness, which consumed her less than the upset and torment occasioned her by Monsieur le Prince, whose constant whims were the curse of all those at whose expense he exercised them, whims which had rendered this princess inconsolable because two inches in stature had led to her younger sister's being preferred as a bride for M. du Maine, thereby denying her an escape from intolerable servitude. All the children of Monsieur le Prince were near-dwarfs, except the Princesse de Conti, his eldest daughter, though she was still small. Monsieur le Prince and Madame la Princesse were small, though not exceptionally so, and the elder Monsieur le Prince the hero, who was tall, liked to joke that if his race were to go on shrinking in that fashion, it would eventually disappear. The cause was put down to a dwarf whom Madame la Princesse had long had in her household, and it is true that in addition to being short and stocky, Monsieur le Duc and Madame de Vendôme had exactly his face. Mlle. de Condé had a handsome face, and a soul more handsome still, with much wit, common sense, reason, gentleness, and a piety which sustained her throughout a less than happy life. She was therefore sorely missed by all who had known her.[35]

Line of descent, blood, nobility form the whole of the semantic field covered by race up to the nineteenth century. Then the social objects implicated in the field changed, and if we are to assess the shift in meaning between the old social universe and our own, we must look at the group which replaced the aristocracy as the bearers of racial meaning, people for whom race was to be, from then on, their social emblem.

The change in the meaning of the term 'race' from nobility, blood, family, household, to Arab, Asiatic, Jew, Israelite, Negro, Black is one which has passed almost unnoticed. A word which in the old days applied only to the aristocracy is nowadays reserved for 'racialized' peoples, two groups which could not be further apart in terms of both economic and political power. From designating an institutional power-group, it has shifted to cover categories of people without any legal definition, who have nothing to do with the exercise of power.

We shall trace the emergence of the racist meaning of the modern semantic field by comparing the old definitions with those of our own day. For while they may not in the past have belonged to any such highly élitist field of meaning, they did already exist at that time.

> **Arab**. *18th c.*: Which is from Arabia; figuratively, one who demands his due with extreme harshness. – Arab(ic): the language of the Arabs; – arabic numerals, our ordinary numerals taken from the Arabs. *20th c.*: Which originates from Arabia. The Arab people. An Arab horse (*See* Nedji). An Arab greyhound (*See* Sloughi). *Subst.* The Arabs, Semitic people, and by extension the indigenous islamicized populations of the Maghreb. *See* Barbary, Bedouin (desert Arab), Moor, Saracen. Arabs refer to Christians as 'roumi'. – Of or pertaining to Arabs.

We might begin by noting that the early stereotype, 'one who demands his due with extreme harshness', is no help in the area that concerns us here. We shall come across such stereotypes again in other definitions, and there are a few things which might be said about them, but in general stereotyping is a marginal aspect of racism, and not even specific to it. In this particular case it is enough to point out that the image of the man who is hard with money seems to have disappeared from modern usage.

In the old definition, the references are: (a) geographical (from Arabia);

(b) cultural (Arabic language and numerals). There is no mention of biophysical characteristics.

The current definition, on the other hand, takes us into the realm of geneticism ('which originates . . .'), and introduces animal associations (Arab horse, Arab greyhound) alongside a reference to the Arab people. This is the only definition where we find such an association with animals through contiguity, but the underlying drive towards bodily hypostasis finds expression in other ways too, as we shall see. Racial vocabulary then follows, with Semitic; it might be objected with some appearance of plausibility that the linguistic, not the racial term is being used here, but if so, we might have expected 'people of Semitic language', to avoid any ambiguity. The same dictionary also uses 'Semitic' in an explicitly racial sense in other definitions. Moreover, the main meaning of a term at a given time encapsulates all its other meanings, whether we like it or not, and that happens here as much as anywhere else. Finally, 'indigenous' further strengthens the racial colouration.

For a group now considered to be one of the 'fundamental races', we find:

> **Yellow (-skinned).**[36] *18th c.*: Colour of gold, lemons, saffron, egg-yolk. *Adj.* of colour yellow. *20th c.*: **1)** One of the seven fundamental colours of the spectrum. **2)** Yellow-coloured object. **3)** Individual of yellow-skinned race. **4)** Blackleg, strike-breaker.

There is one straight fact here far more basic than any shift in meaning or connotations: until the twentieth century, 'yellow' did not serve to designate any human group. Those people who, when the West was seized by the craze for somatic designations and Europe discovered the need to order humankind according to the colours of the spectrum, suddenly found the colour yellow thrust upon them apparently had no specific skin colour before that. Now the term 'race' is applied to them too, without anyone thinking of protesting. It is perhaps this term, which has undergone the clearest and most abrupt development, which best illustrates the change that has occurred. What we see here is the overlaying of a totally new meaning on an old word, and its further crystallization into the notion of 'race'.

After this perfect elliptical synthesis of our argument in a single definition, let us move on to look at two terms which seem at first to suggest the opposite. The ancient roots of their usage, and of the social group they designate, appear to support those who see 'race' as an age-old, if not eternal, notion. However, their very age shows up the inconsistency of this belief.

> **Jew**. *18th c.*: One who professes Judaism. *Fig.* Man who makes usurious loans or sells at too high a price. Rich as a Jew, very rich. Wandering Jew, one who is constantly wandering from place to place. *20th c.*: **1)** Noun. Name given to the descendants of Abraham since their Exile (4th century BC). *See* Hebrew, Israelite. Semitic, monotheistic people who lived in Palestine, and whose dispersal lasted from the period of Exile to the 2nd century BC. Name given to the descendants of this people scattered throughout the world, who have generally remained faithful to their religion and attached to Jewish tradition. *Fig.* One who seeks profit above all else, usurer. **2)** *Adj.* Jewish: of or pertaining to the community of Jews, ancient or modern.

Here again, and by no means for the last time, we find that the old definition is based on a socio-cultural reference, in this case to religion: 'One who professes Judaism'. We might notice in passing the assumption, long since vanished, that being a Jew is a matter of choice, and not, as people now tend to believe, of biology. This old definition certainly contains stereotypes, but there are no geneticist assumptions, unlike in the modern definition, which reflects our western culture's obsession with such things in words like 'descendants' and 'Semitic'. To this is then added the thoroughly coherent racism of genetic continuity, whereby a religious group is essentialized into a genetic monolith which goes on reproducing itself unchanged through time and space: 'Name given . . . since their Exile', 'who lived in Palestine, and whose dispersal lasted from . . . to . . . descendants . . . remained . . .'. The variations on Israelite readily confirm these observations.

> **Israelite**. *18th c.*: Ancient Hebrew people. A good Israelite, an honest, simple man. *20th c.*: (18th century, from Israel). Descendant of Israel, one who belongs to the Jewish community or religion. *See* Hebrew, Jew.

Here again a modern, geneticist definition ('Descendant') contrasts with an older, historical one ('Ancient . . . people').[37]

Prior to the nineteenth century human differences were classified according to 'phenomenological' systems, be they social (appointment to high office, royal favour), religious (one who professes a given faith), or historical (ancient people). Nowadays, geneticist systems are the ones used, as will be confirmed in the case of the term 'Negro'.

> **Negro**. *18th c.*: Black slave employed in colonial work. Treated like a Negro, very harshly. *20th c.*: Used in common parlance to refer to

those of black race, especially Blacks belonging to the so-called melano-African race. *Remark*: the word Negro does not correspond to any scientific anthropological classification. In modern-day speech 'Black' is generally preferred to Negro, seen as pejorative. – Physical type of the Negro: wiry hair, snub, splayed nose, fat lips. – White or albino Negro. Negro dance, customs, music, religion. *Specially*: Black formerly employed as a slave in certain hot countries.

The eighteenth-century definition mentions 'black' as a physical trait, which is particularly interesting as this is the only time that we find such a trait in an old definition. The meaning and function of this detail of pigmentation are important, however. In the eighteenth century defin-ition, 'black' is the qualifier, not the determinant. The determinant is 'slave', a socio-historical designation, which is secondarily qualified by 'black'. In contrast, the word 'black' acts as the determiner in the modern definition because it is the reference: to be a Negro now is no longer to be a slave, it is to be black, and someone who in the eighteenth century was 'a black slave employed . . .' would nowadays be 'a Black employed . . . as a slave'. So the definition has come full circle, with the racial aspect now dominant over the social one. This leaves behind an awkward feeling, however, because why should we worry about the word 'Negro' not corresponding to 'any scientific anthropological classification', unless we have completely lost sight of the fact that it is actually a social, not a scientific, term?

In the current definition there is an abundance of anatomical and biological terminology, but the logic (as opposed to the fantasy value) of such a deluge of physical characteristics remains far from clear, particu-larly as they are totally absent from the antonyms 'white' and 'yellow (-skinned)'.[38] Finally, the sense presented as special is actually, as we have already observed in other cases, the original meaning (here, the socio-historical one: slavery).

The term 'black' itself undergoes the following evolution:

Black. *18th c.*: The colour black. – To see the black side (take a gloomy view) of everything. – To leap from black to white, from one extreme to the other. – Think black (gloomy) thoughts. – Negro (by opposition to white). *20th c.*: **1)** The colour black . . . **2)** Darkness, night . . . **3)** Black (paint, etc.) **4)** Black as symbol of melancholy, pessimism . . . **5)** Black part of a thing . . . **6)** (*mus.*) Crochet. **7)** *17th c.*. Man or woman of black race. *See* Negro. Specially, black slave, black servant.

In the eighteenth-century definition the colours are seen as a relational system, as indicated in 'by opposition to': black is a comparative quality ('Negro, by opposition to white'), which takes us back to Negro as a social designator, because it is necessary to point out that the word can also mean 'black'. Conversely, the definition of 'white' contains the corresponding observation: 'person whose skin colour is white, by opposition to Negroes'; this has totally disappeared from the present definitions, which deal in all-embracing, self-sufficient, absolute realities ('man or woman of black race' on the one hand, 'man or woman of white race' on the other). Furthermore, the modern definition makes use of the term 'race' which, as always, is absent from the eighteenth-century definition. Thus we have two distinct descriptive schemas:

- the relational, eighteenth-century one: colour X 'by opposition to' colour Y; absence of the term 'race';
- the non-relational, twentieth-century one: race X . . . or . . . race Y; use of the term 'race'.

The current perceptual system is both geneticist and absolute, and is definitely the result of a historical process, since it did not exist at all before the nineteenth century, but is universally present today. It is quite a rare thing to observe such regularity in the expression of an ideology, for the coherent use of terms at a given period, and the sharp divide revealed by comparison between periods, are not just limited to 'race' and 'races'. Line of descent, nature, genealogy, all concepts at the periphery of the 'race' field, yield exactly the same results, but to examine them in the same detail would be overly fastidious, and in any case beyond the scope of the present essay.

However, there is one important term which allows all the foregoing observations to be brought together and checked for validity, a word which lies at the heart of the conflict we are investigating, and is the key to all geneticist thinking: inheritance.

Inheritance. *18th c.*: Right of succession, property a man leaves behind on his death. *20th c.*: **1)** Total amount of property a person leaves behind on death. **2)** Hereditary character; transmission by line of succession. *Biol. 1842.* (Mozin). Transmission of characteristics of a living being to its descendants. Specific, racial, inheritance: rigorous transmission of specific, racial characteristics by which two individuals (or a single hermaphrodite individual) of a given race or species can only engender individuals of the same race or species. In common parlance, set of characteristics, dispositions, aptitudes, etc.

inherited from parents, forebears; hereditary inheritance. Unfortunate inheritance; inheritance of physical and mental defects. *By ext.* Characteristics found from one generation to the next in certain geographical, social etc. milieux, as consistently as if they were hereditary . . . provincial, peasant, foreign inheritance.

'*Living being, descendants, racial, hermaphrodite, engender, race, species, aptitudes, forebears, hereditary inheritance . . .*': we are here deep in the black-magic territory of bodily nature, a long way from the modest inheritance of the Age of Enlightenment. The 'property a person leaves behind on death' has become swollen with another, more threatening meaning: 'unfortunate inheritance . . . physical and mental defects . . .' paint a rather curious picture of the term's sinister implications, and it is perfectly clear that it is 'other people' who form a 'race' by virtue of their heredity, for there is nothing particularly narcissistic about such a cheerful catalogue as this!

From one example to another a clear pattern has now emerged. It is hard to deny that the modern senses are indeed based on the old ones, as no new terms have been created. But new meanings have certainly been superimposed on old terms. This has come about largely under the patronage of the natural sciences which, unlike popular, everyday language (which has no objection to lexical creation), prefer to find new meanings for old words, rather than invent new words. That is what has happened here, for the terms we have analysed are the fruit of prolonged scientific efforts to re-describe the world. We know just how successful this vocabulary, new only in terms of meaning, was to be; it quickly took over in the human sciences as well, which became directed towards providing a physical, mechanistic account of human behaviour. These developments are all the more obvious as they involve not a change in the meaning of just a single term, but the drift of a whole semantic field. Without exception, the words in this field are now all markedly different from their older homonyms, showing that the somatic-biological ideology they carry, completely absent from earlier usage, was indeed something quite new.

AUTO-AND ALTERO-REFERENCE

Change of signified group

The internal shift of meaning that we have just analysed is not the only change undergone by the race system. Not only has the descriptive sense of the word, in its religious, historical or social aspects, lurched towards innate meanings and become swathed in an aura of biological inevitability, its field of application has also altered. Thus, in addition to a change in meaning, there has been a change in object. We of course noted in the course of our analysis of the semantic field of the term 'race' that it had been extended from the aristocracy to cover the somatic groupings created in the nineteenth century. The aristocracy now having disappeared from the socio-political stage, no single group can be said to have borne the 'race' emblem without interruption.

Change of referential topology

They may not be the same ones, but there are still groups which bear that emblem. In any system which privileges the race symbol by assigning it a referential role, whether it be the old-style phenomenologically-based system or the modern naturalistic one, the two opposing terms are always Self and Other.[39] Which of these social terms is invested with the racial characteristic depends on whether the old or the new system is in operation. Thus, while race remains the referent, that does not mean that it occupies the same position in the system, for it can be either auto- or altero-referential.

The auto-referential system, centred on the Self, was historically the first to be put in place; it coincided with the pre-eminence of the aristocracy, to whom its race symbolism was specific. The system gravitates around the social Self: all social relations between groups are governed by the definition which those who institutionally control power give of themselves. Their eyes remain fixed on their own existence which, both in their own minds and in reality, regulates the course and the symbolism of social activity. It is perhaps legitimate to see in this system a form of ethnocentrism, in the sense that value is derived from those characteristics specific to the dominant group. However, 'aristo-cratism' is not yet racism because unlike racism, it is not founded on a belief in its own 'naturalness'.

Altero-referential racism is centred on the Other, and seems to arise only in egalitarian societies. A fundamental trait of such a system is the occultation of the Self, of which people have no spontaneous awareness; there is no sense of belonging to a specific group, so the group itself always remains outside the frame of reference, is never referred to as a group. This can be seen clearly in the everyday ways in which groups are designated. For instance, present-day French society designates Jews as a group but not Christians, Blacks but not Whites. Being White,

Christian, etc. 'goes without saying'. This trait is so deeply ingrained in our social universe that it distorts language for its own ends. What conclusion can we draw from the fact that 'Christian' and 'white' are still used mainly adjectivally, whereas Black, Jew ('Juif') and Asiatic ('Jaune') have become nouns, if not that the dominant groups have escaped the process of substantivization which has befallen those whom they dominate?

Furthermore, violence in relations between groups is always explained by reference to the other. We are all familiar with the peculiar logic which produces expressions such as 'the black problem' or 'the Jewish question', but it extends further than is generally realized, because all contact situations (if the use of such a euphemism is permissible) are named by reference to an Other: slave-hatred, anti-Semitism, xenophobia . . . Conversely, none of these words has an antonym: pro-Christianism, pro-masterism, indigenophilia, etc. obviously do not exist, which confirms the one-sidedness of the relationship. Whatever approach one takes to this question, only the Other seems to be present in people's minds as the explicit referent behind the perceived situation. Our social discourse is no longer directed out from a dominant sense of Self, but towards a dominated Other. Race is no longer associated with power, but with lack of power. Whereas in auto-referential societies difference is the declared property of the dominant group, and used to its advantage, in altero-referential societies it is the Other (in the form of the various dominated groups) who is always different. And underlying this difference is the fact that the Other has now become a regulator, rather than a producer, of social discourse; a regulator deprived of power, and so reduced to the status of an object.

In an auto-referential system the subject group, which controls power, makes the assertion: 'We are different'; by contrast, in an altero-referential system that group asserts: 'the Others are different'. With the common factor being that race is the signifier of the perceived difference.

The purest form of altero-referential racism is probably what we are seeing in France today, whereas anti-revolutionary aristocratism is the most typical example of the auto-referential type. But the composite forms of modern racism nevertheless retain large residues of auto-referentialism. Such is the case with Nazi Aryanism, American Caucasianism, and the Celticism and Latinism of the French Far Right. However, modern forms of auto-referentialism all appeal to biological criteria, and, above all, are only secondarily auto-referential; they are mainly, and centrally, altero-referential. An obsession with the Other remains their dominant characteristic. The Nazis' anti-Semitism was more of a driving force than their Aryanism; Negrophobia is far more powerful in the United States than Caucasianism.

It is highly likely that the most serious situations are those in which the two systems occur together. In combination they form a structure of explosive rigidity, all the more so as the proportion of the two types of reference becomes more equal. A case in point is that of the Nazi regime, where the law governed both who was an Aryan and who was a Jew, thereby dictating a substantially equal degree of closure of both groups in on themselves.

The form of racism prevalent in France today represents the ultimate expression of altero-reference in that it recognizes only others and not itself. Ultimately, it shows a complete failure to recognize and define any Self group at all. It offers its own completely adequate explanation of lived experience, one that is literally so blindingly obvious that it prevents its proponents from also seeing, specifying and designating themselves as a race at the very time when they are busy designating Others as belonging to one. We have moved as far as it is possible to go from aristocratism, where the Self group alone had the right to such a definition. This type of racism is characterized by blindness about oneself as much as by an obsession with the Other, two traits which it unites into a single system.

SYNCHRONIC AND DIACHRONIC PERCEPTIONS

We therefore perceive and conceive of race today in a profoundly different way from our predecessors. This difference is not just a result of the introduction of socio-genetic syncretism, a shift in the object designated by the term 'race', or a change in the position of the referent in the social system; it is also marked by a profound modification of temporal perspective. Let us now return to the minimal sense put forward earlier as the semantic core of 'race': a coherent group of people (as defined by whatever criteria, which will obviously vary over time as we have already seen: common legal and administrative status in the early period, common biophysical inheritance nowadays).

The old-style temporal perspective, which for convenience we shall term 'pre-racial', is diachronic. It is organized in terms of line of descent, genealogy, family, as a mechanism for handing down a name. This perception of race therefore follows a line from past to present, in which the individual represents a moment in history. Though essentially a perspective wedded to the passage of time, it can also forge links in space by way of family relationships and alliances, but its main kernel is resolutely temporal. The solidarity between individuals of the same race is that of the passage of time. Moreover, it depends on a legal and institutional system which brings together under one 'family' name a well-defined group of people, 'the Bourbons', 'the Rohans', etc. In this old system, where the term 'race' was only used in the specific context of a family's line of descent, it therefore referred to a set of concrete individuals, limited in number at any given moment, and of ascertainable extension backwards in time.[40] In short, 'race' covered a finite number, graspable by an ordinary person's imagination, of individuals who ensured the continuity of a name through time. A name which was always embodied in the individuals so named, who were generally also known by a personal name distinct from that of the family, and possibly also a number (X, III, V, etc.) or a place in the system of relations (son of . . ., mother of . . ., first cousin of . . .); individuals, in other words, who were listed in various ways and so were easily identifiable. Thus the social reality of race was defined by an extension in time and space that was graspable by everyone's imagination, and the relative individualization of those involved in the system.

In contrast, the present notion of race is characterized by a substantification of time, an enormous extension in space, and the complete disappearance of the individual. Paradoxically, the introduction of geneticism into the picture has broken up the linear temporal perspective specific to the old institution. Biophysical similarity now implies a spatial but atemporal commonality. The perspective has become synchronic and now links together a society composed of contiguous contemporaries, an unlimited number of individuals spread across a huge material space (the whole world). The groups thus formed are vastly bigger than they could ever have been in the past, and a particular physical feature is the only recognizable sign they have in common. The individualized 'filiation' of the old-style races has been replaced by an undifferentiated mass whose obscure origins are lost in the mists of time. The individual does not stand out; he remains unnamed, a mere actualization of the species.

Paradoxically, this takes us into a completely non-concrete domain. Paradoxically, because we would not spontaneously associate the physically dense notion of race, with its litany of somatic and biophysical characteristics, with abstraction. Yet that is indeed the case, for there is nothing more abstract than this undifferentiated mass, floating somewhere outside the passage of time, like an eternal essence from which no single individual stands out in space or time. No name, no number, no family relationship specifies anyone, classes anyone individually, in this mass. A succession of individuals in a family tree has been replaced by a collection of unspecified atoms (Negroes, Jews, Asiatics . . .). The aristocracy were not one race but many (the Xs, the Ys), whereas now we say in the singular 'the black race', 'the Jewish race' . . . We have gone from multiplicity to singularity.

The two perspectives on race thus belong to two profoundly different social topologies. Whatever the characteristics (and consequences) of the old-style view may have been, it did have built into it an evolutionary variable: time. By contrast, the modern system of perceptions has expelled any reference not only to change, but to the very passage of time itself. Time only figures in the form of an immobile archetype, which is eternity. The pre-eminence of succession in time has been broken, to be replaced by juxtaposition in space. Race today is a collection, an agglomeration of contemporaries, brought together under a noun which is no longer the name of a family, but a nominalized adjective. There are no longer any proper nouns, only an undifferentiated and immemorial mass.

CONCLUSION

The characteristics which we have identified above give, we hope, a somewhat broader picture of race ideology and show more accurately what makes it specific. They at least allow us to differentiate clearly between the ideology and its accompanying racist theory and doctrine, which can be regarded as a secondary edifice. A hierarchy among human groups, a system of biophysical causality underlying social and mental forms, are actually rationalizations of the ideology itself. The ideology implies much more than these doctrinal claims, and possesses specific characteristics which are, as we have seen, quite far removed from the field to which the 'race question' is normally assigned.

Geneticism is, of course, part of this field, but the change in the objects designated by the term 'race', the shift from a temporal to a spatial perspective, and the move from a system referenced around 'Self' to one based on reference to 'the Other', are not generally linked to this question. However, it is precisely these things which are specific to race ideology, i.e. to the perception of race and its sociological meaning. They are not secondary or optional characteristics, but essential and differentiating ones.

The old-style, 'pre-racial' notion of race (in the sense that its ideological field was quite different from that of modern racism) was legal and institutional in nature, applicable to a single, powerful social group, and set in a temporal perspective. It acted as a means for the dominant group in society to designate its own membership, and so can be said to be narcissistic.

The present-day idea of 'race', the cornerstone of racist ideology, refers to social groups which are very different from their aristocratic predecessors. They are the members of minorities, the oppressed, those on the margins of society, who have no power. As a mass biological 'entity', race today brings together a collection of undifferentiated elements widely scattered in space. Finally, it allows members of the dominant group to designate the groups to which 'others' belong.

It is this latter concept of race which forms the foundation of racist theory. A theory which exploits, expresses and rationalizes the reversal of a particular type of belief, itself grafted onto a reversal in the sociopolitical situation. The theory took shape during the first decades of the nineteenth century and crystallized around 1850, at the moment when the French monarchy was disappearing for good. Thus it came exactly at the point of junction between two different social topologies: autoreferential aristocratism on the one hand, altero-referential racism on the other. Before, a dominant class which literally did not see other people; after, a dominant class which literally did not see itself.

This was the moment in history when the bourgeoisie became the élite and took over power. In so doing, they also took over the élitist views of the dispossessed class, but without the same means of justifying them: no long-standing genealogical practice guaranteed their status, no divine or royal assent legitimized their situation. They thus carried with them into their new position of power the lack of ideological goods and chattels of the common herd from which they had risen, and to which they did not wish to return. Torn between the nobility to which they did not yet belong and the populace which they had left behind, this aristocracy in function but not in name set about laying the foundations of a new élite which is still with us today. In the absence of coats of arms, titles and great houses, they therefore invented ability, aptitude, merit . . .

They also needed to define a common herd of their own, and they found it ready and waiting at the gates. At the gates of the cities, into which the peasants moved to swell the ranks of industrial workers. At the gates of the nation, where conquered peoples came to pay tribute to their victors. At the gates of a strengthened and newly prominent religion. Workers, Negroes, Asiatics, Jews . . . plebeians, primitives, foreigners . . . Others. The guarantors of the legitimacy of the bourgeoisie's conquest of power.

The theoretical discourse of the bourgeoisie thus managed for a brief period (until its efforts were deflected by the unforeseen need for practical social action) to fuse together the auto-referential system and altero-referential racism. In Gobineau's book of the mid-nineteenth century, the nobility on its way out meets up with the people on its way in: gods on the one side, Negroes on the other . . . Thus racist theory, at the moment of the bourgeoisie's triumph, half a century after the fall of the aristocracy, twenty years after the start of modern colonialism, thirty years before the Dreyfus Affair, bound tightly together an ancient, Germanic nobility and an obtuse Gaulish populace, a demi-gods' ethereal paradise lost, and the solid animality of Negroes and half-castes who were busily corrupting a doomed world. But the gods and the aristocracy had already left the political stage, and thus *de facto* the ideological universe . . .[41] A ruler deposed has no further existence. Enter the Others, who will act as a mirror, an inverted image, for this bourgeoisie anxiously seeking its own identity. Since the bourgeoisie did not know what it was, unlike the nobility which had a very clear view of itself, it wanted at least to know what it was not. The era of positive definition was therefore followed by a time of definition by negation,[42] and auto-reference by altero-reference: the bourgeoisie is not black, nor Jewish, nor proletarian.

So this leads to an apparently paradoxical situation. Racism in the modern sense first arose in a 'democratic' society, a mass society whose expressed ideals were fraternal and egalitarian, one in which individualism was becoming accepted, cultural difference was no longer a hindrance to citizenship, and different forms of popular nationalism were attaining almost religious status. At the moment in history when the murder of the king had opened the door to a 'society of equals', when the night of 4 August 1789 had thrown privilege of all types to the winds, when Catholics, Jews and Protestants were no longer anything but citizens, when slavery was about to be abolished, there lurked behind this rosy picture of egalitarianism (which is, of course, also accurate in its own way) the grim shadow of an unbreakable determinism, a closed world: human groups were no longer formed by divine decree or royal pleasure, but by an irreversible diktat of nature. Frontiers which before could be crossed by dispensation from on high had now become fortified walls, defended by the strongest argument available in the young secular and scientifically orientated society of the day: 'such are the laws of Nature, from which no one is exempt . . .'. The gradually accumulating doctrines of the existence of races, their inequality, the survival of the fittest, progress, the protection of the weak by the strong, the forward march of peoples, all came to take their place in the construction of this fortress.

In this way, the combined forces of atheism, determinism, individualism, democracy and egalitarianism in fact served to justify the system of oppression which was being built at the same time. By proposing a scheme of immanent physical causality (by race, colour, sex, nature), that system provides an irrefutable justification for the crushing of resourceless classes and peoples, and the legitimacy of the élite.

NOTES

1 This irreversibility is not a concrete one: power could, at least in theory, change hands. What remains immutable is the underlying symbolism.

2 Notice that we are not using socio-historical designations here because these are, in the eyes of the ideology in question, all Essences.

3 We might look back in this context to observations of R. Benedict, O. Klineberg, C. Lévi-Strauss, G. Myrdal and L. Poliakov, among others.

4 Hypotheses put forward, for example, by M. Duchet and M. Rebérioux in *Racisme et société*; P.-J. Simon in "'L'école de 1492'", *Cahiers internationaux de sociologie*, vol. XLVIII, 1970.

5 What has passed into the literature, in fact, is the association of the two. But this still leaves the 'concrete reality' in place, and accepted as such.

6 *Journal des Débats*, 17 December 1847. Quoted by F. Ponteil in *Les Classes bourgeoises et l'avènement de la démocratie*, Paris, Albin Michel, 1968.

7 See Noëlle Bisseret, 'Notion d'aptitude et société de classe', *Cahiers internationaux de sociologie*, vol. LI, 1971.

8 Figures taken from Jean Fourastié, *Le Grand Espoir du vingtième siècle*, Paris, Gallimard, 1963.

9 See Pierre Jalée, *Le Pillage du Tiers Monde*, Paris, Maspéro, 1967.

10 Marc Bloch underlines the popular nature of these nationalisms in *La Société féodale*, Paris, Albin Michel, 1939.

11 For an analysis of individualism as a class phenomenon, see Félix Ponteil, op. cit., and for its history as a philosophical concept, see Louis Dumont, 'The Modern Conception of the Individual', *Contributions to Indian Sociology*, no. VIII, Mouton, 1965.

12 Diderot made himself the most impassioned spokesman for equality, not only in the *Encyclopédie* (whose role in bringing about these changes is well known), but also in his many political, scientific and literary writings.

13 This attitude is incidentally often wrongly assimilated to modern racism: we shall see below how great a gulf divides aristocratic narcissism of this type from the racist ideology of the industrial world.

14 *L'Histoire de la langue française*, by Ferdinand Brunot, describes in detail the conquest of French as a common language in the revolutionary period, and shows how motivating and emotive a process it was. What more vivid

illustration of this could there be than the picture of Bougainville [t.n.: Comte Louis-Antoine de B., navigator, author of *Voyage autour du monde* (1777) and member of Louis XVI's Cabinet] taking the examination to become a primary school teacher?

15 The mid-nineteenth century was marked by the birth of the trades unions and the founding of the First International.

16 It was published in 1852, having taken three years to write.

17 It is being over-generous to Gobineau and his followers to credit them with the paternity of such a major development, or suggest a causal role for them. This view, a survivor from an 'élitist' conception of history, with its preoccupation with tracing the cause of events back to a single important political, military or intellectual figure, fails to take account of the ideology behind all social movements. Key figures only succeed in integrating themselves into such social movements to the extent that they fit in with this underlying ideology. They may perhaps be catalysts of events, they can certainly be the spokespersons of a latent ideology, but it is highly doubtful whether they are ever founders.

18 See Lalande, and the standard dictionaries of French.

19 A postulate which is, in any case, fairly imprecise: see C. Guillaumin, 'Aspects latents du racisme chez Gobineau', *Cahiers internationaux de sociologie*, vol. XLII, 1967.

20 This raises the fascinating problem of the unconscious as a sociological trait. Unlike the individual unconscious, which only reveals its objects by way of symptoms (i.e. transpositions), the social unconscious shows itself at face value, without concealment. Society holds up its fantasies just as they are; ideologies, like uncensored dreams, literally speak the obsessions and magic imprecations of their culture.

21 This is where the sociological and the individual unconscious link up again. The practice of negation is a conscious superstructure which can never filter down into the unconscious infrastructure, where the logical mode of negation is unknown. Everything that is said, whether in negative or positive form, is an affirmation. Saying 'that is not true' is strictly equivalent to saying 'that is true'. Hence the bitter disappointments of some anti-racism campaigns.

22 Theory is here regarded as an 'opinion'. Whatever objections might be raised against this assertion (and we would certainly subscribe fully to them), it is sociologically accurate: theory operates on a conscious level, and is shared to differing degrees by different social groups and individuals. It falls within the domain of a sociology of attitudes or doctrines, not one of ideologies. Theory provides answers to questions such as: 'Do you think x . . .?', 'Do you believe that y . . .?'; ideology neither thinks nor believes, it assumes.

23 Sigmund Freud, *Ma Vie et la psychanalyse*, Paris, Gallimard, 1950 (our emphasis).

24 In G. Tomasi di Lampedusa, *Le Guépard*, Paris, Le Seuil, 1958.

25 Incidentally, a group very different (the aristocracy) from those who currently find themselves so designated.

26 By 'coherent' we mean 'symbolically coherent'. The modern notion of race involves a belief in the biological cohesion of racial groups which is

objectively false, for example. The criterion of this coherence is what society believes.

27 In fact, definitions always work in that way, but with one level remaining inaccessible to conscious scrutiny.

28 See Bertrand Russell, *An Enquiry into Meaning and Truth*, London, Allen and Unwin, 1961, who classifies 'no' as a characteristic of 'hierarchic' language, by opposition to the 'object language'.

29 And based on an earlier work: see Colette Guillaumin, *L'Idéologie raciste. Genèse et langage actuel*, Paris-The Hague, Mouton, 1972.

30 T.n.: As the relevant English semantic fields do not always match the French, it has sometimes been found necessary to adapt a definition, and occasionally to omit one or other section.

31 T.n.: This sense, usually applied to animals (= 'breed'), is commonplace in French but very rare in English.

32 Edmond Goblot, *La Barrière et le niveau*, Paris, Alcan, 1930.

33 The old conception remains [in French] in relation to the animal kingdom, where the term 'race' is applied according to the same hierarchical schema as in human groups: animals 'of race' (i.e. thoroughbreds) are supposed to be the best (the aristocrats), while the rest (mongrels and other half-breeds) are said to be 'without race' (i.e. without breeding). We shall see this dichotomy appearing again later in the present study, but reversed, in the fact that in humans it is the 'others' (the rest) who are said to have a 'race'. We might remark in this connection that the practice of intensive 'racial' selection of animals (dogs, and especially horses) goes back precisely to the nineteenth century. The Jockey-Club and other horse-racing societies came into being at a time when 'race' was in fashion. Up to the eighteenth century, memoir writers do not seem to have been particularly interested in this question. As far as we know, Saint-Simon, for instance, says nothing about that passion for thoroughbred animals which is supposed to have been characteristic of the class to which he belonged, and which Balzac, Stendhal and even Proust were careful to attribute to their elegant heroes.

34 This is a clear example of the demotion of a strong (principal or original) sense to a secondary heading ('Specially' or 'By extension'). Thus the senses on which usage is founded end up exiled to the periphery, leading us to think that that was where they had always been. This is particularly striking with the definition of the term 'race', where 'group of people with similar characteristics' is demoted under 'By extension', whereas in fact it forms the basis of the modern meaning. The perception of these groupings underlies the whole synchronic perspective which characterizes modern racism, and in turn the modern usage of the term 'race'. Thus the third estate, the 'Gaulish people' of Thierry, Guizot or Balzac, the 'laborious and rural populations' of Gobineau, the 'Semites' of the linguists and Renan, and 'Negro slaves' (very different from today's Blacks), were the first to bear the race emblem, the first to be given the dubious privilege of being of a particular race. This was not so much on the basis of physical characteristics, as people today think, but rather because of common social characteristics which distinguished them from other groups.

35 This passage forms a single paragraph in Saint-Simon, with his remarks on the paternity of Monsieur le Prince's children occurring as if quite naturally

in the middle of a commentary on the character of Mlle de Condé. Saint-Simon, *Mémoires*, Paris, Gallimard (La Pléiade), vol. 1, p. 768.

36 T.n.: The French noun 'un Jaune' means a person of 'yellow' skin; there is obviously no equivalent nominal term in English.

37 Note also the inversion of meanings between the eighteenth century and our own day, first in the stereotype (the honest Israelite has become a schemer), but particularly in the historical and religious references. In the old days, the term Israelite carried the historical meaning, with Jew being kept for the religious sense, whereas now the situation has been reversed: Israelite [in French] is taking on the religious sense, leaving the historical connotations to the term Jew. With the added difference, of course, that both now carry a racial sense which they did not have in the eighteenth century.

38 We are here adopting modern racial logic, which distinguishes three main races, black, white and yellow (in alphabetical order).

39 Self and Other are obviously being used here to refer to social groups, not individuals.

40 Even if only mythically, by reference to a founding ancestor or a dated origin for the family.

41 They were, of course, still very much a part of the world of conscious images: no class has ever been more fascinated by the aristocracy than the bourgeoisie of the nineteenth century. But it was now merely an object of contemplation; it no longer had a role as a creating subject, or producer of institutions.

42 Something emphasized by Goblot (op. cit.), who shows that the bourgeoisie did not so much define as differentiate itself.

The idea of race and its elevation to autonomous scientific and legal status

INTRODUCTION

The fact that at one point in the history of the last few centuries certain social relationships came to be called 'racial' does not necessarily mean that they are so. For that to be the case, 'race' would have to be a concept with a practical basis, founded in 'reality'. But it is not. What are called 'race relations' refer to two different kinds of facts: either to relationships regarded as racial by those directly and actually involved (Nazi Germany and the Republic of South Africa are two examples of this belief being given legal form), in which case such relationships are indeed, ideologically speaking, 'racial'; or to intergroup relationships described as 'racial' by anthropologists or other outside observers, in which case those directly involved may not see the relationships as racial at all and may interpret them in terms of nationalism, class, religion, awareness of ethnic distinction, and so on. This last was the case of the bourgeois and popular revolutions in France between 1789 and 1793, seen by those directly involved as revolt against a group possessing wealth and political and legal power, and reinterpreted as 'racial' conflict by historians in the first half of the nineteenth century.[1]

We are clearly dealing with two different things: in one instance the idea of race is part of the situation being studied, while in the other it is present in the study itself. Small wonder that people's notion of race relations is so vague, when its derivation is so mixed.

But is there anything to be learned about the facts of race from the slow development and crystallization of the idea in the course of the last two hundred years, at the point of interaction between the economies of colonialism, industrial growth, and progress in the natural sciences? I shall try to point out certain tendencies which show how belief in the physical existence of race is really an archetypal attitude of pseudo-materialism. Authors whose arguments incorporate the idea of race as a fact while pretending to 'allow' for it almost always manage to avoid actually discussing those relations which introduce (or make use of) the idea of natural relationship.

It is vitally important for us to know how and upon what grounds the idea arose that certain social relationships are *natural*, irrespective, in the last resort, of politics or economics, and reflecting only Nature itself together with its constraints and its inevitability. For let there be no mistake: what is urged upon us in the form of racial (or natural) symbols is the great law of obedience to order and necessity, the law enjoined in so many different ways by oppressors upon the oppressed. Whether in its triumphal or in its apocalyptic form, the notion that the power of instinct is the driving force of history is drummed into us over and over again. For the last hundred years dominant groups have brought forward one version or the other according to whether they themselves are going through a period of expansion or of anxiety. If they are winning, that is because, according to the Darwinian interpretation linked to the rise of the middle classes,[2] they are stronger, more capable and more per-severing than others and because the predominance of their group is guaranteed by the natural order; those they dominate are subjects by nature or, in short, inferior. If the dominant groups are, or look like, losing, that is because, according to the Gobineau version, linked to the decline of the aristocracy,[3] they are fewer and of finer quality than the rest, and have been 'overwhelmed' by the once subjected masses whose very numbers prove their coarseness or, in short, their inferiority. Today, we are obviously being treated to the 'apocalyptic' version, linked this time to the 'decline' of Europe. While it is still too soon to identify the most significant form this interpretation will take, we may guess that it is most likely to come from the ethologists, the majority of whom are rapt in a vision of romantic catastrophe.

But both versions are assertions of the notion that social relationships are 'natural', and that the somatic, physiological and genetic context (this is the historical order of the forms assumed by the idea of natural selection) distinguishes superior and inferior, master and slave, man and woman, white and black, noble and commoner, Aryan and Jew, élite and plebs. Although the two versions differ when it comes to predicting the future, they are alike on one crucial point: not on that of 'values' – which is accorded to masters but refused to slaves, for such questions are products not causes of the power relationship – but in the categorical assertion that the groups concerned are 'natural' and not socially created, and that their characteristic features are not merely endogenous but somatically endogenous.

The fixations of somatic determinism were to become more and more sophisticated in later phases of the naturalist ideology. Rooted at first in the body or the blood, this ideology later shifted to the brain and nervous system, and has now taken refuge in the genetic and chromosome potential. But always the social characteristics under observation have been regarded not as deriving from a particular historical relationship, but as a permanent and essential potentiality.

This conception of social relations as being natural relations was both inaugurated and perfected in two works produced in the nineteenth century, Gobineau's *Essai sur l'inégalité* and Darwin's *Origin of Species*: perfected in that the process of giving 'scientific' expression to the naturalness of socio-human relationships had been launched about a hundred years previously and that these two works synthesized and clarified what had hitherto been scattered and fragmentary; inaugurated in that they represented an ideological crystallization of a mode of relationship then developing rapidly and still with us today. The popularity of neo-naturalism in the last ten or fifteen years is fundamentally not unconnected with those nineteenth-century accounts, and the present fashion for introducing biological considerations into the human sciences is not so much a new approach as a survival of the traditional naturalist attitude. Such an attitude makes groups into fetishes, frozen into some intrinsic form of 'being' and possessing qualities which, whether flattering or damaging, are in any case eternal. This is what lies at the heart of the idea that human groups are 'natural' entities or 'races', that these are genetically distinct and therefore, in the context of somatic determinism, politically, intellectually and socially homogeneous, forming closed entities fixed unchangeably both in nature and in law, whatever the superficial incidents that may affect their interrelationships. According to the proponents of naturalism, this deeply fundamental order is demonstrated by the fact that every group is as much 'instinctive' as physical, apprehending itself and the others 'instinctively'. In short, it is a world of certainty. So who needs deeds of ownership? Why wonder that a dominating group should emerge?

In this context, racial (or natural) relations mean relationships characterized by the naturalness of the groups involved. But the fact that such relationships are thought of as racial by those concerned (and sometimes this is as true of the oppressed as of the oppressors) is a *social* fact, and it ought to be examined as carefully and sceptically as any other explanation offered by a society of its own mechanisms. Such explanations can only refer to a particular time and place.

The truth of the matter is that those who produce theories about societies are also directly involved in the action and that the naturalist interpretation is put forward by a dominant group partly because of the very fact that it is dominant; but also because, relevantly but separately, that dominance makes it the observer of social phenomena and the dispenser of 'scientific' judgements. This dual mechanism is both the basis on which the naturalist classification of social relationships is constructed, and the reason why that classification is so difficult to analyse. Whatever the theoretical foundations underlying the various interpretations of 'racial' relations, the very use of such a distinction tends to imply the acceptance of some essential difference between types of social relation, some, somewhere, being specifically racial. Merely to adopt the expression implies the belief that races are 'real' or concretely apprehensible, or at the best that the idea of race is un-critically accepted; moreover it implies that races play a role in the social process not merely as an ideological form, but as an immediate factor acting as both determining cause and concrete means.

Hence the need to understand the real sociological significance of the idea of 'racial' relations in the theory of the human sciences. The idea belongs on the same plane as role-playing theory in the analysis of sexual relationships, or the theory of function or stratification in the observation of class relationships: all of them attempt to analyse social relationships while accepting the existence of problems involved in those relationships. The dominance relationship produces the idea that there are 'different' races (and therefore 'racial' relationships), that there are 'different' sexes (and therefore 'sex' roles), that there is a whole set of functions operating in a continuous society (and therefore continuity between classes). Domination conceals itself behind the idea of 'differ-ence': in other words, the ideal that all belong to the same universe, that all possess the same reference but in terms of different kinds of being, fixed for ever. Such theories tend to show us as being heterogeneous in principle and separate by nature, but linked together in an everlasting higher order, the order of hierarchy, of groups arising out of relationship. Social agents, those who embody social relationships, are brought forth fully armed by the transcendent universe of Nature.

This is not to say that theories of role-playing, of functions or of racial relationships are not sometimes shrewd and illuminating; but they leave out an important fact.[4] By furthering belief in ideas like 'race' and 'sex', by teaching us that groups may exist irrespective of social relationships, they obscure the real social relationships. And strangely enough, even those who claim most strongly (and perhaps sincerely) to believe that human groups and their structures and practices are defined by social relationships still think that somehow, somewhere, these groups are natural.[5] 'Yes, I know, but still . . .' In this stubborn phrase Freudians detect the unconscious, and sociologists ought to detect ideology. In these matters, and especially in relation to the natural determination of sexual groups, suggestive sneers or flat contradiction, offered instead of reasoned argument, are sure signs of self-censorship on the part of the advocates of natural order.

Yet one cannot fail to be struck by the irrepressible mutterings which seek to contradict the theories in which, one after the other, the notion of the naturalness of social groups has decked itself. The murmur may be uncertain and sometimes inconsistent, but it implies a question badly put and an assertion far from self-evident; it indicates that we have to deal here with both ignorance and fiction. We are aware of an anxious presentiment, still somewhat ambiguous, in Max Weber and Franz Boas.[6] It emerges more clearly in de Tocqueville's irritation with nascent racial theory and in Durkheim's refusal to mix the social and biological levels of analysis. It is the only possible guarantee, albeit a fragile one, against the wiles of ideology. It, together with all the nameless men and women whose voices have been drowned in the clamour of dominant groups, all those who have fought for real questions and against the deadly and deceitful excuses which try to disguise the material violence of relationships that are really quite concrete and not 'natural' at all. When new social relationships have brought about a new viewpoint, when some shift has made the unseen visible, what now seems 'self-evident' to many will fade away.

The subject here, however, is not this protest itself but what has provoked it, i.e. the development, and the success in a series of different forms, of the idea that social groups are natural; how the idea came into being, and what has become of it in the course of the twentieth century – a period of its history that has been comparatively neglected since people have generally been more interested in its premises than in its triumph. Probably, too, it is not so easily recognized now that it has become both 'self-evident' and in varying degrees censored or hidden beneath new masks. But the crucial fact is that the present century has seen the idea of race given legal status, alongside the older categories such as property, sex and age. The idea has emerged from the area in which it was still only an *effect* of social relationships (and thus still an ideological form), and become in its turn an independent *cause*. This change has been to some extent underestimated. Moreover, progress in the biological sciences since the 1930s has been closely linked with the ideological form of the idea and its transformation into a legal category, though the increasing sophistication of such research has had a restraining effect. And today the question raised by the notion of race, if not of racialism, is generally thought to have been settled. The notion is supposed to correspond to self-evident physical fact; to be beyond debate, and thus something it is unnecessary or ill-bred to discuss. But the whole point is that race is not a material fact which produces social consequences. It is an idea, a mental fact, and so a social fact in itself. And if we really want to, we can find out where ideas come from. They certainly do not fall out of the sky.

What we shall be examining, therefore, is the transformation of a power relationship into an idea, together with the various modifications and adjustments to history that it has undergone: the way it has been isolated as an almost independent factor, first 'scientific' and then legal, and its subsequent re-introduction into the realm of concrete fact.

> *M*: I was speaking in those days about three things we had to do: appreciate cultural differences, respect political and religious differences and ignore race. Absolutely ignore race.
> *B*: Ignore race. That certainly seemed perfectly sound and true.
> *M*: Yes, but it isn't anymore. You see, it really isn't true. This was wrong because –
> *B*: Because race cannot be ignored.
>
> (James Baldwin and Margaret Mead, *A Rap on Race*, 1971; Laurel Edition, 1974, p. 14)

The idea of race has developed in parallel with that of the diversity of societies and social groups, and the two notions tend to be confused, as can be seen in the enormous difficulty of defining race clearly. The most ardent advocates of the idea of race also underline this by their reluctance to allow too close an identification of a notion that owes most of its social usefulness to its vagueness and the licence that it permits. If the dominant group calls itself 'white' and reserves to itself the right to say who is 'black'; if the Aryan groups follow in the footsteps of Goebbels who said to Fritz Lang, 'Mr Lang, *we* are the ones who decide who's a Jew'; if in South Africa the State decrees that those of Chinese origin are 'non-white', though this does not apply to those of Japanese origin – all this is not inconsistency, but on the contrary a strict equating of categorization to political aims and ends. Politics really defines things in accordance with its own needs and practices, not in accordance with the alleged factual characteristics of the things defined. Whatever the pretence, these characteristics enter into the definition only as signs and not as causes.

The idea, if idea it can be called, that a human social group is a natural formation grew up in the course of the eighteenth and nineteenth centuries. The idea of race as a natural group was given legal status in the twentieth century, especially, but not exclusively, by the countries practising Nazism and apartheid. But it began in the racial classification of the nineteenth century.

TAXONOMIES OF RACE

The history, or rather, the pre-history, of the idea of race began with a legal definition. It was, however, very different from the modern one and dealt with social relationships, not with true or alleged physical characteristics. I refer to the laws on the annexation of human beings, of slavery – the annexation of a whole labour force, as occurred in the period from the end of the seventeenth century to the beginning of the nineteenth, when agricultural production in the West Indies and the United States was being industrialized.[7]

The spread of modern slavery as distinct from the feudal serfdom which attached a man to the soil rather than annexing him as a tool, was intensified by the transition from mixed to single-crop plantations, and was soon reinforced by a classification of human beings according to intellectual and epistemological criteria. And also according to geography: Linné and then Buffon put forward human taxonomies based on territorial incidence: *Homo afer, asiaticus, europeus*, etc.[8] For a few decades slaves were recruited both in Europe and in Africa; but the trade soon concentrated almost exclusively on particular areas (chiefly the Gulf of Guinea and East Africa). Is it pure chance that this exclusivity was soon followed by an attempt to divide human beings into categories? One may doubt it.

After several earlier efforts of a sporadic nature which were not pursued,[9] these attempts at classification began to take shape in the middle of the eighteenth century. And it was in Europe that this happened, where modern science was being created and where men were working out a set of rules and laws concerning the material world. For these attempts at classification were only part of a whole system of taxonomies dealing with everything that was 'thinkable', not merely the morphological and geographical aspects of the animal and vegetable kingdoms but also inert matter, legal systems and social forms, both historical and contemporary. The study of peoples distant in space, like the Polynesians and the American Indians, or in time, like the ancient Greeks and Romans, played an important part in the social analysis then being carried out.[10] After several centuries of normative or Utopian accounts of humanity and the world, the establishment of the power of the bourgeoisie introduced a new kind of account claiming to be objective, classificatory and impartial (the latter because it was allegedly governed solely by intelligence and virtue). The views and attitudes of Buffon and Montesquieu on social relationships were quite different in nature and aim from those of More, Machiavelli or Pascal. The object of the eighteenth-century thinkers was to impose an intelligible order upon a disorder no longer capable of interpretation as the decrees of Providence or the will of the Prince. In a way, the analysts of the Age of Reason were more concerned with imposing order than with finding a meaning or revealing some transcendental power.

The order they gradually introduced hierarchized and classified the elements that went to make up the world and that received much more attention than did the relations between those elements. It was an age more interested in varieties and species than in mechanisms, an age fertile in entities, or what we today would call beings or essences. Not only were particular things like sulphur and vital fluid, *Homo americanus* and *europeus*, the legislative and the executive, the objects of its thought, but also virtue, childhood, barbarism and so on, all regarded as clearly distinct essences with intrinsic qualities. Every sphere of inquiry was like a set of dominoes tumbled into confusion because it was no longer held together by divine order – or as if an immense heap of pebbles were lying about for man, now Man with a capital M, to appropriate and annex.

There were immediate practical reasons for trying to organize and name the pebbles. The terrain they lay in was not a desert waste, but a field being feverishly explored and manipulated, the object of fierce competition. By classifying mankind into groups, Linné and Buffon multiplied the possibilities of annexation, ranging from commerce in goods to commerce in human beings, which were being extended through war, exploration and the partitioning of the globe and its inhabitants – an operation still going on today in different forms. At the same time as the world of objects, Man himself and his political systems were to be subjected to the scrutiny – and the analysis – of the bourgeoisie's surveyors, who measured not only the world and the labour force, but also the body of the labourer. It was thus that men came to be classified, together with the uses that could be made of them and the study of those uses.

But was it a racial classification? Not exactly, and not at first. As we have seen, Linnaeus and Buffon, the two great pioneers, tended towards localization of human groups in space rather than in endogenous class- ifications. Moreover, Buffon attributed somatic characteristics to the effects of climate and thought that they changed with geographical movement. Localization in space was specified, however, in terms of physical traits like skin and growth of hair. But these were only the secondary terms in which taxonomies were expressed: classification actually based on somatic characteristics was not to come until later. The eighteenth century adopted it enthusiastically if vicariously, but while it made use of the physical characteristics of types of men it did not regard them as the foundation of human categories. As yet, taxonomies were not in themselves racial affirmations in the modern sense. They did not extend to the belief that race is a factor of social movement, because the idea of relationships, if not absent altogether, was then much less im- portant than the intrinsic characteristics of groups. In any case, the thought that historical relationships might be determined by characteristics endogenous to each relevant group never crossed the minds of social analysts like Diderot (*Supplément au voyage de Bougainville*) or Condorcet (*Tableau des progrès de l'esprit humain*), whereas half a century later it was the central preoccupation of Gobineau and Spencer. In short, no one dreamed as yet of looking for the driving force of history in somatic characteristics: early taxonomies were more concerned with separating in order to distinguish than with linking in order to explain. The nineteenth-century idea of race, on the other hand, was, like our own, dominated by relationship. True, it dealt in relationships between natural entities, but it did deal in relationships: both natural entities and relationships between them are necessary to a conception of the world in terms of race.

It should be noted that while these taxonomies were being devised, the individual did not yet exist legally. The world was divided into social groups (States, castes, etc.) rather than individual units. In a way it might be said that pre-bourgeois holism conceived of a reality transcending the existence of individuals, who were seen as mere elements. Nevertheless, in this pre-racial period, social and political science did begin to describe social forms on the theoretical basis of the idea of contract. Rousseau's *Contrat social* (1762), the first attempt to describe the way societies come into being, is an example of this, and so are Montesquieu's *Esprit des lois* (1748) and Rousseau's own early work, the *Discours sur l'inégalité* (1754). The individual is here being introduced into social analysis, but still only at a theoretical level. In practice, social structure remained that of the State, which did not recognize the individual at all. The bourgeoisie expressed its individualism in works which were abstract and not descriptive of concrete social facts. In the social philosophies of the time all processes derived from consensus between individuals, idealized parties to free contracts. The middle-class *philosophes* were dreaming up the Republic. Rousseau and Itard place at the centre of their politics the individual-king: whether influenced by his environment or the originator of policy, he is the ultimate theoretical reference, while social organization remains syncretic, States alone having real existence.

THE EMERGENCE OF THE IDEA OF NATURAL GROUPS

Colonization as it existed in the seventeenth and eighteenth centuries – a commercial activity, a search for trading posts and trafficking in labour – assumed or implied an ideological naïvety or brutality which was reflected in a practice that felt no need for naturalistic justification. 'What trade', asked the Nantes Chamber of Commerce, 'can compare with that which exchanges men for goods!'[11] Men in the mass were simply held equal to merchandise. The current taxonomies were part of a general arrangement of the physical world, and were accompanied by, though not based on, a system of somatic characteristics later to become inseparable from them. But it should be noted that at the time this bracketing together was not compulsory. Taxonomies did not yet assert that social relationships were governed by natural causality. It was only at a later stage that bourgeois thinkers came to invent the idea of race in its modern sense.

For this to happen it was necessary to gain some knowledge of social antagonisms, and this knowledge derived from the Age of Enlightenment's discovery of individuality. Social functioning had somewhere to produce autonomy and liberty if human groups were to rise above the status of mere 'things' and knowledge of distinct social forms arose only out of revolutionary conflicts and the contradictions they contained. More accurate knowledge of definite social groups, together with observation of their antagonisms, relationships and separate practices, gave rise to the modern conception of history as a study of relationships between a multiplicity of human groups.

It was this awareness of multiplicity which produced the first phase of the modern system of interpretation which embodies the notion of race, or the *belief that groups are naturally diverse, because of endogenous characteristics which are determining factors in themselves, independently of history or economics*. This attitude developed at the same time as military forms of colonialism at the beginning of the nineteenth century. Though these enterprises were primarily concerned with territorial conquest, they involved social formations, already national in character, which were more extensive and coherent than those relevant to the commercial conquests of the previous centuries. French colonization of Algeria began in 1830; in 1833 the British Government took over the monopoly of the East India Company; and the wars arising out of this kind of policy brought peoples as such face to face with one another.

The first half of the nineteenth century produced theories which tended to interpret revolutionary upheavals – the storms of which had not yet subsided – as the results of competition between groups 'naturally' different from one another: examples were the struggle between conquerors and conquered (as in the case of the Teutons and Gauls), or that between nobles and commoners (Franks and Gauls). Though political philosophy was no novelty, science was relatively new and was regarded as a description of facts followed by investigation of the laws governing their interrelationships. The idea that relationships between human groups could be approached scientifically was also new, and this was one of its earliest manifestations. But to the assertion that reality as a whole, and human relationships in particular, were not governed by an order hidden from and incomprehensible to man, came the tempting answer of an interpretation based on 'natural' order. The idea of determinism in Nature was the chief victory of the new scientific spirit; it was to develop slowly and have many consequences.

In the nineteeth century, then, social amalgams became groups of individuals – individuals linked together by their natural character.[12] The expression of the group idea in such terms as 'Aryan' or 'Negro' was something quite different from its expression in terms of slaves or nobles. It is irrelevant that the term 'Negro' came to be used in relations involving slavery: eighteenth-century dictionaries give 'slave' and 'Negro' as equivalents; or that the use of 'Aryan' is derived from linguistic analysis and the classification of languagues into Indo-European and Semitic. Both terms soon came to form part of a naturalist conception of social groups, and to signify what had just been invented, namely the idea that social groups were 'races' or 'natural amalgams'.

It should be noted in passing that the word 'race', itself ancient, acquired a connotation of naturalness. Before the eighteenth century it did not possess the taxonomic meaning that it has today. In feudal and monarchic society it merely signified the 'familial unity' of the ruling class, though the notion of procreation was not insistently dwelt on. The word was just a name in strict terms of class, applying only to those who could hand down seigneurial property, and not to the common people. But at the beginning of the nineteenth century its meaning changed completely: it came to be applied to various human groups of a certain size, and to involve the idea of somatic cohesion, together with the notion that such groups were naturally constituted.

Meanwhile, as the idea of Nature came into being, so did the idea of 'society' and of separate and different societies, instead of the one great Society of Man. In place of the single human society subject to and contrasted with God, there were many different human societies scattered through time and space. From now on the world consisted of finite groups in relation with one another, no longer of one united and continuous humanity. This was the great idea produced by the nineteenth century, the age which saw the creation of the sciences. Whether we ascribe it to the historical school which includes Guizot and Michelet, or to what might be called the 'societism' that ranges from Proudhon to Marx, or again to the line of social philosophers from Gobineau to Comte and Durkheim, the dominant idea of the century was that social groups and societies are varied, that they are characterized by their relationships and to a certain extent are modified by them.

Montesquieu and Rousseau presupposed a society closed in on itself and ending with itself, having in a sense no history, its only possible relationships being external, such as those of war and trade, deemed not to involve its real substance. Victory and defeat could not change that society, even though they could affect the way it lived. While the eighteenth century saw only the finiteness of society, and saw it as a totality, the nineteenth began to discover rifts, relationships and antagonisms. The bourgeois revolutions had had their effect. And the idea of race only came into being through awareness of profound social changes.

Paradoxically, the idea of race, an over-simplified notion if ever there was one, emerged, like the idea of class, out of a complex and manifold set of factors and involved many different elements. It is not to be confused with the idea of *estate* or *status*. It does not derive from a static and hierarchical view of the world. On the contrary, it strains towards that view, which is very different. Its source lies in an awareness of the antagonisms and power relationships which disturb the very organization of society.[13] Marx was to regard Thierry as the father of the class struggle. The idea of race came into being as a premonition of structure.

Hence the practical ambiguity that has caused it to be accepted – with alacrity or with considerable reserves, but still accepted – by the great majority of historians and social analysts of the nineteenth century and of today.

Bourgeois or industrial society was to replace the ideology of estates and hierarchy by that of an economic system of antagonistic groups, a system of exploitation. This same society, having invented the 'rational' appropriation of things both material and human, also invented the idea of a reservoir of material and human objects to be marshalled and described by science and exploited by labour. This reservoir was Nature. But the exploitation of human groups, now liberated by bourgeois revolution and rendered more mobile by being broken down into free individuals, themselves so tangible, having emerged from the world of objects, was ascribed to a form of Nature invented in the same way as those other ideas – Nature no longer a mere reservoir as it had been in the eighteenth century, but an efficient power discernible through the frenzies of romanticism and in process of being systematically developed by science. The best modern embodiment of this idea of efficiency is the belief in the genetic determinism of social behaviour. No sooner was the individual freed than he was imprisoned again, this time in the chains of somato-genetic determinism. Thus the dominated or oppressed were explained in terms of natural constraints.[14]

Also during the last two centuries, in parallel with their pursuit of the 'scientific' interpretation, the thinkers and activists of the rising class, soon to become the ruling class, developed their ideas on inequality and the influence of groups upon one another.

LEGAL EXPRESSION OF THE NATURALNESS OF RACE, AND THE APPROPRIATION OF HUMAN BEINGS

From the subject and the period with which we are concerned – the idea of natural groups from the eighteenth century up to the present day – the chief factor among those affecting social relationships consists in ownership of oneself. This is the more easily understood because it found legal expression, probably as a simple variant of property in general. Specific cases apart, one could be excluded for life from ownership of oneself by slavery, serfdom or sex. Partial or temporary exclusion arises from being under the age of majority, from hiring oneself out, from enlistment and from certain kinds of contract; but such partial and temporary exclusions do not carry with them a total naturalistic sentence against the groups in question.

Citizenship, also a legal category, is derived from ownership of the self, and nationalist movements have accorded it only to those supposed to enjoy complete possession of themselves as well as property in land or chattels. Subject peoples, wives and servants have, at various times since the category of citizen was invented, been excluded from it. Race, which became a legal category after citizenship, is also related to ownership of the self.

In the period of history with which we are dealing there was a general change of focus in the legal rules reflecting and governing relations between people. The law, which in the first instance consisted of rules governing relations with things, was supposed to deal with their possession and exchange. There was little room for the organizing of individual status, which in any case scarcely existed. To take an example, members of the Assembly of the States-General which immediately preceded the Revolution of 1789 were, in the case of the two chief estates, the nobility and the clergy, recruited on the basis of material possessions, actually in the form of land. The envoys of these two proprietorial estates – whether agents, stewards, legal owners or administrators, and whatever their age or sex – could sit in the Assembly because of what, not whom, they represented. Individual status (apart from the fact of actually belonging to the estate in question) was completely disregarded, so that women might be found in the Assembly representing the Church or the nobility. This was rare, but it did happen in the primary Assemblies. Any such situation became unimaginable after the institution of the Code Napoléon in the early nineteenth century, when individual status became central and decisive, involving criteria of sex, age (majority) and personal property. And so individual status – class, sex, and today race – came to take the place of the status of the estate or group to which the individual belonged irrespective of his or her fundamental personal characteristics. Groups were defined by their possessions, not by their relationships with other groups.

In those days some people were still things and not the possessors of things. Serfs belonged to the land they were attached to, in the same way as crops, trees and game (in France the last serfs were emancipated in 1770). In the organized slave trade the human tools of the plantation economy were sold by the ton and not as individuals. At the end of the eighteenth century the constitutional documents of the United States distinguished between men who were imported (Afro-Americans) and immigrants (Euro-Americans).[15] Another century had to pass before the first were emancipated.

Bourgeois individualism – the belief that an individual exists independently of his social relationships, exists in himself with his own personal characteristics – had not yet emerged clearly. For that to happen, another kind of appropriation was necessary – the annexation of man's labour power in place of the annexation of his whole physical body. Then came the legal expression of individuality, which in turn gave rise to the legal expression of membership of a race. The process of rationalizing the exploitation of human beings started with the seizure of bodies and the use of their power to work and reproduce, and culminated in the enunciation of an intrinsic physical quality which sanctioned appropriation. As the degree of formal liberty accorded to the appropriated workers increased – i.e. their interchangeability and mobility – so too the ideological rationalization of this situation was reinforced. Their condition was no longer held to be due to a state of dependence, as in serfdom or slavery, but to their very nature.

This nature, which could be appropriated by anyone, became an inner characteristic, a natural and everlasting specificity, a genetically derived ability to be always and everywhere available for whatever use the dominant group chose to make of one.[16] Appropriation no longer involved the personal element of a certain place or a particular master; it was no longer explicable through a given social status; it was one of your specific qualities, not merely constraining you, as before, but identical with and inseparable from you yourself.

Early evidence of this can be seen in the seventeenth century, when certain American citizens had to prove that they were free although their skins were black. The fact that a black skin implied slavery was not yet a symptom of 'race', but it was a harbinger of the 'nature' soon to triumph, first in literature and politics, then in science, then in law. Legally speaking, slavery was not a racial distinction: whether one was deprived of one's rights or able to exercise them fully depended on one's place in the system of economic relationships. This place was seen in terms of possession of one's self. It was only later that the ability or inability to exercise one's rights came to be explicitly ascribed to 'nature', and somatic characteristics came to occupy a central (though not, of course, a causal) place in the practical and legal determination of the rights of social groups. Studies in heredity and biology during the second half of the nineteenth and in the twentieth century transformed the somatic into the 'genetic'. It was a change, vivid today, that did even more than the legal acceptance of race to reinforce the effects of the domination and exploitation of dependent groups.

The more the methods of appropriating people's bodies or labour came to be rationalized and systematized, the more, at the same time, the ideologists sought for a natural explanation of social groups. And the ideological explanation tended to be transformed into scientific and legal categories. Also, and the paradox is only an apparent one, the dominant groups now tended to think of themselves as belonging to a race, i.e. to attribute to themselves supposedly natural characteristics. Racialization, or the attribution of race, at first exercised *vis-à-vis* dependent and exploited groups, was only applied to dominant groups later, usually at the stage of legalization.

Hence the establishment of a system of human 'races' was a somewhat intermittent affair in the nineteenth century. The imputation or denomination of race might be applied to one only out of the several social groups involved in a relationship. To begin with they were applied by preference to groups which were oppressed, and the dominant group might well think of itself as unaffected by the system and unmarked by the brand of 'nature'. 'Race', applied only to dependent groups, was a category invented in the breeding of domestic animals; to themselves the dominant groups applied the more general term of humanity, explicitly free of animal connotations. It was not until the first half of the twentieth century that the term 'race' came to be applied to all groups and not only to those under domination. But even today the old doctrine remains plainly visible: it is still the dominated groups which are most often referred to in racial terms, not only, as might be expected, by the person in the street, but also by science, which persists in trying to define and enclose with indelible markers the groups which do not dominate. Dominant groups never quite believe that they themselves belong to a race, even today.

The ideology of race probably reached its climax when the notion came to be extended to dominant as well as dominated groups. This was the point at which racial category was given legal expression, and each social agent held to belong to an unchangeable category which was at once part of society and determined by something outside society. The development of naturalist theory produced racial-type distinctions applying to dominant groups (whites within apartheid, Aryans in the Nazi system, men in the system of the sexes), as well as others applying to dominated groups (women, Jews, blacks in those same systems). The law proclaimed the racial distinctness of both dominant and dominated groups. Unlike everyday racialism, its legal expression forced dominant groups to apply a racial criterion to themselves in order to ensure the juridical isolation of the oppressed, the ultimate phase of physical oppression. Most European countries are still at a pre-juridical stage of racialization in that they still apply racial criteria to dominated groups only.

By the turn of the century the naturalist beliefs developed in the preceding decades had been transformed into legal rules, thus institutionalizing at the State level the constricting relationships already slowly built up in practice. The notion of race has thus become a basic legal category alongside such other qualifications of the individual as those of age, sex and nationality. Restrictive laws in some industrial countries excluded subordinate groups and what were regarded as racial minorities according to various criteria: historical (length of time the group had been established in the country); cultural (literates versus illiterates); economic (considerations of income and property). These rationalizations were long in use, and still are today for the same purpose, though rationalized from a somewhat different angle. But it was not until this century that the criterion of race came to be expressed deliberately and society held to be conditioned by the 'physical nature' of its members and in accordance with the somato-biological groups they belonged to. The criterion became explicit in the Jim Crow laws in the United States at the end of the nineteenth century; in the Nuremberg laws in Nazi Germany in 1933; and the South African laws on apartheid passed in and since 1948. The Nuremberg laws limited citizenship to Aryans and excluded non-Aryans from certain professions, certain forms of ownership, government service, public life, and so on. The laws on apartheid made race the legal criterion of individual rights.

Nothing fundamentally new emerged in the two centuries regarding the content of intellectual and scientific discussion of physical appropriation, but they did take on increasingly sophisticated forms, as the methods of appropriation acquired more technical efficiency. Such strictly operational phenomena as the exploitation and extermination of Jews by the European Nazis or the exploitation of the Africans by apartheid in southern Africa demonstrate that legalization is a technical device paving the way to social practices. The apparently super-structural effect of a practice becomes in its turn an active element in that practice and in its systematization.

Legal ratification of practices already in existence is, of course, a standard process, but there is something special about the racial laws of the twentieth century. Laws usually express some factual reality of an economic character: property, history, age, and so on. But with the racial laws the legal criterion became overlaid by the ideological one of 'natural' affiliation. The alleged 'fact' is always related to a mythical past. Let us take the divisions black/white and Jewish/Aryan as examples of 'natural' legal categories. A person is regarded as Jewish if both parents or three grandparents were Jewish (but what made *them*

Jews?). A person is regarded as black if one parent is black (but what made that parent black?). Contrariwise, a person is held to be Aryan, or white, if he is not Jewish, not black. In fact, however far back one pushes the origin of the physical or 'race' criterion, one ends up face to face with the social criteria underlying the invention of the idea of 'race'. Going back in time one finds the social relationships which preceded the modern imputation of race – the slavery of the pre-industrial age, or the religious community of the *ancien régime* – in other words, something quite different from what we are led to believe. We are asked to regard social characteristics as natural and endogenous – to snap our fingers at history and practical relationships, and place our hopes in a natural order. The great advocates of the naturalness of human groups are always great advocates of law and order.

The legal enunciation of the physical (somatic, genetic, etc.) characteristics of citizens, nationals, individuals, and so on is the present stage in a history which has crystallized social relationships into fixed notions, the notion now in question being that of the natural social agent as member of a natural group.

In the various stages through which the attribution of naturalness has passed, what was really at issue? The law proclaimed a right, or in other words, ratified a practice already established in fact.[17] In this context of natural order, the right was the right to the appropriation of labour, which does not necessarily imply the right to immediate use but does imply the right of availability, or postponed manipulation. But this appropriation is 'natural' only when it does not involve a transformation of the forces of production. (When it involves not transformation but only development, it corresponds to industrial development rather than to the birth of industry, which did not go any further than mere taxonomy.) The appropriation of labour was part of a process of which the transfer of labour constitutes a good example: in the European factories of the nineteenth century, in the mines of modern South Africa, and in the Nazi concentration camps, forced labour was taken from the primary and tertiary sectors (subsistence agriculture and the service industries) and transformed into the secondary. The German war effort, mining, and industrial rationalization are not technical novelties but the rationalization of already existing forms, specially adapted uses of labour.

But should the notions of 'race' and 'sex', taxonomic to begin with and then juridical, be regarded without further argument as a reflection of actual exploitation, or as its intellectual rationalization? The question is inevitable, and no doubt both answers are to a certain extent present in these scientific and juridical formulations. But fundamentally the problem does not seem to present itself in these terms. The practices involved can develop without undergoing a process of rationalization while, historically speaking, the legal aspect of the idea, as we have seen, has often emerged from previously existing social forms. In such cases there is a transformation rather than the creation of an idea. Domination, a power relationship, may be established without appeal to rationalization: while fifteenth- and sixteenth-century speculations on the nature of the North American Indian brought to heel by the conquerors gave rise to theological debate as to whether the Redemption applied to them, there was no such debate about the nature of the Africans, though what was at stake was their subjection by the very people who rallied to the Indians' defence. But their presence on American soil, and hence their real enslavement, still lay in the future, so that the relationship was potential rather than real. The importance of this distinction lies in the fact that rationalization came after and not before the initiation of practice. The idea of 'nature' underlies appropriation only when it has become actual practice, not when it is still at the planning stage.

We are thus dealing with a practical logic of domination, its intellectual, mental or symbolic aspect, rather than with a real everyday relationship. Nothing could be less abstract than the idea of a natural social group, or it never occurs except in the context of an existing power relationship, and that is the crux of the matter. An ideology or interpretation of reality which balanced the *right* of the oppressors against the *nature* of the oppressed, each conceivable only in terms of the other and both belonging to the actual practice of appropriation, could hardly be described either as reflection (which presupposes the separateness of the practical and symbolic levels) or as rationalization, which presupposes not only the same separateness but also an intellectual ingredient in the exercise of domination which is not always present in hard fact.

Domination and exploitation on the one hand and the idea of natural groups on the other are two sides of the same coin, and both can be discerned in scientific interpretations. Dominant groups can be explained in terms of social (or human) laws, or the general laws governing the animal kingdom. The effect of domination, of the rights exercised by some people over others, is thus paraphrased in scientific works which completely ignore their own epistemological asymmetry,[18] obvious though it is. The notion of race is a scientific invention of this sort; and theories of racial relationships may perhaps be accounted for in the same way, for some of them assert that there is a 'natural' element in certain social processes – in short, that some human groups are more natural than others. Otherwise it is hard to see how this 'special case' in social relationships came to be invented, where the speciality consists in the 'natural' element of race.

SCIENTIFIC EXPRESSION ON THE NATURALNESS OF SOCIAL GROUPS

We should begin by noting that, implicitly or explicitly, the social sciences are here mainly concerned with relations of conflict – those of antagonism or confrontation. 'Relationships' is a euphemism at which one hardly knows whether to laugh or wonder. So-called 'race' relations are relations of exploitation, domination and violence. Other kinds of social relationships do not resort to naturalistic camouflage: they are explained in terms of politics and economics without appeal to nature. The word 'relationships', usually associated with adjectives like 'friendly', 'social', 'intimate', 'professional', 'personal' and so on, has little to do with the power conflicts involved in so-called 'race' relationships. For in fact, what is the real context of the theorists' observations and treatises? The real context is conquest, ordinary or colonialist, the voyages of 'discovery', plantation society, industrial concentration, crisis economy, war economy, and so on – all of which have nothing to do with 'race', a term that is hypocritical rather than technical. It leaves out the very element which contributes most of its own use in a racial context: technical and economic power. This is no accident, since description in terms of race denies or disguises the real relationship and holds Nature responsible for it.

The point is not merely academic, since the joining of the word 'racial' to 'relationships' leads straight to that specific category of social relationships which in turn calls up ideas of Nature and 'inevitability' affecting both the groups and their interrelations.

Between the mere characterization of human groups in somatic terms (first stage), the enunciation of the idea that their 'natural' characteristics are subject to endogenous reproduction (second stage), and the belief that physical characteristics are the cause of social relationships with other groups (third stage), there lies a whole historical and ideological development. The idea of race as we know it combines the last two stages. Today, even though some people deny it, the idea of race cannot be separated from the whole of which it is an active part. That whole no longer consists in a naturalist view of social groups themselves, but in a naturalist view of their behaviour.

What are the changes which have caused the idea of race to develop from the taxonomic to the active stage? The earliest explicit stratum of the ideology in question (first half of the nineteenth century) was the idea that a group's socio-mental qualities were closely linked to its physical characteristics. Negroes' brains were black, women's brains were small, in the same specific way as these same groups had a special form of intelligence to go with their special skin or sex. It went without saying that there was a fundamental likeness or interpenetration between somatic and mental forms, though this did not quite amount to determinism, or to causality in our modern sense of the word. Strange as it may seem, at this stage race was still emblematic, and closer to medieval symbolism than to would-be scientific determinism. Social groups were conceived of in terms of homogeneity and syncretism rather than of determination and causality. The group was thought of as an immediate datum from nature – somehow without a past and without relationships with other groups. The fact that it had a natural cohesion, whether ante-social or a-social, was, as we have seen, connected with the belief that social and mental characteristics emerged directly from this naturalness without any other intervening process than that which materialized their essential and immutable potentialities. This technical and intellectual invention was regarded as a genetic potentiality, actualized at a given moment in accordance with circumstance and individual 'genius'. The 'spontaneous' invention of agriculture, of genetic origin, was one example of this type of reasoning among others.[19]

There still remains the obsessional linking of physical characteristics with social relationships or, more accurately, the invention of physical characteristics to go with the social relationships of domination. Wherever there is a power relationship, a somatic trait is found or invented. The classifications of physical anthropology are a 'scientific' application of this mechanism.

'Scientific' in inverted commas, indeed, because the social origins of the notion of race are clear. In social history there is always a time-lag between the invention of certain categories of thought and their adoption by the exact or natural or social sciences. This is particularly marked in the case of naturalism, at least as applied to the human race.

I have already said that the early idea of 'race' in the sense of a large human group was a recording, written in terms of physical characteristics, of social divisions such as slavery. The second stage, at the beginning of the nineteenth century, linked socio-mental and allegedly physical characteristics on the basis of factors which might be historical (bourgeois revolutions), linguistic (the study of the Indo-European and

Semitic languages), cultural, and so on. This pre-Darwinian idea of race, as enunciated by Thierry and Gobineau, arose out of social observations and preoccupations with history, and *preceded* the establishment by the natural sciences of an idea of race which involved the notion of the temporal continuity of characteristics. Natural science inherited the view of the world arrived at by the *philosophes*, the historians and the men of letters, and not the other way round. The linking of somatic and mental traits was given a scientific and determinist basis, and chronological continuity, first by the invention of the notion of the heredity of somatic traits during the second half of the nineteenth century (Mendel, 1865), then by progress in genetics in the late 1920s and 1930s (Morgan won the Nobel Prize in 1933), and then by the birth of molecular biology (Watson, Wilkins and Crick, 1962). For whatever reservations geneticists in the strict sense of the word may express, the ideological bracketing together of the two kinds of characteristics derives a façade of legitimacy from research on the processes of transmission of somatic characteristics.

The modern idea of race derives not from observation in the field of the natural sciences but from the instigation of society and politics. Political and social theories, not only those of professional thinkers, but also popular ones of which the latter have taken advantage, raised questions to which the natural sciences sought to find the answers, in the form of roots or traces, during the years that followed. The racial theories of the end of the nineteenth century and the beginning of the twentieth, those of Spencer, of the social Darwinist school – and those of Hitler – preceded intense activity on the part of the biologists during the 1930s and great efforts by physical anthropologists in a Europe obsessed by 'race'.

It is only comparatively recently that practical research has been undertaken in the recording of genetic characteristics and their chromosome location, and not until the last few years have there been practical experiments in artificial genetic translocation. The first group of genes was isolated in 1962, though the idea of the genetic basis of intelligence dates from the beginning of this century. While genetics proper still concentrates on somatic characteristics (as in the age of Mendel, though animals have replaced plants and fruit flies are used instead of peas), there is a large mixed area of biological research which links social characteristics (aggressivity, intelligence, performance, alcoholism, etc.) with traits that are morphological (stature, sex, colour, and so on) or physio-chemical (uric acid, lactose, G6PD, etc.), either through the postulate of 'self-evidence' or by drawing up sets of statistics supposed to prove that some social or socio-mental characteristic is genetically determined. In any case, the context is one which identifies morphological traits with social ones, holding that the former symbolize and express the latter, though this relationship is never even analysed.

The history of 'intelligence' is significant in this factual situation. Intelligence tests were developed as an aid to educational policy, and the Binet-Simon scale initiated a long series of IQ measurements which were used and improved upon for some fifty years, chiefly in the United States. But they have done much to add to the misunderstanding. Such tests, which are still in use, have given rise to the invention of the 'g factor', which might be said to represent intelligence as a natural characteristic. Though specialists deny that the use of these tests amounts to genetic prediction, the denial is formal and superficial. Implicitly the notion of intelligence is still imbued with that of naturalness, and much of the biological research just referred to treats it explicitly as a genetic trait. Indeed, the revival of the theory that every social group has its own specific natural characteristics has laid much stress on IQs, which have played a large part in the empirical research underlying the recent reassertion of the genetic character of social traits.[20]

Most biologists, and especially geneticists, adopt an attitude of reserve, if not of hostility, towards the 'fictions' of the philosophers and the human sciences, but they themselves do not hesitate to make use of social criteria in their own work, for example in selecting a field of inquiry, and seem unaware that their deep analyses are often no more than 'common sense'. They seem not to realize that such criteria have no place in their own science. What meaning can be attached to 'intelligence' or 'aggressivity' in biology or genetics? Or rather, what meaning can they have outside a context of social relationship? In a recent interview concerning some research he had carried out on a certain genetic trait (sickle-cell anaemia), a scientist said: 'This trait is specific to Blacks (it was first discovered in Afro-Americans, and then found again in Africa), but strangely enough it is also found in India, among white people'. Strange indeed, and the scientist could only say such a thing because he *accepts* a social distinction between black and white. So ingrained is the belief in the existence of race that this scientist can say with a perfectly straight face that a certain trait is specific to one race and then immediately contradict himself: social imperatives are so much stronger that he can declare that races exist and in the next breath put forward the contradiction as a curiosity, an exception, an oddity. Such aberrations, though frequent, are not usually so obvious, and as a general rule the empirical categories of the natural sciences coincide with social divisions. One may even find religious or national groupings being taken as explicit fields for biological research.

Ever since it first began, and as it developed and became more sophisticated, the classification of human beings has adopted – with a certain time-lag – the ideological notions arising out of social relationships between groups. The gradual confining of social relationships within a finite and inflexible 'Nature' is evident throughout the whole process, from the taxonomies of living beings (including man) (1750), through the heredity of anatomical characteristics (1865), to molecular biology and the genetic determination of separate traits (1960), into which relational traits such as aggressivity, intelligence, docility, and so on have been gradually reconciled and incorporated.

It is also evident that beneath the formal protests, both ethical and political, it is social relationships that still foster the ideas of Nature and of the natural character of human groups. The great interest devoted nowadays to the biological sciences bears witness to this: such studies are accorded a predominant place in the human sciences and in science in general. The growth of this tendency in the course of the last ten years has given rise to controversies which reveal quite clearly what is at stake behind the scientific options, though no attempt is made to identify the reasons why such choices are made.[21] The growing diversification of the biological sciences helps to explain why their adherence to a racial conception of society is not clearer, except to a small periphery of scientists. Whether it is a question of the genetic code, of the definition of genes themselves, or of less recent chromosome research, the focus has now become so fine and specialized that the links of this kind of research with human behaviour are rarely expressed except in relation to 'psychological' traits, deviant or marginal behaviour, such as madness or crime, psychic weakness or alcoholism, all regarded as individual forms except by that minority of social scientists who see them as the effects of social relationships.[22] In any case, the direct association of somatic or physiological traits with social groups *taken as a whole* has become more rare, though it is still encountered.[23] The genetics of human population, for their part, have moved away from naturalism, and in some cases are in the process of breaking away from the traditional categories dictated by social relationships.[24]

But animal ethology (metaphorically applied to humans), biosociology, biochemistry, etc. still characterize and analyse according to naturalist attitudes; taken all together, such projects amount to an extension and refinement of the idea of natural order beside which the early racial theories and the old physical anthropology were random thoughts.

The basic postulate of all the present forms of thinking is the idea that a human group may be physically (or as common sense would put it, 'objectively') specific *in itself*, independently of its relationships or practices. Practically speaking, theories of racial relationships rest on the postulate that there are biologically specific groups within the human race, and that these are separate from one another and recognizable by somatic, genetic and physiological criteria – in short, by criteria which can be measured physically. All the rest really stems from that notion.

Nowadays classification rests on genetic criteria that are 'invisible' but derive directly from those of skin colour or sex. I say 'rests' rather than 'is based' because as they grow more sophisticated, the new criteria lose their comprehensive discriminatory force and instead of applying generally to each (or every) individual of the group in question apply only to the majority or even merely to some individuals. But this does not weaken the belief that groups are genetically determined. On the contrary, the characteristics which are now specific instead of general define the groups involved even more efficiently than before.[25]

Homo afer, asiaticus, europeus, etc., once defined by his geographical origin together with the colour of his skin, is or might be classified today by a genetic peculiarity. For example, in the case of *Homo afer* (and it is no accident that he is the subject of research and propositions in the United States), the distinguishing feature might be sickle-cell anaemia, which originated in the Gulf of Guinea. A certain Nobel prize winner has suggested that it should be indicated by a tattoo mark on the person's forehead, which would make the distinction even more 'visible'.[26] Thus the African origin of a haematological characteristic is made the justification for the branding of members of a social group, all of whom would be potentially threatened. The transition reflects the whole history that runs from geographical taxonomy to genetic determinism and its specific expression in the idea of race. Much of modern research in human biology is devoted to the search for 'genetic markers': discriminatory factors are still sought after and socially desired. It is not surprising that this research includes studies in legal medicine.[27]

The idea of natural groups marks the birth of the modern proletariat, first slave then wage-earner, transferred first from Africa and Europe to America, then from the outskirts of Europe to this or that industrial metropolis. This process is not finished: the nineteenth century's colonization by territorial conquest, which succeeded the opening of trading posts and impressment of labour characteristic of the eighteenth century, was itself followed after 1914 by a new phase in the appropriation of labour – the current of migration was reversed when the people of what was not yet called the 'Third World' started to move towards the big towns.[28] So it is no surprise to see that the science born in the metropolis and nursed by the dominant groups is in hot pursuit of the physical specification of human groups.

The category of 'race' and its invention reflect a kind of relationship between human groups. It is not an empirically verifiable category (though many attempts are made to make it appear so) nor a concept (close scrutiny has always been carefully avoided), but a practical relationship which has been crystallized in a pseudo-scientific form, the form of racial taxonomy and its successive historical implications.

Here some observations are called for on the 'self-evidence' of physical characteristics, which is supposed to go without saying. In fact characteristics are not as significant as is currently supposed. Are black and white, red and yellow, immediate data of perception? These crude colours have a history; they did not spring from the brow of Nature fully armed. They appear and disappear at definite historical moments. Moreover, they have played a comparatively minor role in the process of 'scientific' construction which led from geographic labelling to genetic markers. In terms of taxonomy, they represent only a brief moment – but that brief moment has had an enormous popular success. If we now see these characteristics as a self-evident means of classification, the reason is that they exist through the social use which is made of them and its significance.

The process did not arise spontaneously out of some impartial view divested of all practical experience. On these perceptions, slowly arrived at but very efficiently made to seem 'self-evident', rests the 'spontaneous' notion of human race.[29] We thus see a social practice becoming an unquestioned postulate in two major scientific fields, the natural sciences on the one hand and the social sciences on the other. For the notion rests on a presupposition; it is not something which has been demonstrated or explained (it has always been regarded as beyond proof). Unlike a truly operational notion, it has neither empirical nor conceptual foundation. Its ideological nature is revealed by the fact that it is derived from evidence: thus to talk about somatic or racial classification is paradoxical.

That the paradox is not obvious on a superficial approach, and that its provocative nature is not clear, is classically typical of all ideological propositions. They seem so spontaneously true, people take them so much for granted as pure platitudes, that few think of questioning them. Is it not true and self-evident that day is day and night night, a woman a woman, a white a white and a black a black? What is the point of examining what is beyond dispute, especially when anthropology and biology back up the evidence of our senses and act as scientific guarantors of our common sense?

Yet all this is to take as a factual datum what is merely the ideological result of certain social relationships. It is to accept as eternal entities what are really derived substances, the transitory form of particular relations. It means believing that between the eternal categories of 'black' and 'white', of 'men' and 'women', there are relationships which are secondary and adventitious. A modicum of attention to history or to the world around us shows that it is relationships themselves which create and crystallize those categories; which give rise to a belief in the naturalness of the groups involved; which set up a whole science of naturalness. No doubt it is no longer easy to understand fully (and not merely on the epistemological plane) what actual relationships are reflected in the idea of nature; or what constraints have produced the idea of an uncrossable frontier; or, in short, what links of physical or economic dependence, what conflicts or antagonisms, have crystallized into the notions of 'colour' and 'sex', and how those notions can be applied not merely descriptively but substantively to social groups involved in relationships with one another.

For while the idea that there are relationships between men is an old one, the idea that there are races and 'racial' relationships is new. Similarly, the differential study of human physiology (the specification of groups in accordance with sex or race) is also a recent phenomenon, dating perhaps from the second half of the nineteenth century. The basing of human classification on physical characteristics derives directly from social relationships and not from some universal abstract giving rise to 'pure' taxonomic categories and a-historical 'self-evidence'. The notion of race corresponds to an ideological analysis of social relationships and not to categories existing as concrete physical objects. In other words, there is no such thing as race in itself, but only the notion of race which is a product of industrial societies, only social relationships interpreted in racial terms.

NOTE ON THE TWO COUNTER-CURRENTS

The individualist and ethical counter-current

After the First World War there appeared a current of opposition to the racial interpretation of social phenomena. To a large extent this movement was set off, at least in its public expression which emerged between

1930 and 1940, by the racialist postulates and practices of European Nazism. It had a certain kinship with the individualist philosophies of the Age of Enlightenment and with such post-revolutionary analysts as de Tocqueville. It was also to a large extent linked to culturalism, and put the individual in the centre of the stage, as against the totalist syncretic system of the Nazi and Fascist ideologies. This individual, while of course formed by society, constituted the ultimate meaning and the ultimate actor in the socio-human process. What are the different personalities that go to make up human groups? And on the other hand, what effect do these personalities have on human history? Such questions lay at the centre of the discussions opened by a school which rejected the syncretic approach adopted by the believers in racial-social determinism, and which endeavoured to fight against what it regarded as a pathological or deviant attitude.

In this perspective, social facts depend on people's minds, and social matters take on a personal tinge. The universalist argument, an intellectual effort emanating from the liberal bourgeoisie and expressing the values which had accompanied its rise to political power in the previous two hundred years, took account of, and for a while supported, interests which really were 'universal', as Marx observed of the first bourgeois revolutions. And at the time it represented the only attempt at scientific opposition to the proclamation of the Natural Order.

This ethical current arose directly out of the terror caused by the results, in Europe itself, of racial logic, which had its deep roots in the colonial relationship and was now seen in one of its practical and legal forms. Although this current did not call into question the invention of race itself, it refused to accept such a concept as a means of analysing and understanding social relationships, and by showing that it had no influence in socio-cultural matters, tried to limit it to the field of physical anthropology. The brief exchange between Margaret Mead and James Baldwin quoted at the beginning of this paper shows the former expressing attitudes typical of the trend we are now considering: broadly, a rejection, and a very incomplete dismantling of the position hitherto occupied by the notion of race in the various social philosophies. A large section of the scholarly ranks, at that time and up to about the 1960s, was bent on demonstrating that physical and socio-mental characteristics were not inter-determinant but independent of one another.

But this rejection did not develop into a real challenge. The taxonomic racial system itself was not called into question; only its implications were denounced. This was largely due to a belief in the independence of science, a faith very deep-rooted in scientists themselves. It is apparently difficult for any scientist to admit that he can only ask a question in so far as his society, and his group within that society, allow or force him to formulate it – or indeed to conceive it. The failure to make such a distinction probably also underlies the illusion mentioned in the introduction to this paper, the illusion according to which 'racial relationships' exist absolutely and in themselves, without any distinction being made between 'racial' in the minds of the actors and 'racial' in the minds of the observers (the latter are, of course, also actors in the play, but somewhat differently so).

In the context of this neo-individualist trend, somatic traits were no longer used to predict and explain behaviour and social relationships, and came to be regarded as straightforward observations of fact, allegedly neutral. In a way, this was giving autonomy to the notion of race. The transformation of the traditional physio-somatic category into an independent characteristic was first attempted at the beginning of this century by Franz Boas, who tried to invalidate the causal links between somatic and socio-mental characteristics but only succeeded in reversing rather than destroying them. According to Boas, socio-mental traits help to modify somatic characteristics. The causal links were only really broken by the neo-individualism we have just been considering, and then in a distinctly ethical context.

But while naturalism had abandoned, at least in theory, the *human* social sciences, it had not altogether disappeared. Somatic classifications of human groups did not only continue, they spread and grew more and more attractive and intricate. This happened not only in the wake of the various new orders in Europe, but also in science, now less politically marked and more traditionally bounded by the requirements of bourgeois republics. Scientific research was directly angled by relationships of class colonialism. Naturalism remained the ideological choice of physical anthropology, and subsequently of biology, which has grown steadily in significance since the 1930s. In these fields there still persisted a more or less open belief in the parity, whether syncretic or causal, between identifiable (and fragmentary) somatic traits and social characteristics. Socio-Darwinism was still alive and well, and though it had abandoned sociology and social anthropology it still served as a semi-theoretical, semi-implicit basis for the development of the natural sciences as applied to man. Here it became a kind of sub-argument or postulate. At the same time, the piecemeal legal enunciation of racial affiliation, in other words of legal racialism, was closely allied to a system of somatic classification. And culturalism, by setting aside social relationships, failed to criticize a notion which was itself a manifestation of certain social relationships.

It was probably a combination of several factors which confined neo-individualism to a half-hearted protest, although it was the only theoretical form of argument which had any influence. The trend was reinforced in the 1930s by the fashion for psychoanalysis, which also proclaimed the individual genesis of mental and social forms, and even cultural forms in the case of the 'primary institutions' of Kardiner, Benedict, Linton, and so on. Psychoanalysis concentrated on the process by which the individual acquired characteristics supposed to be statistically frequent; there reigned a kind of psychological atomism indifferent to social structures.

But above all the influence of Horkheimer, Adorno, Reich and Bettelheim, who focused explanation on individuality and its own history and thus produced a kind of freeze at the individual level, contributed to the fact that when racial logic exploded on the continent of Europe, it came as a kind of surprise, devoid of historical preparation, because the birth and development of that logic in colonial relationships was still unknown, or at best regarded as belonging to some other analysis. The only explanation of the explosion seemed to be madness or disease, or complex processes ultimately concerning only individuals.

By its influence on the human sciences this trend, while it helped to counter the arguments of the traditional physio-somatists, also helped to obscure a societal counter-current which, though it constituted an older criticism of the racial interpretation of history, was also, as we shall see, in some ways more ambiguous. It took account of a gulf which is superficially regarded as political but which is also theoretical.

The societal counter-current

This current was older than the first just considered: it was contemporary with racialist logic itself, and developed alongside it in the first half of the nineteenth century. It did not crystallize so clearly as the individualist current into a definite and historically datable opposition. Further, it was ambiguous, in that its development was closely linked to that of naturalist ideas themselves, which were as little individualist as the societal current itself.

During the nineteenth century, and following the economists of the eighteenth, the syncretic somatic-cum-social postulate (which led to the idea of 'natural groups') came to be rejected, and an attempt was made at conceptual clarification. This developed side by side with the so-phistications of naturalist pseudo-materialism. The resulting attitude was to 'explain the social in terms of the social'. From their different points of view Marx, Comte and Durkheim all endeavoured, with the aid of economics, history and the example of the exact sciences, to describe social facts without presupposing an endo-determinism rooted in un-changeable assumptions. It matters little whether we call this sociology or sociometry: what it means is that all analysis is based on encounter between human groups, and not between individuals as such. Moreover, human groups were not apprehended or analysed in terms of their essence. It was a limited approach, both common sense and the pre-vailing and dominant, scientific attitude still tending to what came to be called socio-Darwinism at the end of the nineteenth century. This latter view, which itself had little use for individualism, deliberately adopted a kind of bio-social syncretism.

In actual fact, resistance to the dominant naturalist version of social relationships came into being only later, as we have seen, and because European social structures were themselves directly involved, as objects, in the social relationships which introduced and made use of the idea of a natural order. And this resistance expressed itself in neo-individualist terms, 'values' serving as a battle position. But at the time, the contra-diction between naturalist presuppositions and the analysis of social relationships was not clearly articulated, and probably not often clearly perceived.

Nor can it be perceived easily, for in practice the knowledge that there are social formations is, in the awareness which social agents have of the world in which they live, hostile to the perception of individual processes. As has already been shown, the idea of race is closely associated in its historical development with the description of social groups, not of individual processes, and with the (non-analytical) obser-vation of conflicts and confrontations between groups. This being so, the societal trend must include a naturalist branch which regards social groups as natural entitites naturally programmed. Within the societal current this was always a strong temptation, even with Marx and Weber, perhaps even with Durkheim, and one always present in the minds of those analysts who regard social groups as something more than the simple aggregate of the individuals of which they are composed. So the defence against naturalist 'self-evidence' continued to reside in values, through which the individual in his 'humanity' ranged himself against 'irrational' mechanisms. For two hundred years endo-naturalist ide-ology had been so strong that even those who rejected it were forced at the same time to accept it – that is, to regard nature as a finite entity and not as the limited creation of certain social relationships; to accept it as a datum with mechanisms that could be classified quantitatively, whereas it is in fact a formal approximation of reality, its form being determined by the social relationships of here-and-now.

These two trends coexist – the neo-individualist which sets humanist values against the pillars of the various 'natural orders', and the other which, while it analysed social relationships, was still at the mercy of naturalist pseudo-materialism. It is as if some unthought-of factor made the contradictions between these trends insurmountable. While the neo-individualists rejected the belief that somatic forms influenced social and mental processes, this did not lead them to criticize the introduction of the idea of race or of natural groups. Indeed, such a step would have been difficult for advocates of a theory which did not consider that there were such things as specifically social relationships, and believed still less, if that were possible, that definite intellectual categories arise out of such relationships. For the neo-individualist, Science was just Science, independent of and apart from social relationships. 'Societism' also accepted the idea of Nature without too many questions asked, regarding social relationships as part of the natural world, and at best, like Engels, looking on them as one of nature's methods of operating. At worst, 'societists' tended to regard social formations themselves as natural, and as long as social groups were studied as entities the resulting explanations and descriptions were always influenced by this underlying naturalism. Social and anthropological conceptions of race relations reflected the ambiguity: somehow, somewhere, social analysts continued to think of human groups as natural.

The syncretism which connects knowledge of social formations with an explanation of that knowledge in terms of endo-naturalism is still with us. And while traditional anti-racialism refuses to accept somato-physiological traits as a cause of mental or social phenomena, it can put forward only individualist explanations and suggestions, such as respect for individual rights, the fight against amoral individual trends, the fight against ignorance, and so on. But what individualist humanism is confronted with is not deviant individuals but a State apparatus and its economic, military, legal and police powers. Until quite recently, the currents of thought which rejected naturalist causality, whether they were neo-individualist or sociological in character, rarely gained a true idea of the material and social imperatives behind the 'rights' of the racialized and biologized, oppressed and, today, dominated minorities.[30]

It is difficult to say what is the predominant tendency now. Since

1965, a school seems to have emerged, allied, like anti-racialist neo-individualism, to cultural anthropology, and using as its central argument culture and the right to cultural identity. Contacts between societies and social groups are interpreted in terms of culture. This trend of thought has produced an atomist concept of social forms, according to which every social group exists in itself, its identity defined by a specific culture and moreover formed and transmitted chiefly through language. Every social group possesses substantial intrinsic qualities, a sort of essence. In this approach social relationships appear to be *external* to the groups themselves, and unconnected with their 'essence'.

These assumptions are reflected in the decision-making bodies of the dominant groups who, when preoccupied with 'minority problems', now stress first and foremost the 'right to be different' – a view which is shared by some members of the dominated group themselves.

In fact, the theory underlying this stress on the cultural specificity of dominated groups is not so very far removed from the traditional racialist belief in the existence of somatic barriers radically differentiating human groups. But while the idea of a somatic barrier is a typical, unambiguous racialist belief, there is some ambiguity in talking of 'cultural differences' in the abstract, apart from the relationships by which groups involved are constituted. That means postulating some *being* specific to human groups, and it is of minor importance whether that being is to be encouraged or saved: the fact remains that groups are being regarded in the light of essences and not of relationships. The question of the history of different cultures is not raised. So in certain respects this modern anti-racialist trend is only a continuation of the old traditional racialist attitude.

In practical terms also the refusal to see that history and social relationships are constituent elements of so-called 'cultural' forms may be dangerous: it may, for example, lead to the defence of social traits which are merely an expression of dependence and domination, and thus tend to perpetuate certain consecrations of inferiority. The inability to speak the (or a) dominant language, the inability to acquire techniques, and so on, tend to prolong helplessness and oppression, or at least to leave people still exposed to manipulation, defenceless against the very weapons of domination they reject. In fact, the famous 'specific cultural characteristics' are often, perhaps usually, mere crystallizations of domination, setting oral against written culture, 'natural' knowledge against 'scientific', traditional language against the language of mass communications and technology. It is interesting to note that a group which finds itself in a dominating position in a given relationship shows little concern if a dominated group refuses to acquire some of its own cultural traits, whereas the dominating group is extremely favourable to any action on the part of the dominated which lessens their opportunities for contacts, decreases their potentiality for struggle, or in general reduces them to the level of folklore. When the children of the bourgeois classes are taught several languages, we do not hear them (multilingual as they are) complain or talk about the psychological evils of bilingual-ism, though the latter is supposed to do irreparable damage to dominated groups. The same kind of thing is true in many different fields. When people are confined within one type of technique or a single language, when their inability to acquire knowledge puts them at everyone's disposal, this helps to maintain a system based on dependence, exclusion and exploitation. To be kept within one enclosed area, whether it is your birthplace or elsewhere, is a similar kind of confinement. To be domin-ated is to be kept within these limits – or, as they sometimes say, within this 'culture'.

It is this which brings so much ambiguity to the belief in the 'right to cultural difference' which is such a contemporary form of anti-racialism. This attitude is bound to be ambiguous because those who adopt it will not accept that it is relationships which make groups; they do not, therefore, take these relationships into account; and they cannot free themselves of the idea that groups exist *per se* and are the expression of some eternal essence.

NOTES

1 Thierry, A., *Lettres sur l'histoire de France*, Paris, 1840; Guizot, F., *Histoire de la civilization en France*, Paris, 1930.
2 Darwin, C., *The Origin of Species by Means of Natural Selection, or the Presentation of Favoured Races in the Struggle for Life*, 1859.
3 De Gobineau, J.A., *Essai sur l'inégalité des races humaines*, Paris, 1852. While Darwin's book was based largely on plants, birds and insects, and thus had a metaphorical rather than a direct bearing on race, Gobineau's essay was centred on man.
4 Like conjurors who draw our attention to what their right hand is doing whereas the real transformation is being effected elsewhere, leaving us astounded and perplexed.
5 Witness the definition of 'white' and 'black' by those who know very well that in a society divided up in terms of race, the 'blacks' are often white; and yet these people do not want to hear about it – they probably, literally, do not see it. One is also reminded of sociology's staggering invention of 'bio-social' classes.
6 Max Weber, confronted with socio-Darwinism, asked for proof (Confer-ence of German Sociologists, 1910. See Guillaumin, C., Poliakov, L., 'Max

Weber et les théories bioraciales du XXième siècle', *Cahiers internationaux de sociologie* (Paris), vol. LVI, 1974. Franz Boas was interested in variations in physical characteristics in acculturations (see *Changes in the Bodily Form of Descendants of Immigrants*, 1912). The two attitudes show a mixture of uneasiness and doubt in which, though the conclusions of the naturalists are challenged, their actual approach is accepted, since a search is being made for proof and counter-proof. We are here in a world in which questions are pure and independent of their social background, of the social relationships which produce them, and of the social significance of their formulation. The petulant indifference shown by Alexis de Tocqueville in his correspondence with Gobineau is more marked when it comes to the inadequacy of an approach to the analysis of social relationships which he compares to 'horse-trading'. This, though usually regarded as a mere witticism, is the most accurate commentary on Gobineau's theories, since it reduces them to their origins and true meanings; what they are really dealing in is the appropriation and exploitation of human groups. While Emile Durkheim, like all his contemporaries, was fascinated by organic metaphors and perhaps even inclined to accept biological causality, he was at least perfectly clear about the analysis of social facts themselves (*Les Règles de la méthode sociologique*, Paris, 1894).

7 At first property in human beings was limited to, say, four or seven years, but it later become unlimited – in fact, for 'life' – and culminated in the additional appropriation of the power of reproduction: a slave's children were themselves slaves.

8 Linné, C. von, *Systema naturae*, Leyden, 1735; Buffon, G., 'De l'homme', in: *Histoire naturelle . . .* Paris, 1749.

9 Like that of François Bernier in the seventeenth century or, at the beginning of the eighteenth, the Marquis de Boulainvilliers's attempt at a racial theory (see Poliakov, L., *Le Mythe aryen*, Paris, Calmann-Lévy, 1971). Boulain-villiers was also a devotee of astrology, a kind of interest, we may note in passing, which often goes with the representation of the world in racial terms.

10 Montesquieu, Diderot, Voltaire, l'abbé Raynal, Condorcet, etc.

11 Williams, E., *De Christophe Colomb à Fidel Castro: L'histoire des Caraïbes*, Paris, Présence africaine, 1975.

12 Dumont, L., 'Caste, racisme et 'stratification', in *Homo hierarchicus*, Paris, Gallimard, 1966. The author analyses the historical change of perspective between 'holistic' and 'democratic' societies.

13 Guillaumin, C., 'Caractères spécifiques de l'idéologie raciste', *Cahiers internationaux de sociologie* (Paris), vol. LIII, 1972.

14 Even when domination does not lead to the development of *racial* theory, it probably does produce an idea of *nature*, not necessarily with a 'naturalist' connotation. After all, Aristotle presupposed a slave 'nature', but this was not somatic-natural in the modern sense.

15 Marienstras, E., *Concept de race et de culture dans l'Amérique des Lumières* (Roneo, fasc. 10 of the RCP *Histoire du racisme*), Paris, 1975.

16 The invention of the notion of race as a set of somato-hereditary character-istics is rooted in the systematic development of animal husbandry in the first half of the nineteenth century – the crossing and selection of domestic

animals, especially cattle, sheep and horses. The development of this idea, and the practice of rationalized *exploitation* of the world's resources throws a harsh light on the modern use of the word 'race', first applied, as far as human beings were concerned, to exploited groups and above all to 'the masses'.

17   Technical novelties, on the other hand, disturb rather than develop law. Consider legal changes, for example: emancipation, decolonization and divorce all mark a change in the form of exploitation, introducing *mobility of the exploited*. In this they may be compared with the abolition of feudalism and the introduction of free contract, as Engels and Marx have shown. These examples all involve the interchangeability of the contracting parties. The example in the text refers to the transition from agriculture to industry as a predominant activity. For the devolution to women, as a group, of child-raising, institutionalized by divorce and involving a change from the status of spouse to some other states (see Delphy, C., 'Mariage et divorce, l'impasse à double face', *Les Temps modernes* (Paris), no. 333/4, 1974.

18   Mathieu, N.-C., 'L'homme-culture et femme-nature?' *L'homme* (Paris), no. XIII (3), 1973; and 'Paternité biologique, maternité sociale', in André Michel, *Femmes, sexisme et sociétés*, Paris, Presses universitaires de France, 1977. These papers show the one-sidedness of the ethnological writing, the disparities in levels of analysis and the absence of explanatory reference.

19   Darlington, C.D., 'Race, class and culture', in J.W.S. Pringle (ed.) *Biology and the Human Sciences*, Oxford, Clarendon Press, 1972.

20   The first explicitly racialist theories, formulated at the beginning of the nineteenth century and referred to in the 'Introduction' of this chapter, were based on the observation of a class antagonism, that of European feudalism, which involved such dichotomies as lords/serfs, noble invaders/non-noble peasants or villeins, and so on. This interpretation of social relationships belonging to an earlier period than the bourgeois revolutions – though the interpretation itself was contemporary with those revolutions – was the earliest form of clearly expressed racial theory. It referred only to social relationships in Europe.

The idea that there is a racial difference between social classes, though less widespread today than in the nineteenth century, is still encountered, sometimes explicitly, in writings on the psychology of intelligence and on the notion of aptitude (Bisseret, N., *L'Idéologie des aptitudes naturelles: Les inégaux ou la sélection universitaire*, Paris, Presses universitaires de France, 1974). The discussion has been revived recently, and two different branches of the racial approach, i.e. traditional or based on class, show their similarity in the interpretation of Arthur Jensen on the distribution of IQ in the United States according to class and race (Jensen, A., 'How much can we boost IQ and scholastic achievement?', *Harvard Educational Review* (Cambridge, Mass.), no. 39, 1969.

21   The protests aroused in the human sciences by theoretical delimitations such as sociobiology, the controversy in 1975 over E.O. Wilson's *Sociobiology: a new synthesis*, and the slightly earlier protests over publications by

Eysenck and Jensen, show that the 'natural' and 'human' sciences are to a certain extent epistemologically concerned over the meaning of such scientific options. In France, criticism has been less vociferous, but see *Discours biologique et ordre social* (Achard, P., Chauvenet, A., Lage, E., Lentin, F., Nève, P. and Vignaux, G.), which tries, though implicitly, to show the social unity of a project in which ethology, ecology and biology combine.

22 Among articles which have appeared in recent years are the following: Gedda, 'Aspetti genetici dell'omosessualità, *Acta geneticae medicae et gemellologiae* (Rome), vol. 12(3), 1964. Carney, Feldman, Wei Ping Loh, 'Sex, chromatism, body masculinity and smoking behaviour', *Psychol. Rep.* (Missoula), vol. 25(1), 1970. Reich, Clayton, Winokur, 'Family history studies, V: the genetics of mania', *American Journal of Psychiatry* (Washington), vol. 125(10), 1969. Hopkinson, Ley, 'A genetic study of affective disorder', *British Journal of Psychiatry* (London), vol. 115(525), 1969.

23 For example: Reed, 'Caucasian genes in American negroes', *Science* (Washington), vol. 165(389), 1969. Walsh, 'A distinctive pigment of the skin in New Guinea indigens', *Annals of Human Genetics* (New York), vol. 34(4), 1971. Kalla, Tiwari, 'Sex differences in skin colour in man', *Acta geneticae medicae et gemellologiae* (Rome), vol. 19(3), 1970. While the whole of a group is not always regarded as being explicitly involved, however, it continues to be involved implicitly. Somatic or chromosome research may be presented as dealing with 'individuals', but these individuals belong to a definite group. See Flatz, Saengudom, 'Lactose intolerance in Asians: a family study', *Nature* (London), vol. 224(5222), 1969; Boulard *et al.*, 'Le retard du développement dystrophique du Musulman algérien: Syndrome génétique', *Annales d'endocrinologie* (Paris), vol. 24(6), 1963; Shaper, Lewis, 'Genetic neutropenia in people of African origin', *Lancet* (London), no. 7732, 1972.

24 At present there seems to be more interest in historical vestiges traceable in specific characteristics of peoples than in traditional classifications; or with the gradual transitions to be seen in variations (see Ruffié, J., *De la biologie à la culture*, Paris, Flammarion, 1976; and *Leçon inaugurale au Collège de France*, December 1972), which shows that the idea of race is not an empirically verifiable category of classification.

25 The idea of specificity (proper to, unique to a species) is central to the system of racialist thought. Denials are worthless and meaningless – they are not listened to.

26 Linus Pauling: 'I have suggested that there should be tattooed on the forehead of every young person a symbol showing possession of the sickle cell gene or whatever similar gene . . .' ('Reflections on the new biology', *UCLA Law Review* (Los Angeles), vol. 15(3), 1968).

27 For example: Hartlage, 'Sex-linked inheritance of spatial ability', *Perceptual and motor skills* (Missoula), vol. 31(2), 1970; Boyd, 'Genetics and the human race: Definition of race on the basis of gene frequencies supplements definition from morphological characters', *Science* (Washington), vol. 140(3571), 1963; Blanc, Gortz, 'Identification of a new factor Gm 'Bet' in blood stains: applications in forensic medicine', *Vox sanguinis* (Basel), vol. 20(3), 1971.

28 Miège, J.-L., *Expansion européenne et décolonisation de 1870 à nos jours*, Paris, Presses universitaires de France, 1973.
29 In current usage 'human race' signifies both 'race' and its opposite: in the plural to show that humanity is divided, or in the singular to suggest that there is only one race, the human race.
30 For an analysis of this strange blindness see O'Callaghan, M.G., *On Human Rights*, 1975, not yet published.

Chapter 3

'I know it's not nice, but . . .'
The changing face of 'race'

The idea of race is one of the most contradictory and violent in our world today. Having been for so many years, probably more than a century, a sort of first truth, something so obvious that no one ever thought to call it into question (in much the same way as sex today), it has become over the last few decades an explosive topic. As something which was part of, and exploited by, a world becoming increasingly efficient technologically, and more and more centralized, race became transformed in the middle of the present century into a means for states to achieve their goals of domination, exploitation and extermination. This is a matter of simple fact.

RACE IS NOT A NEUTRAL IDEA

No, the term 'race' is not just one banal, harmless designator among others. Nor is it a 'given', a word which in itself is neutral and can be used socially in a way which is either 'good' or 'bad', indifferent or pernicious, according to the circumstances. The notion of categorizing humankind into closed, anatomical and physiological entities is a strange one, and it seems astonishing that as it grew and became more complex it was not greeted with greater suspicion. At a time when the whole idea of 'race' was becoming socially accepted (essentially around the beginning of the nineteenth century), de Tocqueville was virtually alone in sensing that there was something shameful underlying its use. No doubt the same thing was seen by other, less famous people whose voices were not so widely heard, but among the notable intellectuals and politicians of the day, precious few showed any reticence.

At the very time when the idea of race was acquiring such social importance, during the first half of the nineteenth century, the anthropologist Franz Boas was already aware of the unreliability of anatomical measurements, which varied from one generation to the next according to living conditions, so that the shape of the bones in our skull was influenced by that most vulgar of commodities, the food we ate . . . Today we know perfectly well (as we probably always did, but what we know and what we are prepared to acknowledge are not always the same thing . . .) that any physical characteristic whatsoever can be made into a 'discriminator' in some socially or politically motivated system of classification (by opposition to a disinterested, scientific one). The choice of somatic criteria is symbolic of the intentions of the classifiers, and nothing more. The Nazis deciding who was (and was not) a Jew, as they put it more than once (when offering Fritz Lang an important role in the cinema industry of the Third Reich, for instance), or the government of the Republic of South Africa classifying Chinese people as belonging to one race and Japanese to another, are sufficient illustration that these things are a matter of politics rather than objective reality, and that the users of such distinctions are well aware of the fact.

'RACE DOES NOT EXIST'

What is the position today? For about the last ten years we have clearly been at a crucial stage in the development of the notion of race. A number of voices have been raised claiming that 'race' does not exist. They are not very numerous, but their importance is considerable. While the meaning of the term has been constantly changing since its emergence, this is the first time any attempt has been made to destroy the very concept itself, which is extremely important. It is certainly crucial in that it marks a break with one of the most untouchable sacred cows of our time, but it becomes even more so when we look at the real significance of this attempted rejection. A number of researchers are currently working to ensure that 'race' is shelved away among other notions which, in the history of science (and natural science in particular), belong firmly to the past. This tendency developed progressively through the period 1965–75, beginning with the questioning of the idea on theoretical and conceptual grounds. The physical anthropologist Jean Hiernaux remarked at the time: 'Race is not a fact, but a concept'.[1] This apparently simple observation in fact represents a turning-point. It acts as a logical introduction to the statement made by the haemo-typologist Jacques Ruffié in his inaugural lecture at the Collège de France in December 1972:

> In our part of the world, in most Latin countries, physical anthropology has gradually become separated from the sociology of culture

. . . Now, in man, there is no such thing as race. That is why, despite numerous and rigorous studies, nobody has ever been able to agree on how humanity should be divided up into races.

This position and its variants underlie the critique of race advanced by population geneticists as well as by physical anthropologists in the strict sense of the term.

How is it that the scientific community should have arrived at a position so startlingly opposed to the common-sense view of our age?

What we today call a race was not, contrary to widespread opinion, something self-evident to people of earlier centuries. While there may be arguments among historians, sociologists and researchers in all the other disciplines that are concerned with the role of race in society about the precise historical moment when the notion emerged in the form in which we know it today, when both the term and the idea were born, there is no debate about the thing itself.

The word 'race' (which came into French only relatively recently, in the sixteenth century) originally had a very precise sense: it meant 'family' or, more accurately, 'family relationship'. Moreover, it was only ever applied to important dynasties (the race of the Bourbons, the race of David, etc.). In no way was it applied at that time to large groups of people with no legal link of kinship between them. From referring to legally circumscribed, noble families, it shifted to being applied to much wider groups, the attribution to whom of some common physical trait served as a pretext for designating them as a single entity, now called a 'race'. This shift from surname to skin colour is a considerable one: from narrow legal link binding family groups together, to complete geographical dispersion, the term underwent a semantic journey of extraordinary proportions. However, it took a long time, and a major change in our ways of thinking, before 'race' became applied to groups of people lumped together according to some common physical characteristic, rather than just a shared surname.

The evolution of the term then went through another important stage. During the first half of the nineteenth century, other, quite different characteristics began to be slipped in alongside the physical (or supposedly physical) common denominators of human groups: these were social, or cultural, traits. Philological research had identified specific groupings (Indo-European languages, Semitic languages, etc.) among the language-forms then known, and these were quickly absorbed into the systems of somatic classification which were then sweeping all before them. It was a short step from there to suggesting the existence of

Indo-European and Semitic races. We all know what that lead to a century later.

BUT WHAT ACTUALLY IS 'RACE'?

The concept 'race' was formed at a historically determined (or determinable) period, as the result of an oscillation between meanings generated from diverse sources, and the combining of several different types of classification (legal, anatomical, linguistic . . .). Heterogeneous lines of thought came to be fused in the single claim that human groups were differential by nature, and that there was a natural line of separation between them. This has now become the *de facto* everyday meaning of the term 'race'. But, however irritating it might be to go on repeating it, we should never forget that 'race' is not a spontaneously given product of perception and experience. It is an idea built up (and slowly, at that) from elements which might equally well be physical traits as social customs, linguistic peculiarities as legal institutions, lumped together and homogenized according to the precept that they must ultimately all be biological phenomena. This idea carries a great deal of weight in a society obsessed with the sanctity of 'Science', which has been invested with the power not only to unveil and understand natural phenomena, but to establish what actually constitutes those phenomena themselves.

Jacques Ruffié's assertion that no such physical category exists within humanity certainly marked a turning-point. At the same time, though, it fell within a critical tradition which was not new, but had been expressed quite differently in the middle of the present century.

This was the period when race, which had originally been a purely descriptive notion, became transformed into a legal one. From being an 'idea' it was turned into a concrete social fact. The scientific community in the 1930s, particularly people working in the social sciences, made strenuous efforts to oppose this and to defuse the legalization of the notion of race which the Nazi regime was bringing about. They proclaimed the complete inadequacy of such a 'purely physical' notion to account for, describe and influence those aspects of human life which were dependent on society and culture, although they did not challenge its relevance to the physical domain. Many different stands were taken at that time. In December 1938, for instance, the American Psychological Association declared that:

> In the experiments which psychologists have made upon different peoples, no characteristic, inherent psychological differences which

fundamentally distinguish so-called 'races' have been disclosed. [. . .]
There is no evidence for the existence of an inborn Jewish or German
or Italian mentality. [. . .] The Nazi theory that people must be related
by blood in order to participate in the same cultural or intellectual
heritage has absolutely no support from scientific findings.

But these warnings could never be more than symbolic, since the legal
and political systems which exploited the notion of race were already in
place.

So a critical attempt was made to break the syncretic link between
physical and socio-cultural traits which had been forged and developed
over the preceding centuries. But it did not call the notion itself into
question. It was a statement of principle as well as a moral protest. Both
are necessary, but not sufficient. The idea of race was left very solidly in
place, and in the end went absolutely unquestioned as such. There had
been an attempt to limit the damage, it had failed, and in 1945 the state
of South Africa in its turn adopted legal categories of race.

These stands were to influence various declarations of the international organizations throughout the 1950s. Their concern was still the
same: to demonstrate that the material, physical fact of 'race' (which
still went unchallenged except by the occasional isolated researcher)
was quite separate from social or psychological characteristics. The
intention was to show that race, still assumed to exist in itself, had no
connection with or influence over the way in which human beings
behaved.

The UNESCO 'Statement on the Nature of Race and Race Differences' of 1951 provides a good illustration of this position:

Since race, as a word, has become coloured by its misuse in connexion with national, linguistic and religious differences, and by its
deliberate abuse by racialists, we tried to find a new word to express
the same meaning of a biologically differentiated group. On this we
did not succeed, but agreed to reserve race as the word to be used for
anthropological classification of groups showing definite combin-
ations of physical (including physiological) traits in characteristic
proportions. [. . .] National, religious, geographical, linguistic and
cultural groups do not necessarily coincide with racial groups; and
the cultural traits of such groups have no demonstrated connexion
with racial traits. Americans are not a race, nor are Frenchmen, nor
Germans; nor ipso facto is any other national group. Moslems and
Jews are no more races than are Roman Catholics and Protestants;
nor are people who live in Iceland or Britain or India, or who speak

English or any other language, or who are culturally Turkish or Chinese and the like, thereby describable as races. The use of the term 'race' in speaking of such groups may be a serious error, but it is one which is habitually committed.[2]

TALKING ABOUT 'DIFFERENCE'

Looking back on this from our position today, we are struck by the pathetic aspect of a protest so resolute and yet so far removed from a reality of repression and violence. It is also striking to see that we are forgetting here – and when I say 'we', I mean all of us who work in the human sciences and are reduced to exasperation and despair by this notion so difficult to tie down – that the idea of race did not belong exclusively to the natural sciences, either historically, or socially, or ideologically. Despite that, however, the idea was challenged as if it did. Moreover, as if that were the only way in which race could, and should, be envisaged.

And yet, while it had become a geographical classification in the work of Linné, and was extrapolated into linguistics in the first half of the nineteenth century during the triumph of philology, race was also a subject for debate in the streets, in political quarters, in the salons, where it came to represent what was 'peculiar' about each human group. It was the equivalent of our 'difference', and that is certainly how it was understood. A case in point was Balzac, the first major novelist to make extensive use of the idea. The current vogue notion of difference is so ambiguous that it is often defended just as much by traditional racists as by anti-racists, whilst even the victims of racism themselves invoke it as something they wish to cultivate. This is because difference has come to inherit all the connotations relating to the specificity of human groups which in the old days were carried by the notion of race. It is true that the idea of difference is an attempt to get away from the imperative of physical naturality imposed by race, and in that sense its aim is certainly to break down the rigidity of the racist system of thought. But at the same time it attracts those who persist in thinking in racist terms, but no longer dare use the word 'race'. When, for reasons of censorship, political prudence or simply cynicism, these people choose 'difference' instead of 'race', they know that they will still be understood as saying something about the 'natural' specificity of human groups. For it is impossible to destroy the deeper strata of a system of thought simply by taking away a particular element; its configuration needs to be modified by adding some new trait.

So, the social sciences forgot the circumstances in which the idea of race came into existence and developed, and failed to take account of the fact that the great theorists of race were from their own camp, rather than from the natural sciences. Gobineau was not a scientist, nor were Vacher de Lapouge and, later, Chamberlain and Rosenberg, and so on.

Today, a few people in the human-related sciences are awakening from this lethargy and trying to reject a notion whose origin is clearly to be sought in socio-intellectual modes of thought which have nothing to do with experimental scientific practice. But this awakening has come as a surprise for the social sciences, which thought that they had discreetly disposed of a category for which they were largely responsible by pushing it off into the domain of the natural sciences. If the responsibility is indeed theirs, it is less because they had a part in the invention of 'race' than because they are the very disciplines on which the study of the phenomenon depends: as a social trait, it falls within their sphere of understanding and analysis. Sociologists, historians and epistemologists were perhaps unwilling to see that this hot potato was their problem, but that is certainly the case. And the natural sciences keep reminding them of it by denying that race has anything to do with them.

WHAT IS THE POSITION OF 'RACE' TODAY?

We now find ourselves at a stage where the pertinence of the notion of race in the natural sciences of man is being refuted on grounds of scientific reason and intellectual honesty (not to mention logic and common sense). This is quite an event, something new in these fields of research. As we have seen, however, it is not an isolated move, for race has been analysed and challenged by other disciplines for some decades now. But this stand is unlikely to achieve its desired aim of eliminating the idea that human beings are 'naturally' different, and that the great divides in society (national, religious, political, etc.) reflect 'natural' differences. For negations are not recognized as such by our unconscious mental processes. From this point of view, a fact affirmed and a fact denied exist to exactly the same degree, and remain equally present in our affective and intellectual associative networks. Just talking about race means that it will always be there in residue. 'Race' is about the least conceptional, cold and abstract of notions, so it appeals from the start to the unconscious side of the mechanisms we have for acquiring knowledge and relating to other human beings. The ideologues of racism have always been well aware of this, which is why they are still peddling their views today.

In other words, simply showing that a category of this type has no scientific basis is insufficient to remove it from the mental universe not simply of the majority of people, but even of those who are intellectually convinced that it does not exist as a 'natural' reality. It is a necessary operation, but not a sufficient one.

The human sciences began by saying: 'race' is a matter for the natural sciences, it is none of our business, it has no influence on cultural and social phenomena, and so on. Today, the natural sciences are replying: 'race' does not exist, it is not a pertinent criterion of classification. Each of these two propositions is partially true, but they hide a third which comes much closer to fitting the real facts. And if ever one revolution or one proposition could conceal another, this is certainly a case in point. Whether race is or is not 'a fact of nature', whether it is or is not a 'mental reality', it is today, in the twentieth century, a legal, political and historical reality which plays a real and constraining role in a number of societies.

(a) That is why any appeal to race (even under the pretext of a love of different cultures, or the search for 'roots', etc.) is a political move which can never be neutral, given the facts. For it is a question of facts, and not one of intentions or opinions, as some people would once again have us believe.

(b) That is why simply rejecting the notion of race is not enough. Denying its existence as an empirically valid category, as the human, social and, ultimately, natural sciences are trying to do, can never, however correct the intention, take away that category's reality within society or the state, or change the fact that while it may not be valid empirically, it certainly exerts an empirical effect. To claim that a notion which is present in a society's vocabulary, i.e. in both its way of organizing the world and in its political and human history, can be negated in this way is a paradoxical position, because that which is negated has *de facto* existence. It is perhaps also an attempt to take away the horror of that reality, its unbearable brutality: it is impossible that something of that kind should exist. Precisely because its existence is unbearable.

However, while the reality of 'race' is indeed neither natural and biological, nor psychological (some innate tendency of the human mind to designate the other as a natural entity), it does nevertheless exist. It is not possible to argue that a category which organizes whole states (the Third Reich, the Republic of South Africa, etc.), and which is incorporated into the law, does not exist. It is not possible to claim that the category which is the direct cause, the primary means, of the murder of millions of human beings does not exist.

But the slow path to intellectual understanding traced by successive and cumulative attempts to elucidate the concept shows that race is a social category of exclusion and murder. Its real nature has gradually been unmasked. The process has not been a simple one, for it is hard not to believe that 'race does not exist' when the idea that it is a 'natural' category has been proved false (as indeed it is), while at the same time that idea was all that was left after the patient critique undertaken by the social sciences. And when, above all, that celebrated 'natural' definition was the very same one which 'legitimized' the legal inscription of 'race' in racist regimes.

Yet the legal inscription of race and the practices that accompany it certainly do exist. And they are precisely the reality of race. Race does not exist. But it does kill people. It also continues to provide the backbone of some ferocious systems of domination. And in France today it is rearing its ugly head once again. Not in the shameful margins of our society, but behind the honourable mask of 'opinion' and 'ideas'. Let us be clear about this. The idea, the notion of race is a technical means, a machine, for committing murder. And its effectiveness is not in doubt. It is a way of rationalizing and organizing by murderous violence the domination of powerful social groups over other groups reduced to powerlessness. Unless anyone is prepared to claim that, since race does not exist, nobody is or can ever have been repressed or killed because of their race. And nobody can make that claim, because millions of human beings have died as a result of their race, and millions of others are now dominated, excluded and repressed for the same reason.

No, race does not exist. And yet it does. Not in the way that people think; but it remains the most tangible, real and brutal of realities.

NOTES

1 See J. Hiernaux, 'De l'individu à la population: l'anthropobiologie', in *La Science face au racisme* (re-edition of the first issue of *Le Genre humain*), Brussels, Editions Complexe, 1986.

2 In A. Montague (ed.) *Statement on Race*, Oxford, Oxford University Press, 1972 (3rd edition), pp. 139–47 (p. 141; p. 143).

Chapter 4

'Wildcat' immigration
(*Immigrationsauvage*)

Ten years or so ago, the walls of Paris suddenly became covered (were covered by someone) in moderate-sized posters in two high-contrast tones, white and something approaching black (dark navy?), shouting out the slogan: 'Halte à l'immigration sauvage!' ('Stop wildcat immigration!').[1] They were striking and brutal, and spoke of an everyday reality, one of those commonplace situations which had yet to find public expression in words. They crystallized in a single formula what was still just a mosaic of concrete acts of exclusion or aggression, conversations and comments made around the tables of cafés, or at family and other private gatherings, within the dominant population.

More importantly, they transformed what until then had been a half-spoken social attitude, made up of individual actions and words, into a collective utterance, a doctrine, a political (and therefore public) slogan. Which is not to say that 'immigration problems' did not occasionally, though rarely, find themselves in the spotlight of current governmental and political affairs. But that is just the point: 'immigration problems', or 'problems relating to immigrants'; not 'Halte à!', not 'sauvage'. The law against racism had recently been passed and the anti-immigrant movement was still on its knees, though very much alive and kicking.

It is fair to point out that this formula as it stands did not meet with the same success in the media and in everyday parlance as, for example, 'the threshold of tolerance', which has now become an untouchable part of the vocabulary, to the extent that subsequent attempts to refute or clarify it have been like so much water off a duck's back. Nevertheless, such a clear shift in perceptions, and such a radical reformulation of social relationships, was not to be without consequence for the future, because a few months ago, some ten years after the original event, a politician took up the same theme of 'uncontrolled immigration' following the municipal council elections of 1983.[2]

On the one hand we have the language of the political poster, on the other, that of the post-electoral speech. They are not the same. While the denotational sense of the two expressions is identical, their meaning is not. If the meaning of 'uncontrolled immigration' is entirely contained within that of 'wildcat immigration', the reverse is not the case, for the latter expression means far more: 'wildcat immigration' overflows the bounds of its denotation and sets off echoes by association across a wide range of different domains.

Some of these associations are clear and conscious, others only partially so (they are, as it were, semi-conscious), and others again completely unconscious. It is not impossible – though unlikely – that those who coined the expression *immigrationsauvage* were fully aware of all of them.

So what are these associations? Before going on to examine the mechanics of what appears to be a single unit of meaning, a seme,[3] it is important to establish the broad outlines of its various senses by separating them out from each other, although they all function together and so to unravel them in this way is a rather arbitrary operation.

THREE LEVELS OF MEANING

'Immigration sauvage' [1]

On the first, explicit level of denotation it means the same as 'uncontrolled immigration'; the two are rigorously equivalent, with no need of paraphrase. This is incidentally the form in which Le Pen re-used the expression when commenting on the results of the March 1983 municipal elections: 'I said out loud what people here are thinking silently to themselves: that uncontrolled immigration leads to disorder and insecurity'.[4]

'Immigration sauvage' [2]

On the second, sub- or semi-conscious level, which is already moving beyond denotation into the realm of connotation, 'wildcat' (sauvage) implies wildness and savagery. An immigration of savages, savages coming into the country. It was certainly this obvious allusion which made the poster such a striking and imperative vehicle of hatred. The inductive association was intentional: immigrants are savages.

The term 'savages' as such does not figure in political speeches, but it is often heard in the street, and also implied or induced in many contexts which actually call for a greater degree of reserve. For example: 'You have to have lived in a block where Moslems are slitting sheep's throats in the courtyard before you can know what it's like'.[5] And, in borderline political discourse: 'Immigrants . . . go home to your hovels'.[6]

These two levels of meaning operate in a domain somewhere between simple denotation and pure connotation. However, they have one thing in common: the logic of their meaning is immediately perceptible, or at least comprehensible; the signified is homologous with its verbal expression, and the meaning flows straight from the grammatical links between the terms. In all these cases, *sauvage* relates directly and logically to *immigration*.

'Immigration sauvage' [3]

Yet these two levels by no means exhaust the available senses, and therefore the overall meaning, of the expression. The latter is also informed by the cultural and sociological colouring of the words used: why one, rather than another? One word with its core sense circled by the halo, specific to it, of its successive historical senses, of which some may have been forgotten but all are still present, although the speaker might not be aware of them, and listeners may perceive them more or less clearly. As one example among many, the meaning of *sauvage* undoubtedly includes its sense (classified as 'old-fashioned' in contemporary dictionaries) of 'exotic' (exotic peoples, exotic customs). Thus meaning rests to some extent on a series of senses which are in fact a combination of the different historical senses.

But certain words also carry an additional colouring specific to a particular moment in history, social class, generation, group, or simply culture in the broadest sense of the term. This additional colouring makes the term into a sort of password, able to establish a feeling of complicity among its users. Some of these words enjoy a brilliant, if at times ephemeral, success; popular with advertisers, they are used to create an impression of modernity, efficiency and irresistible novelty.[7] There are dozens of them, some still current, others having already slipped out of usage, and they in fact signify virtually nothing except the modernity which they seem to herald, since their denotational content is in many cases so slim as to be evanescent.

Immigration, although much used at the present, is not one of these; its violent emotive charge has nothing in common with such vogue words. But *sauvage* is, and has long been so. When, in the halcyon days of the 'New Right', it was pointed out that 'far from being . . . obscurantist', this was a movement which showed 'all the signs of modernity',[8] even before the ideological current (or 'school of thought', to use its own terms) which it represented had even acquired a name, its use of the word *sauvage* (particularly when associated with the poster style of design) was calculated to signify its modern intentions, and give it a 'young' and challenging look. The post-1968 use of *sauvage* by the 'autonomous' 'ecological' Left (in connection with sit-ins, strikes, natural vegetation, masculine odours and mushrooms, all of which were interesting because they were 'wild'/*sauvages*), as a combined image and slogan in close semantic proximity to 'spontaneous', 'free' 'pure', 'non-adulterated', turned it into a symbol of social indocility, dynamism and innovation. *Sauvage* belongs to modernity through its anarchistic and libertarian connotations (the opposite of 'domesticated'), but at the same time its reactionary element (as the opposite of 'civilized') allows it to serve as an appeal to the superiority of the dominant group.

Thus the seme *immigrationsauvage* seems to pull in two different directions, towards everyday racism on the one hand, and modernity on the other.

From the strict point of view of meaning, *sauvage* does not function here in dependency on *immigration*, but independently, as a pure signal: *sauvage* is 'in'. Since it has nothing to do with immigration on the logical level of ideas, it can operate as the semantic guarantor of the freshness and vitality of what in the old days used to be called racism, a word still viewed as dishonourable. 'There is now a need, an urgent need, to expose the profound wrong-headedness and power for evil inherent in racist attitudes, to stop any future confusion between them and the legitimate self-defence of collective specificities and identities'.[9]

Finally, it is worth pointing out another aspect of our slogan which operates in a manner similar to what we have just seen, in that it is far removed from the literality of signs: the use of a negative copula, as in '*Stop* wildcat immigration!', '*un*controlled immigration'. We shall not dwell on this point because it is not critical for our understanding of *immigrationsauvage*, but in one case this verbalized refusal and rejection applies to immigration itself (Stop), and in the other to the idea of control (un-). The focus is therefore evidently different, although the effect on meaning is similar in both examples, adding a negative, antagonistic colouring to the utterance.[10]

THE SEME 'IMMIGRATIONSAUVAGE'

Paradoxically, it is the polysemic nature of *sauvage* that makes *immigrationsauvage* into a single seme, rather than, as in the case of 'uncontrolled immigration', two linked semes. *Immigration* is neither specified nor restricted by the use of *sauvage*; on the contrary, it is extended and diversified.

Indeed, the uncertainty surrounding *sauvage* implies that it needs to be illuminated by the context, and the context here is *immigration*. If restricted to its denotational sense, immigration is at best a neutral term; it seems impossible for it ever to be positive. Yet this best case is only a possibility, and appears to occur only in books on human geography. In practice, however we choose to approach it, immigration always carries negative connotations. But it is not a complex term, unlike *sauvage*. The complexity that has become a structural part of the meaning of the expression as a whole is not (is no longer) a function simply of the addition of the different senses, something which is only possible when the two words have neighbouring or related denotations. This complexity, or diversification, gives a special texture to the resulting composite, in that it integrates signifiers with different colourings, from divergent domains, signifiers which remain present and coexist, without the possibility of any of them being eliminated. The juxtaposition of *sauvage* with *immigration* produces a syncretic meaning which is grasped as a whole as soon as the words are spoken, and which can only artificially be analysed into its component parts. We have just seen a quick inventory of the most prominent of these, but they really cannot be separated. The three levels of meaning function simultaneously and together; their fusion forms an overall meaning, which makes the expression into a single seme.

The creation of a seme is not a simple operation. Once it has been made, it seems self-evident, but initially that is far from the case. Fusing together social realities of different orders is a difficult exercise at which to succeed. In the case of *immigrationsauvage*, if the first two levels (denotation and connotation, for simplicity) express one aspect of the commonplace (so-called dominant) ideology, the third, 'expressive' level (because it is detached from literal signification) is actually political. It is this level that provides the dressing-up necessary for an unselfconscious show of renewed interest in a discredited thematics. Such jumps in level are always a feature of any creative verbal manipulation performed in an effort to endow old actions and old words with an appearance of legitimacy, novelty and dignity. They came about either because those old words are simply worn out, i.e. have ceased to have any effect on their intended audience, or because they are burdened by a dishonourable history, as was the case for twenty years or so with racism.[11]

Thus the association of *immigration* with *sauvage* produces more than just the sum of their meanings. And that was very evidently what the inventors of the phrase had in mind. It was an important achievement because it crystallized a nebulous set of emotive responses which were beginning to boil up around that time. A range of emotions of which some might have been thought unsuitable for re-use even by politicians seeking to exploit racist sentiment. But re-use them they did.

THE SEME, THE LEFT AND THE RIGHT

It nevertheless remains the case that in people's immediate perceptions, this seme is centrally connected with hatred and fear. More precisely, it attempts to convert hatred into fear; real hatred, into a purely induced fear. And not just for reasons of political appeal. For fear is actually a more decent feeling than hatred, and can serve as its acceptable mask. *Immigrationsauvage* is fuelled by hatred but legitimates itself though fear, which is a better vehicle of self-justification than hatred. It has always played an absolutely crucial role in the political exploitation of racist and xenophobic attitudes. But for my part, I am not at all convinced that this fear is genuinely felt by xenophobes. In fact, I very much doubt it. (Whereas the fear felt by immigrants is certainly real enough.) But it is a fact that when politicians start taking this supposed fear into account and making political capital out of it, they thereby legitimize racist and xenophobic attitudes.

This of course raises the question of the transmutations which the attention of politicians brings about, whether insidiously or in more spectacular fashion, on the 'spontaneous' attitudes and actions which they set out to to exploit. This process of drift – or transformation – is relatively well known in connection with the political exploitation of 'social discontent', but much less frequently pointed out as a factor when relations of dominance are being interpreted: it is not generally recognized that the political exploitation of xenophobia, misogyny and racism also creates distortions of this type in the original material.

In the case which concerns us here, the Far Right formalizes (gives form to), and verbalizes, in and through its political discourse, particular tendencies, realities and attitudes, extended to implicate a considerably greater number of people and strata in society than was initially intended.

The same mechanism can be seen at work on the Left. While different left- and right-wing sensibilities certainly do exist, they should each be regarded as a core, a centre, around which gravitate much less stable and politically well-defined elements. These elusive elements, ambiguous in that they can be latched onto and verbalized by differing political sensibilities, are picked up in political discourse, sometimes by Right and Left at the same time, as we saw with the theme of 'difference'.

In one sense, political discourse filters out and schematizes a certain number of themes and goals (but by no means all) which are potentially present in the common ideological background, which is, after all, the dominant one. This is something which pragmatic politicians are perfectly well aware of, and turn to their advantage. The Right's racist discourse is an expression of a much more widely-held attitude than its explicit constituency might suggest, and certainly extends way beyond the proponents of a conscious racist ideology.

Thus political discourse on both sides picks up themes from the dominant, shared ideology, radicalizes them in order to prevent their use by political opponents, makes them coherent – which in everyday practice they are not[12] – and turns them into a driving force for political action. But in so doing, in bringing about this ideological reduction, politicians take their newly coherent, radicalized propositions beyond the point where they are counterbalanced by any reality, either factual or ideological.

NOTES

1   These posters, which, as Annie Geffroy pointed out to me in the course of a discussion, were graphically reminiscent of those produced by the Académie des Beaux-Arts in 1968, were put out by the Ordre Nouveau ('New Order') group, which was at that time running a campaign on this theme with posters, postcards and a rally held on 21 June 1973 at la Mutualité. Attempts by the Communist League to have this rally banned led to numerous incidents in central Paris on 21 June. Ordre Nouveau and the Communist League were both dissolved by decree on 29 June 1973, on the proposal of interior minister Raymond Marcellin. P. Gilbert's *Dictionnaire des mots nouveaux* (Paris, Hachette, Tchou, 1971) dates this use of 'sauvage' to around 1965. It gives an example of the expression 'immigration sauvage' from *L'Express* of 13 April 1970: 'We need to select the geographical origin of our foreign workers: 'wildcat immigration' cannot be allowed to continue'.

2   We should remember that 'immigration' was the central theme of the Far Right in these elections, so that there was nothing peripheral or accidental about the way the topic was raised.

3   I use this term deliberately, bending its meaning somewhat in order to stress

the fact that this 'fixed expression' (my fusing together of the two words is also deliberate) has one single, syncretic meaning, although it retains the original colouration of each of its parts.

4   *Le Monde*, 9 March 1983.

5   Interview in *Le Monde*, 9 March 1983. Just for the anecdote, when I was a child living in a medium-sized French provincial town, people in the town centre would kill their pig in the street, in full view; this did not particularly seem to bring anyone out in spots.

6   Jean-Pierre Stirbois, quoted by *Le Monde*, 15 March 1983.

7   T.n.: Out of context, it is impossible to render the 'trendy' force of the examples given (*crédible, créneau, pêche, dur, valable* and *flipper*) without extensive recourse to paraphrase. They have therefore been omitted.

8   Guy Hocquenghem, *Libération*, 5 July 1979.

9   A. Benoist, *Le Monde*, 7 October 1980. [T.n.: 'Légitime défense' has long been a theme of the French Far Right, generally invoked in cases where extreme violence has been used in defending personal property against theft, often when this is by 'immigrants'.]

10 Negation has a specific status in the unconscious, where it does not exist as a literal signifier. There is no such thing as negation in the universe of the unconscious, only (possibly) denial, which is not suppression, but rather an amplification and an admission that something exists. For the record, 'I am not a racist' is part of this problematic of negation – but that is another story.

11 The type of dressing-up of an old term to look new proved very successful around 1975 with people near the centre of the political spectrum, and in some cases even those on the Left, when 'difference' was introduced in place of 'race', and associated with phrases like 'the right to . . .' and 'respect for . . .'. They were quickly joined (surprise, surprise!) by the word 'roots', and the list is still growing.

12 At times of danger, but also in everyday life, certain people's practical behaviour is more complex than their words would lead one to expect. Racist language can in some cases be accompanied by non-racist behaviour (which in no way excuses the use of racist language). The converse, unfortunately, is also true.

Chapter 5

The rapacious hands of destiny

> Looking to the future, the sad thing is not death, but the certainty of the degradation that will occur before we die; this shame which awaits our descendants might perhaps leave us indifferent, could we not already feel, with secret horror, the rapacious hands of destiny closing around our own throats.
>
> (Joseph Arthur de Gobineau, *Essai sur l'inégalité des races humaines*, 1852)

Linguistic irony has it that 'order' is followed by 'ordure' in the dictionary, and these two terms stand at opposite extremes in the affections of the Right, one, order, being its highest value, the other, ordure, referring to everything it detests, whether in people or regimes. The thematics of the Right revolve around a limited number of notions which recur often and insistently enough to give a particular colouring to its discourse. Such themes leave a deep impression on social practices, even when the State is not actively involved in applying them politically. Some are well known[1] and will only be mentioned here as a reminder, before going on to look at the one which directly concerns us. They include belief in, and emphasis on, the *inequality* of human beings and the disparity of human groups; the natural inheritance of social, mental and physical traits, perceived as a syncretic whole (see Guillaumin, *L'Idéologie raciste*); the cult of, and search for, roots – mythical ones, more often than not; the cult of the *élite*, in whatever terms it may be defined – of strength, perhaps, or cunning, success, refinement or brutality, nobility as a class or as a symbolic attribute, etc.; the *sexual character* of the world, where every gesture, relationship, opinion or form of conduct is virile or effeminate (rather than masculine or feminine); the claimed need for a *hierarchy*, and all forms of reverence for strong leadership (in warfare, gangs, business, the family, political parties, etc.). These are all constant right-wing themes, recognized as such, and although one or other of them might be emphasized at a particular moment to suit the topic of debate or the personality of the speaker, they are always associated and easily link up together.

The gulf between the world views of Right and Left is not unbridgeable, in the sense that individuals are not rigid ideological entities. Although each position will always contain certain fixed values, such as order on the Right and contentment on the Left, quite a few traits from one side can turn up sporadically on the other, in contradiction to their overall system of values and references. *Decay*, a theme which we shall discuss below, is an obsession of the Right, and even if certain left-wing politicians and individuals do sometimes use it, it remains a right-wing notion. Anti-Semitism, the backbone of the Right in all its forms since the early nineteenth century, is also found among certain left-wing groups in the nineteenth and early twentieth centuries in the strict sense of 'anti-Semite', and since the Second World War, as 'anti-Zionist'. Sexism is even more of a basic ingredient of right-wing thought, but is also so widely shared by men on the Left that few if any political groups – with the exception of feminists – even imagine that it might be a matter of political concern. This is not to support the contention, which has been fashionable for a while now, that 'there is no such thing as Left and Right any more', for the two political conceptions and directions are not the same, and the division between them can be seen constantly at work in both politics and everyday life. These broad ideological tendencies are however only synthesized into coherent systems and enunciated as doctrine within 'political' formations proper, and then only the Right does it in a uniform manner.

For it is important to remember that these two intellectual universes are not symmetrical: one has behind it the weight of tradition, common sense, habit, and especially the rigidity and complacency fostered by a long period of legitimacy, when efforts have been directed towards 'reconstruction' and 'hard work', rather than channelled into inventive and creative alternatives. The other undertakes a constant critique of the established order and its primary assumptions; its perspective is not one of recovering a 'lost order', but of questioning the basis of that powerfully established *dis*order by which the right of some to decide the fate of others is instituted.[2] Hitler's hatred was particularly directed against this 'corrosive' cast of mind: 'Marxism too had an aim . . . but it nevertheless began with seventy years of critique, destructive and caustic critique, which continued unceasingly until the corrosive acid had eaten away the old State'.[3]

In summary, we shall not be discussing a closed body of doctrine, even if the key right-wing notions are always found among right-wing groups, whereas few characteristically left-wing ideas ever stray in that direction.[4] Nor will we be talking about individuals, with the exception of major politicians and theorists whose discourse is carefully calculated and so presents an acceptable degree of homogeneity (to the extent that such a homogeneity exists in right-wing ideology). For various forms of anti-Semitism and misogyny are far from rare on the Left, whereas such perceptions of human relations belong in essence to a right-wing world view.

We shall be looking at a number of key concepts, running through linked semantic fields, which paint a picture of a society ordered by, and subject to, so-called 'natural' laws.

To grasp this particular vision of the world, we do not even need to try to uncover the ideas underlying its general thematics, for its vocabulary and field of reference are already explicit enough: decomposition, decadence, decline, bastardization, effeminate, degradation, decay, ordure, stench, debasement, trash, degenerateness, corruption, filth, detritus, dirt, dustbin, rubbish-tip, mud, slime, debauchery, dung-hill, downward curve, weakness, death, etc.

Among these terms, which have recurred with absolute regularity in right-wing discourse since the nineteenth century, the one which occupies a key position and is probably the most significant, is *ordure*, for as well as being [in French] a term of abuse, it carries the heaviest weight of derivatives in the field of 'decay': it expresses and synthesizes degradation (social or moral), stench (organic or human), and betrayal, all aspects of the pessimism complex which so often surfaces, sometimes allusively, sometimes with convulsive and belligerent violence, in right-wing ideology.

VIOLENCE?

Belligerence and social convulsion are often associated with violence to the point of being synonymous with it; indeed, such extreme and emotive states are not just violent, they are actually brutal. But violence is not in itself a right-wing phenomenon, it can also characterize left-wing discourse; whether in the form of an explosion of anger, a practical plan of action, or the condemnation of an unacceptable state of affairs, it is often present there too. Projects for revolutions, which are rarely conspicuous by their mildness, are the prerogative of the Left even more than of the Right; and right-wing revolution takes as its frame of reference the revolution of the planets, whereas the Left's is the overthrow of the established social order. From the 'Eternal Return' theme on the Right to the 'more just society' on the Left, the violence involved is not the same. Incidentally, one aim of the Left is to remove the violence inherent in the present social order, an intolerable, unjust, unacceptable violence which is already built into the system, and which all human effort must be directed towards relieving; for the Left, then, violence is primarily a function of the established order. The Right, on the other hand, sees violence as one means of restoring a decadent or degenerate order, but also as a fundamental, essential characteristic of reality, which is leading the world inevitably towards its final catastrophe; thus for the Right it is both a metaphysical characteristic of the prevailing order and an expression of the way in which that order is being dragged towards its end, its great defeat.

Therefore, the term 'violence' does not seem a very suitable one to describe the Right's catastrophic or apocalyptic perception of life, human relations, the world and history. This vision is characterized less by vehemence and belligerence than by a more or less explicit pessimism, which is shared by intellectual and more popular currents alike. The precise form which it takes will vary according to the social background or intentions of the speaker: the 'pessimism' expressed by a member of the upper bourgeoisie operating in an explicitly 'doctrinal' idiom might well turn into insults and obscenities in the mouth of a muscle-bound security 'heavy'. But from the accusation that it is a 'pals' Republic', to the cry 'they're all rotten apples!', the Right is saying essentially the same thing. This theme surfaced yet again in the European elections of 1984, when a member of the Socialist government in France was called the 'minister for crooks'.[5] A semantic field, by definition, does not play on just one word, and there is no direct equivalence between the terms it contains, so that the use of one rather than the others is a matter of choice. 'Rotten apple' and 'crook' belong to the same field (whereas 'incompetent fool' or 'gangster', although still political insults, do not, for they lack the key connotations of conspiracy and corruption). Equally, in the semantic field of words designating the hierarchy of individuals, one a man might be referred to as a 'leader' and another as a 'boss', terms which are not identical, though both express the ideology of the strong man, the 'élite individual' who 'has what it takes'.

The terms used may vary, but what remains constant is the sense of an insidious malady eating away at the world from within; the obsession with rottenness and decay is shared by all on the Right. This disillusioned and yet belligerent pessimism sees the course of events and of people's lives through the filter of organic decay and putrefaction. From the popular cry of 'they're all rotten apples', already quoted, to Shakespeare's 'something rotten in the State of Denmark', the notion of physical corruption joins together the two ends of a chain linking betrayal and sickness on the one hand with defeat and death on the other.

This belief (if one may use the word) runs right through French literature from the nineteenth century on, from Barbey d'Aurevilly to Drieu La Rochelle, feeding into both its aesthetic and its political concerns. But it is not just a matter of words (whether in literature, politics or banal verbal exchange), but rather of a much wider sensibility beyond explicit, verbal expression. It can also be seen in paintings such as *The Death of Sardanapale* and *The Massacre at Chios* by Delacroix (as is confirmed by reading his diary and correspondence). After Sade, an obsessive preoccupation with 'decay', a fascination with cruelty mixed with force, a conviction of the world's being ground down from without and rotting away from within, gradually came to form the backdrop to a sensibility shared by dandies and storm-troopers, as well as a widespread current of popular opinion which hardens at moments of crisis such as the present. So it is not so much a question of violence as of apocalypse, of a world which contains the seeds of its own destruction.

THE RAPACIOUS HANDS OF DESTINY . . .

For the game is always lost in advance, and a profound belief in the final plunge into the morass, in Death and Nothingness, characterizes rightwing thought in general. Much more common among doctrinal theorists and ordinary people than politicians, who can hardly go into battle shouting slogans of defeat (although the famous 'Long live death!' certainly gives pause for thought), this gloomy preoccupation constantly returns to reiterate its threat: 'when that great evening comes . . . which will cloak in the shadows of death and cast into lonely silence the ruins of what once was France', prophesied Drumont, lamenting '. . . by what sly and cunning enemy France had been invaded, corrupted, stupefied'.[6]

Gobineau in the nineteenth century and Julius Evola in the twentieth have in common a desperate fear that human society is, slowly but surely, slipping towards its inevitable decay and final destruction. If they do believe in the evolution of social forms – or rather, of historical beings – they see a movement not towards increased gain and complexity, but towards death, after a period of agonizing decomposition. Politicians and pragmatists who are fighting on the ground tend to call for a stiffening of resolve and a 'leap into action' in the battle for honour which must be fought in a world without hope, dominated by terrible internal forces of destruction. Dandies and aesthetes merely condescend to look down on the whole business.

This inherent Evil, which has such power over everything, is constantly turning up in the form of conspiracies, betrayals, invasions, moral and physical disease ('Love, a word that needs disinfecting' was the title of an article by Louis Pauwels in the *Journal du Dimanche*),[7] and against it is ranged the sole power for 'good' that still survives in this world under sentence. The only hope lies in the triumph of the strong, whatever form that triumph might take. Political *programmes* take the approach that the world must be purged as far as possible of the evil that is undermining it. And by antiphrasis, words like 'clean', 'healthy', and even 'pure' (in the sexual sense used by religious moralists and directed at women, who need to be kept 'pure' for the benefit of men[8]) figure prominently in electoral speeches and other power-seeking forms of discourse: 'a man of rudimentary cultural knowledge but sound in body . . . is more useful . . . than an invalid, however intellectually gifted he may be' (Hitler, op. cit., p. 54). But the main subject of preoccupation remains the negative side, the infirmity, sickness, impurity which 'have tainted the blood of our people, and corrupted not only their blood, but also their very soul' (ibid., p. 51). These are themes which recur spontaneously, without recourse to any practical consideration. The fascination with death, decline and degradation (to be countered with scorn and condescension), with leprosy and (one of the populist Right's favourite terms, in both literal and figurative usages) venereal disease, with effeminateness and/or emasculation, remains the point of reference for a political vision obsessed by the betrayal of a moral and pragmatic order which in fact only exists *because* of its corruption. Evil occupies centre stage, it alone is worthy of interest, and the fight against it – or to find a way of living with it – is the only conceivable fight. There is little enough trace of any 'good', and certainly not of the type that might concern real people. That probably explains why, for the Right, it is not appropriate to try to bring about a 'better world', but rather to look beneath the world as it now is for an eternal essence, and the strength to go on living.

SCIENCE?

Paraphrasing, I think, Drieu La Rochelle ('tout est foutu': 'everything's gone to hell'), Plumyenne and Lassiera sum it up like this: 'Alas, nowadays everything's gone to hell! It's the end of the world. Read

Minute. Everything's cracking up!'[9] The squares on a snakes and ladders board running from enfeeblement (Start) to death (Finish) and strewn with invasion and loss of honour, sickness and inter-breeding, have been in place since the nineteenth century. There is a striking continuity in these topics, something which did not escape the notice of those who, when the New Right started making waves, set out to gather together and compare notes on their various recollections of the past, and saw at once that the same themes, though disguised in modern dress, were coming back again. The fact that they were wrapped around with scientific terminology was nothing new, contrary to what many people believed or wanted to make others believe. Proof by science is an old habit on the Right, and Gobineau went even further than the social Darwinists, who themselves are very keen on this type of formal justification, in equipping his *Essai sur l'inégalité* with a heavy-handed academic apparatus. Incidentally, it is worth noting in passing the ironic fact that the Left, which used to be accused of having an old-fashioned and out-of-date faith in science, has now found itself accused of failing to listen to 'scientific fact'. For order can only be discovered in facts, and it is science that decodes the facts. Actually, it is all too easy to discover whatever order you choose in facts, but that is perhaps another story.

From a right-wing point of view, therefore, society is *already* corrupt, and it is not so much that the world is perverted by people despite their intentions, as that its *natural* tendency is to express a fundamental evil of which people are only one element among others. Yet this mixture of pessimism and cynicism is accompanied by a respect for the 'natural order', an order which is both cruel and good at the same time, characterized by brutality, force and cunning, but which allows the Ego (of the Stoic, dandy, aristocrat, pragmatist, politician or realist) to create a fantasy bubble of cleanliness within which it reigns supreme (the family, a group of comrades, an élite above the common herd . . .), or is embodied in some mystical or military 'leader' in whom complete trust can be placed. The love of order in a perverse world is, then, clearly a difficult option which can only be pursued in the tragic posture of hero or dandy.

Ethologists claim that man's misfortune and imminent decline are caused by a failure to remain faithful to his instincts (see Chapter 12), a proposition which denies instinct at the very moment when its importance is being proclaimed. Since man's instincts are 'straight' (but not 'good'), betraying them means betraying the order of the world, whose obvious cruelty, repressing or destroying the weak and allowing the strongest (the fittest, the best . . .) to triumph over their inferiors, is a fact of nature. The natural order, proclaimed as the most desirable model, knows no pity, which is its great virtue. The death of the weak and the poorly equipped, the submission of women (the females of the species), the 'marvellous instinct towards slavery' (to quote Darwin), the taming of the young, are all in line with this much-revered order. It is an order not so much of everything in its place as of everything *put* in its place, under duress, with human beings 'trained' like performing animals; a world in which the spirit is broken by harsh rules, one in which what is euphemistically called a 'training' is handed down, by generations of those who have 'been through it' and 'become men', to the young who must not be allowed to get away without doing the same; without going through war, sexual violence, enforced child-bearing, military service, all of which are 'noble' and 'part of life', in the minds of the elegant set and the political Right no less than in the morality of the man in the street, both of whom consider that no one else should be allowed to avoid doing the things that the speaking ego, for its part, has been through.

Schematically, an original order, which is either coded in instinct but not yet properly actualized, or somehow betrayed, is under threat from various elements which operate by insidious contamination rather than by open antagonism. The ultimate consequence of this slow and at times chaotic penetration is, or will be, the end of civilization and of the world. Between an original or potential founding order and the final apocalypse, sickness, vermin and cross-breeding all gnaw destructively away at the world, dragging it towards the abyss from which only a drastic and general return to solid values can preserve it, and then only temporarily. Failing that, honour, condescension, stoicism and contempt provide the élite individual's only answer to the prevailing decadence.

Whatever happens, therefore, the world is heading for *catastrophe*, whether through betrayal of the natural order or through *conformity* with it, as a result of the massacres and the repression which merely serve and maintain that order, which is legitimized by Science. We live in a state of necessary violence and terror which removes the possibility of life being in any way pleasant, and only the spineless and degenerate Left could still imagine and wish for it to be just and 'humane'. Even moderation and humour among those on the Right are unable to temper this pessimism: 'love and friendship must be extended to the whole of humanity and . . . we must love our human brothers without any discrimination. This is by no means a new commandment. Our reason is quite able to understand its necessity, and our sensibility to appreciate its beauty. And yet, constituted as we are, we are unable to obey it'.[10]

SOME 'POLITICAL' WORDS

Northern League
Defence of the West
Group for a European Cultural Renaissance
The 121
The 343
League of the Rights of Man

These are the titles of some groups which have participated in political life in different ways and at different times. The oldest goes back to the Dreyfus Affair and the most recent was active fifteen years or so ago. It is obvious that some of these names express aims and sensibilities which are clearly on the Right, others on the Left. The League of the Rights of Man was born out of the Dreyfus Affair and still exists today, unlike its anti-Dreyfusard opponent of the time, the League of the French Nation. The Group for a European Cultural Renaissance (GRECE), founded in 1968, marked the official resurgence of the traditional preoccupations of the 'non-political' Right. These groups are of interest to us here not for their goals, but for their chosen names and what they imply. Our selection was made at random; many others might have been chosen which would show the same characteristics. On the Left we find groups named after the number of like-minded individuals who made up their membership (the 121 intellectuals against the Algerian War, the 343 women who declared publicly that they had had an abortion) or groups which proclaim the rights of each human individual; they are all concerned with people, social actors, human beings, and their consciences or rights of conscience. But this left-wing sequence is only there to point up the specific feature of names on the Right, which is that they all relate to a space or territory, and lack any reference to actors in society.

As is well known, references to the soil, without being exclusive to the Right, nevertheless play a special role in right-wing ideology in that the soil of itself engenders legitimacy. Pétain claimed that his own legitimacy derived from the fact that he had remained on French soil, and a current right-wing leader, in an interview going back some time now, mimicked in front of the cameras the action of trampling the soil which was supposed to guarantee the correctness of his political position. These entities of space, soil and territory join others ('culture' nowadays, 'blood' not so long ago – and in fact still today in some cases) in standing as ultimate referents, under whose overwhelming influence individuals are generally reduced to the state of insignificant pawns and either crushed or carried along on the wave. These entities, for the Right, exist to a greater degree than human beings ever will, for one day 'vigorous Nature will regain its universal dominion over the Earth, and human creatures will no longer stand before it as its master'.[11] In short, concrete reality means something quite different according to whether we seek it on one side of the political spectrum or the other. For the Right, that reality is non-human and transcends individuals, whereas for the Left it is first and foremost a human matter, to be found in all the particularities of human life.

But the political vocabulary itself, in the restricted sense of the term, can be common to both. We have already noted that the word 'Revolution' has long since been adopted by the Right. Paired up with 'national' (as in 'National Revolution'), it was the slogan of the *État Français* of the Forties, the so-called 'Vichy Regime', one of whose official objectives was a return to the soil. This re-use of the word was justified on grounds of meaning by the idea that a revolution is, literally, nothing but a return of the same, making it an excellent expression of the 'Eternal Return' theme so dear to the Right, particularly as it could be interpreted not just as a simple return, but as a complex trajectory able to take in new domains as it went. It was the strange fate of the expression 'new order', the title of a newspaper (*L'Ordine Nuovo*) founded by Gramsci and Togliatti in 1919, to become the name of a Far Right group in France half a century later. But the word 'order' is, of course, evocative of right-wing sensibilities, in which it plays a central role in all its forms (from 'order of knighthood' and the 'natural order' of instincts, to 'order' on its own), even if the idea of novelty and 'the new' does tend rather to belong (though not exclusively) to a left-wing thematics.

A vaguer, less precisely delineated notion is currently undergoing a similar adventure: that of man as his own maker. The first theoretical expressions of this idea appeared on the Left in, among other places, Engels's *Dialectics of Nature*, which characterized the human race as being the producer of its own nature. This, linked to and blended in with its traditional dandy-istic morality, is widely echoed in the so-called New Right's concept of the 'individual as his own maker'. The coincidence of terms remains superficial (human society as the producer of human nature on the one hand, the élite individual constructing his own being on the other), but it does give pause for thought, particularly as a large sector of ethology with explicit right-wing leanings has taken a neo-Engelsian line on the origin of social formations.[12] The exceptional individual's construction of his own self as tragic hero or dandy, conqueror or aesthete, was an aspect of right-wing morality so much taken for granted (see, for example, Gobineau, Barbey d'Aurevilly, Barrès) that there was absolutely no need to mention it: any élite being would by nature remain aloof from the common herd. Today, the most distinguished voices on the Right are telling people of the need to surpass themselves by deliberately cultivating the superior man's instincts, thus confirming the inferior status of the other poor fools.

ENTITIES, FANTASIES AND HUMAN BEINGS

In the eyes of the Right, an internal sickness is eating away at the most precious values, and if corruption and decomposition are obsessionally associated with the things that it hates the most, they can also affect those that it holds most dear. 'France' has become a 'dustbin' and a 'rubbish-dump', expressions which are paradoxical to say the least in the mouths of people who revere their country and make such a point of saying so. Corruption is inherent in material 'possessions' and for that reason they are despised, although ownership is not, for there is no doubt that it is unavoidable and essential. It is both good and necessary to have children, a wife (or wives), money (not to be confused with detested 'capital'), a house (not to be included in the category of 'merchandise'), and of course land, a concept rendered completely abstract to the point where it has become a symbol of itself. We saw above the importance of territory, geographical space and references to the 'soil' (which for its part seems to escape all taint by decay or decomposition). So ownership is taken for granted, but possessions themselves are immoral, 'capital' and 'merchandise' are evil incarnate, children are difficult to control and need to be tamed, corruption seeps out to poison the very air we breathe, money 'stinks' and so do women.

Anti-capitalism has been one of the most constant features of right-wing discourse for the last century and a half, and one of the lengthiest anti-Semitic pamphlets in French presents itself as a work of anti-capitalism.[13] This anti-capitalist discourse is sufficiently ambiguous to create a zone of uncertainty such that it can be acknowledged and adopted by individuals on the Left, as 1968 and its political repercussions once again showed. Yet we should note the fact that Left and Right do not mean the same thing by capital (though that should be self-evident). For the Right, capital is money as essence, money as fetish-object, a solidified monetary mass which can corrupt merely by contact; for the Left, capital is a social relationship – after all, Marx wrote *Das Kapital* in order to describe a process, and his subject is not money but human work; the book is a critique of money as essence.

The unhealthy essence which, in the eyes of their owners, characterizes certain material possessions, whether inanimate or human, is most clearly revealed in situations of uncertainty or conflict, and only occasionally comes to the surface in everyday life. Belief in this essence is perfectly compatible with a discourse of approval, and even of praise, as women know to their cost, for they, like money, can be alternately despised and complimented, and they too are made out of something slightly dubious. They are necessary, but contemptible. Contemptible because they corrupt, as well as being themselves corrupt, unless they are first tamed by techniques which the Right knows all about, from rape to close protection. Their corruption is ultimately that of all beings and things, with the speaker alone able to rise morally above the universal disaster.

This obsessive, omnipresent, menacing corruption is therefore carried by human beings; doubly so in that they themselves are eaten away by it, while at the same time acting as its means of transmission. A group of people, a set of concrete individuals become the embodiment of an obsession with evil which runs all through right-wing thinking. And a person's skin, a human life, is a fragile thing. There is a terrifying mechanism by which obsessional imaginings and fantasies to do with evil, corruption, betrayal, sickness, apocalypse . . . are foisted onto real human beings without their having any power to prevent it. A murderous form of collusion is thus produced which allows one group of people to transfer their worst nightmares onto the bodies of others.

The theme of poisoning is one of the oldest known examples of this mechanism. Recently a famous psychiatrist well known for his right-wing opinions railed against psychoanalysis (we shall not become involved in that debate here) in terms which assimilated it to a form of poisoning. Anyone with some knowledge of history will know that poisoning and corruption, which are such frequent elements in right-wing discourse, are laid preferentially at the door of the Jews; everything from corruption of the mind, of which the *Protocols of the Elders of Zion* purports to contain the programme, written by the victims themselves, to 'poisoning' by 'Jewish science' (i.e. Freudian psychoanalysis). This provides a good opportunity to bring out another, much older accusation, one voiced more frequently in earlier times: that of poisoning wells, which cropped up regularly in anti-Jewish attacks throughout the medieval period. By manipulating the accused, the accusers strip away the humanity of those whom they are oppressing physically. When

Darquier de Pellepoix, a former high official in the Vichy government, speaking in an interview with a weekly magazine, used the term 'lice' in connection with the extermination of Jews in the Nazi camps, when Himmler earlier used the same term to say explicitly what Darquier was denying, that 'anti-Semitism has been for us a question not of world-view but of hygiene, and one which will soon be resolved. Soon we shall have no more lice',[14] they were both doing far more than just using a word. Whenever human groups (religious, cultural, historical or of any other type) are referred to in terms of lice and vermin (a trait of right-wing discourse if ever there was one, even if the speaker claims to be on the Left), they are deprived of their humanity as a prelude to, or at the same time as, being deprived of their life. Jews are no longer even the *agents* of evil, they are evil incarnate.

Then suddenly the endemic evil embodied in real human beings becomes eradicable. The Right has the answer to the problem of un-employment: this far from imaginary evil is embodied in immigrants who have 'stolen' the jobs which, without them, would surely be avail-able for others. Just get rid of them and unemployment will go away. Evil can be got at directly, in the shape of real human beings. The themes of vermin, filth and incarnate evil are components of fully-fledged racist discourse, which itself is one of the Right's most consistent character-istics: its system of reference is based on 'allogeneity', as represented by immigrants, foreigners, anyone who does not fit the myth of the 'typical' Frenchman, and its political effectiveness is being demonstrated once again in France today. The people who are picked on in this way become filthy vermin as a result, so guaranteeing by antiphrasis the healthy humanity of their accusers, those who speak and then decide, those whose speech itself decides.

Whether the evil in question be something identifiable and localized, tied to a particular point in history (as with unemployment), or some-thing metaphysical and eternal (such as the malice in men's hearts), it must be made tangible, perceived as and proclaimed to be co-extensive with specific, real, human beings. If that is not always the case (for something as grand as evil does not always condescend to embody itself in particular people, and in any case a share needs to be kept back for apocalyptic events and the ups and downs of the aesthetic cycle), con-crete carriers of evil are still necessary: people who can be pursued, put under duress, hunted down, and killed. The human beings chosen for this deadly honour, the groups selected, are those in a state of depen-dency, those who are 'at the mercy' of others.[15]

CONCLUSION

It is difficult to treat in isolation a single element of a thematics whose different traits all reflect and point back to each other, forming a homogeneous ideology. Thus it would be artificial to separate out the theme of corruption and the inherent evil of the world because it is explained and justified by many others, the most striking of which were mentioned at the beginning of this chapter. Most of the writings based on this ideology in fact make use of many of them together, so that a careful reading allows us to trace its overall configuration.

The evil which inhabits the world is its very essence, insidious, endemic, ultimately fatal, and it characterizes what might be called the *involutionism* of the Right. For a long time *evolutionism*, now outdated, was the keystone of a view of the world in which change was usually regarded as synonymous with progress, however that notion was defined. It was generally, though not always, a left-wing phenomenon. But alongside this 'scientifically' inspired evolutionism, there continued to exist a different way of looking at people and the world, history and nature, one which the Left never shared and which today is exclusive to the Right. Believers in this approach maintain that decadence and decay are the keys to history. They assume that things can only turn out for the very worst, that even at the height of the golden age the characteristic manifestations of evil and corruption were already working away, and that their increasing spread as perceived by contemporaries (of whatever period) is but an expression of death's inevitably expanding role in history, and a sure sign of the end of the world. The passionate and preferential search for the signs of decomposition, putrefaction and decay finds its ultimate justification in this pessimistic credo.

NOTES

1 This thematic has received frequent coverage from different angles. See, for example: A. Rollat, 'Le P.F.N. et la Nouvelle Droite' (relations between a party and a 'movement of ideas'); C. Capitan-Peter, *Charles Maurras et l'idéologie d'Action française* (the case of an important right-wing leader); B.-H. Lévy, *L'Idéologie française* (from the Dreyfus Affair on, as embodied by influential politicians from all sides); J. Plumyenne and R. Lasierra, *Le Complexe de droite* (humorous look at twentieth-century writers).

2 This is something which does not always please the 'others', whatever we might be told about good bosses, good fathers, good husbands, good dictators, in short, good leaders (and dispensers of the wealth which they cream off from the work of their subordinates).

3 *Mein Kampf*, p. 63.
4 However, we are seeing the gradual adoption by the Right of certain left-wing words (rather than ideas), such as technology and modernity, or, as we shall see below, 'revolution', man 'as his own maker', the 'New Order', etc.
5 *Le Monde*, 8–9 July 1984, p. 8.
6 *La France juive*, vol. II, pp. 573, 577.
7 24 October 1976.
8 *Front National* rally on 20 May 1984. As far as I know, these statements were not reported in any of the newspapers.
9 From the publisher's blurb for Plumyenne and Lasierra, op. cit.
10 K. Lorenz, *Aggression*.
11 J.A. de Gobineau, *Essai sur l'inégalité*, vol. II, p. 561.
12 I allude here to the line of thinking popularized by Lionel Tiger, Robin Fox, etc. which sees the origin of civilization in co-operation between males for the purpose of hunting.
13 E. Drumont, op. cit. Incidentally, Marx's reply to Bruno Bauer, *The Jewish Question*, one of his most controversial books and one generally regarded as anti-Semitic, is about 'economic' ideology.
14 Quoted in J. Gabel, *Réflexions sur l'affaire Faurisson*, p. 82.
15 At the same time, by some sinister form of humour, formidable powers will often be ascribed to them: it is well known, for instance, that the world is dominated by women and Jews. But they must live among their pursuers, unarmed. People attribute to immigrants, in addition to the privilege they share with women and Jews of being carriers of disease (sexual and other), an almost occult power derived from their numbers, supposedly sufficient to overrun the host country.

Part II

Chapter 6

Race and Nature: the system of marks

The idea of a natural group and social relationships

THE IDEA OF RACE AND OF A 'NATURAL' GROUP

The idea of race

The idea of race. What is this self-evident notion, this 'fact of nature'? It is an ordinary historical fact – a social fact. I deliberately say *idea* of race: the belief that this category is a material phenomenon. For it is a heterogeneous intellectual formulation, with one foot in the natural sciences and one foot in the social sciences. On the one hand, it is an aggregate of somatic and physiological characteristics – in short, race as conceived by the physical anthropologists and the biologists. On the other hand it is an aggregate of social characteristics that express a group – but a social group of a special type, a group *perceived as natural*, a group of people considered as materially specific in their bodies. This naturalness may be regarded by some people as fundamental (a natural group whose nature is expressed in social characteristics). Or it may be regarded by others as a secondary fact (a social group that 'furthermore' is natural). In any case, in the current state of opinion, this naturalness is always present in the approach which the social sciences take, and which the social system has crystallized and expressed under the name of 'race'.

So apparently it's all very simple. A purely 'material' approach to observed characteristics on the one hand; and on the other hand, a mixed approach, more interested in socio-symbolic traits than in somatic traits, all the while keeping the latter present in the mind, in the background in some way or another. But with no profound clash between the two approaches; it is indeed a matter of the same thing in both cases. And equilibrium seems assured with the natural sciences referring to physical forms and the classical social sciences referring to social forms.

Nevertheless, one might expect from the latter that their classifications and commentaries, even if they render discreet homage to the natural sciences, would still declare their specificity, first by defining with precision their concerns, and then by questioning the meaning in social terms of the fact that certain social categories are reputed to be natural. In fact, the social sciences are fascinated by the natural sciences, in which they hope to find a methodological model (which at the very least is debatable), but in which also (and this is the most serious matter) they believe they find an ultimate justification.[1] This attitude is not unrelated to the social reasons which lead to the usage of the idea of nature in the classification of social groups.

But, to proceed, let us accept for the moment that the division is effective and that equilibrium is realized between the disciplines, and let us take for established fact a separation between them, at least in their explicit concerns. So we have, on the one hand, a *supposedly natural* taxonomy, that of physical anthropology, population genetics, etc., declaring the existence of 'natural' groups of humans, finite and specific (whites, blacks, brachycephalics, dolichocephalics, etc.); and on the other hand, a *social* taxonomy, that of history and sociology, taking into account the relational and historical characteristics of groups (slaves, the nobility, the bourgeoisie, etc.). The two types of classification can overlap or not, can have common areas or have no meeting point.[2] An example of *non-overlap*: The blacks of the American social (read racial) system obviously have nothing (or very little) to do with the blacks and whites of physical anthropology in the anthropological meaning of the term. An example of *overlap*: The whites and blacks of the apartheid system are indeed what anthropology designates them as. But let us note that this is only at the price of another category, which is, if you wish, non-existent, or out of consideration – the 'coloureds' – bringing together both an aggregate of socio-economic criteria (an aggregate without which and outside of which this group would literally not be *seen*) and an ideological *denial* – the denial of the non-existence of naturally finite groups. The denial is constructed as follows:

First step The fantasizing initial position postulates that an unbreachable barrier separates human groups, that races are radically dissimilar from each other.

Second step The reality nevertheless is that this barrier does not exist, since the continuity between groups is proven in action by individuals who, belonging to two (or several) 'races', show that there is only one.

Third step Then comes the denial: 'I do not want to know that there is no barrier, because I assert that there is one, and I consider null and void any contradiction of that barrier. I don't see it, it doesn't exist'. In other words the constitution of a 'coloured' group says that *it is not true that there is no* unbreachable barrier between 'blacks' and 'whites'. By the creation of this 'non-group' no evidence exists of the continuity between groups, for the evidence of it is turned into a particular and independent entity. That class formed by people belonging in fact to one *and* the other group is declared to belong to neither the one nor the other, but to itself.³ And thus the system proclaims that human groups are natural, and that in one's natural materiality one can belong to one *or* the other of these groups (or to some other *group*) but in no case to both one *and* the other. But the reality meanwhile is that people do belong to one *and* the other (or to some other groups).

A first questioning can already begin. The two preceding statements – that certain (social) blacks are whites (in the United States) and that a group belongs to both one *and* the other group (in South Africa) – are exactly the opposite of what is implied by the idea of race itself, which is supposed to be a *natural closed category*, and which thereby certifies the status of a group that is first of all fixed and secondly hereditary. In the impassioned proclamations of the social system there is the fantastic and *legalized* affirmation (we will return to this) that the boundaries between the groups are beyond the reach of, and anterior to, human beings – thus immutable. And, in addition, these boundaries are considered as obvious, as the very avowal of common sense ('You're not going to tell me there are no races – surely?' and 'It's plain for everyone to see!').⁴ And on the other hand, one cannot but charge such affirmations with lack of reality when one looks at what actually goes on and when one tries to apply the most ordinary rules of logic to it. For what goes on is the opposite of the impossibility that they affirm to us – no barrier nor separation, but a close association, a deep social and material imbrication which far outstrips the simple somatic continuity between the groups so violently denied.

The idea of a 'natural' group

Material 'imbrication'? Social 'imbrication'? Yes, for supposedly 'natural' groups only exist by virtue of the fact that they are so interrelated that effectively each of the groups is a function of the other. In short, it is a matter of social relations within the same social formation. One does not care to assert naturalness when there is economic, spatial and other independence among groups. Only certain specific relations (of dependence, exploitation) lead to the postulation of the existence of 'natural heterogeneous entities'. Colonization by the appropriation of people (traffic in slaves, later in labourers) and of territories (that of the last two centuries) and the appropriation of the bodies of women (and not solely of their labour power) have led to the proclamation of the specific nature of the groups that endured or still endure these relations.

In fact, the groups concerned are *one and the same natural group* if one accepts this classification in terms of nature. The social idea of natural group rests on the ideological postulation that there is a closed unit, endo-determined [determined from within], hereditary and dissimilar to other social units. This unit, always empirically social, is supposed to reproduce itself and within itself. All this rests on the clever finding that whites bear whites and blacks bear blacks, that the former are the masters and the latter the slaves, that the masters bear masters and the slaves slaves, etc., and that nothing can happen, and that nothing does happen, to trouble this impeccable logic. The children of slaves are slaves, as we know, while the children of slaves can also be – and often are – the children of the master. What 'natural' group do they belong to? That of their mother? That of their father? That of their slave mother or that of their master father? In the United States in the eighteenth century the person who was on either side (the mother's or the father's) the child of a slave was a slave. The child of a slave man and a free woman was a slave (in Maryland as far back as the seventeenth century); the child of a slave woman and a free man was also a slave (in all the slave states). What 'natural' group did they belong to? It was said (this line of argument developed in the United States) that the child of a slave woman was a slave 'because it is difficult to dissociate a child from its mother', but what becomes of this argument when the slave child is the child of a free woman? If it is 'difficult to dissociate a child from its mother', should it not be free? In Maryland a free woman who married a slave saw her children born slaves.

We can move one step further if we take into consideration the social relationships of sex in this matter. They clarify the relationships of 'race' (theoretically involved in slavery) better than considerations about 'maternity'. The child and the wife are the property of the husband-father, which is forgotten. A woman slave is the property of the master as a slave; her child is therefore the property of the master; a free woman is the property of her husband as a wife and – her husband being the property of the master as a slave – her children are the property of the master, thus slaves. She herself, moreover, was obliged to serve the master as long as her husband was living.

In addition, the sexed division of humanity is regarded as leading to and constituting two heterogeneous groups. The fantasy implies that men make men and women make women. In the case of the sexes, emphasis is more and more placed on intragroup homogeneity: men with men, women with women, in their quasi-speciation. This can be seen in the scientized expressions used in discussing parthenogenesis and in the half-reproving, half-condescending attitude which surrounds fathers who father 'only' girls. But, for the time being, men are the children of women (a fact which is well known, perhaps too well known). What is less known seems to be that women are the children of men. To what 'natural' group do they belong? Being a man or being a woman, being white or being black means to belong to a social group regarded as natural, but certainly not to a 'natural' group.

And moreover the American system – first a slave system, later transformed into a racial system in the nineteenth century with the abolition of slavery – has well and truly defined belonging to a 'race' according to class criteria, since the whites who had (or might have had) a supposed slave ancestor were (and still are) 'blacks'. Thus, a great-grandparent – that is, one out of eight direct genitors (since we have eight great-grandparents) – or even one ancestor out of sixteen makes you belong to a determined social group, under the mask of naturalness – the most adulterated naturalness in this case. For logically if one takes the suggestions of natural realism literally (and not figuratively), having seven white great-grandparents certainly means being white. But this is not so! You are not white, you are 'black', for it is the social system that decides. The social situation is that you are black because that is the way the (social) definitions have decided it. Why then speak of pre-social, outside-of-society, 'scientific' classification – in a word, of 'natural' classification? It is this which makes us ask ourselves about this 'natural' that claims to be natural while being something else than what it claims to be, a natural that defines a class by something other than that which is effectively at work in constituting a class. In short, beneath this single notion there stretches a network of relationships covered with a justifying mask – that of Nature, of our Mother Nature.

The denial of reality in the apartheid system illustrates this extra-ordinary operation of masking. This system claims – having found another, more subtle means of defining membership in a group – that there is no material mixing between groups. There are supposed to be two races, one white, the other black, each exhibiting its own characteristics and its own nature, *and* another race, completely different, without any relation to the preceding ones, a pure product in and of itself. Institutionally separate, the 'coloureds' constitute the 'other' race, the third element that renders any questioning of the system irrelevant.

These two examples of naturalist false consciousness have been taken from western industrial society and refer to two historical extreme points: the sequels of the period of capital accumulation (plantation slavery) and the contemporary technological society of South Africa. This is not by chance, for the development of the idea of race is co-extensive with that spatial and temporal zone. But it is more than doubtful that this idea still has spatial limits today.

THE SYSTEMS OF 'MARKS'

The conventional mark

During the two preceding centuries, the geographical localization of productive forces has been the determining factor in the *form* taken by the imputation of naturalness to social groups. The European labor force, in Europe itself, produced a certain number of products (metal ingots, cloth, weapons, etc.) which served as the means of exchange in Africa, especially in the Gulf of Guinea, for a labour force directly transported to the Americas (the South, the Caribbean and the North) to cultivate the land by 'industrial' (or intensive) exploitation. This agriculture, which at first had been extensive and devoted to luxury products (tobacco, indigo, etc.), rapidly became intensive, with the growing first of sugar-cane and then of cotton to be exported to Europe. This triangular traffic, as it is called, maintained the European labor force in Europe for mining and manufacturing, and exported the African labor force to America for the industrial-agricultural production of tropical products. But the recruitment of the labor force was not immediately so neatly divided. During the seventeenth century, the American agricultural slavery system recruited in both Europe and Africa; the indentured slaves of that period came from the two old continents.[5] It is then as a by-product of, and in a manner dependent on, geographical origin that skin colour acquired a role, in so far as the occasion presented by the search for a labor force and the extension of the triangular traffic offered the possibility for 'marking'. For if the idea of naturalness is modern, written into the industrial-scientific society, it is not the same, on the other hand, for the socio-symbolic system of marks put on social groups. This latter system concerns a large number of historical and contemporary societies. It is not linked, as the race system will be, to the position of the dominated as such. It comes into play at all levels of the relationship, dominating and dominated, although the mark has specific characteristics according to the level, as we shall see.

Distinct from the idea of nature,[6] and even in a sense contrary to it, since it bears witness to the conventional and artificial inscription of social practices, the system of marks has been present for a very long time as the accompaniment of social cleavages. It still exists, although it is not always noticed, and in its most constant form it is too familiar to be seen. The fact that men and women dress differently, with clothes that are not cut in the same way (draping persists to some extent in women's clothes, while it has disappeared from men's) is an example of marking that continues to be generally recognized.

Nevertheless, people recognized the dress differentiation between the bourgeoisie and the nobility during the feudal period of the eighteenth century which gave the nobility the right to furs, jewels, bright colours and metallic cloth, and gave the bourgeoisie almost a monopoly on the wearing of black.[7] This distinction disappeared when the noble class melted into the bourgeoisie during the nineteenth century, after the bourgeois revolutions. These latter, by abolishing clothing prohibitions, are the source of so-called peasant 'regional' costumes, in which colour, lace and embroidery express a newly acquired right. It is well known that during the Middle Ages the members of non-dominant religions wore a clothing mark such as the yellow pointed hat or the yarmulke (varying according to regions and period) of the Jews, the yellow cross for the Cathars, etc. The nobles marked their various family groups (groups that, from the fifteenth to the eighteenth century, were called 'races') with 'coats of arms' on movable objects such as harnesses, shields, armour, vehicles, paintings, servants (objects like the others), or on their buildings, on the porticoes, gates, etc. In the sixteenth and seventeenth centuries, the galley slaves, the deported prostitutes, and then the slaves until the nineteenth century, were marked by an *immovable* sign, directly inscribed on the body (physical marking of slaves was abolished in 1833 for France), as in the twentieth century deportees were marked by the Nazi state; this same state imposed a cloth badge on Jews before it started to exterminate them. We know that today military personnel and street cleaners (among others) wear a uniform, but we have forgotten that only a short while ago (in the nineteenth century) a man's shaving his beard was a sign of being in domestic service; the tonsure of Catholic priests, ringlets of very orthodox Jews, and long hair for women and short for men were (or still are) some of the many signs and marks, either external or inscribed on the body, that expressed (and imprinted) the fact of belonging to a definite social group. And there is a very long list of such signs and marks.

The characteristics of the mark vary, and its indelibility, as well as its more or less close proximity to/association with the body, is a function of: (1) the assumed permanence of the position that it is a sign of; and (2) the degree of subjection that it symbolizes. The convict under the *ancien régime*, the contemporary concentration camp victim and the American slave bore the mark on their body (tattooed number or brand), a sign of the *permanence* of the power relationship. The dominating group imposes its fixed inscription on those who are materially subject to them. The mark of status is inscribed in a reversible fashion when it signifies *contractual* subordination: transitory bodily adaptions, such as shaving the beard or not (domestic service), the wearing of a wig (marriage), the tonsure (religious vows), the length of hair, etc. Marking by clothing, much more subject to change in one sense, is without doubt the zero expression of belonging to a *social station*,[8] or, if you prefer, the expression of place in social relations. It is only in the division between the sexes that the clothing mark persists in a permanent fashion today. For although a person puts on a uniform (professional, military or other) for work – that is, for a specified time and in a limited area – a person is, on the contrary, at every moment when dressed, and in all circumstances, in the uniform of sex. In short, the idea of visually making known the groups in a society is neither recent nor exceptional.

Naturalization of the system of marking and development of the idea of a natural group

However, the idea of classifying *according to* somatic/morphological criteria is recent and its date can be fixed: the eighteenth century. From a circumstantial association between economic relations and physical traits was born a new type of mark ('colour'), which had great success. Later developments turned it from the traditional status of a *symbol* to that of a *sign of a specific nature* of social actors. Then began the fabrication of taxonomies that were to be progressively qualified as 'natural'. This naturalness was not obvious at the beginning, when the concern for form unquestionably overshadowed it.[9] The taxonomies were transformed into classification systems based on a morphological mark, in which the latter is presumed to precede the classification, while social relationships created the group on which the mark – because of the social relationship – is going to be 'seen' and attached. The taxonomies thus served as anchoring for the development of the idea of race, but the idea of endo-determinism spread little by little onto the schema of marking, which was completely classical at its beginning.

However that may be, the morphological 'mark' does not precede the social relationship, any more than branding or the tattooing of a number do. I alluded above to the triangular traffic and to the role played by the spatial/temporal extension of this process. At the end of the seventeenth century and at the beginning of the eighteenth, the capture of a labor force for the Americas from just one region of the world – the Gulf of Guinea and East Africa – to the exclusion of Europe, played the role of catalyst in the formation of the idea of race, which was done through the means of the class 'mark'. The accidents of economic history furnished in this case a ready-made form. But in fact the process of the appropriation of slaves had already been going on for around a century when the first taxonomies that included somatic characteristics appeared: the mark *followed* slavery and in no way preceded the slave grouping. The slave system was already constituted when the inventing of the races was thought up.

This system developed from something completely different from the somatic appearance of its actors. It is heart-rending to hear so many well-intentioned people (then as now) question themselves about the reasons that could exist for 'reducing the blacks to slavery' (contempt, they think; visibility; who knows what else?). But no 'blacks' *per se* were reduced to slavery; slaves were made – which is very different. All these strange reasons are sought and advanced as if 'being black' existed in itself, outside of any social reason to construct such a form, as if the symbolic fact asserted itself and could be a cause. But the idea of 'reducing "the blacks" to slavery' is a modern idea which only came about at a specific historical juncture when the recruitment of slaves (who at the beginning were blacks *and* whites) was focalized. People were enslaved wherever they could be and as need dictated. Then at a certain historical moment, from the end of the seventeenth century on, slaves ceased to be recruited in Europe because their labor power from then on was needed there, with the development of industrialization. Consequently they were taken only from a specific and relatively limited region of the world, constituting one of the poles of the triangular traffic. During the period of European/African recruitment, there was not (not yet) a system of marking other than that used for this purpose (branding). So, *a fortiori*, neither was there any reflection about the somatic/physiological 'nature' of slaves. This reflection, moreover, only appeared after the marking by the somatic sign itself. The taxonomics preceded the racist theories.

The 'nature' of the exploited

During the nineteenth and twentieth centuries there have been (and moreover still are) many scholars looking for a 'naturalness' in classes and exploited groups. For example, the presumption and affirmation of a genetic and biological particularity of the working class, expressed in the form of a lesser intelligence, was – and still remains – one of the strong points of the naturalist discourse. It must also be said that this approach is strongly opposed; it may even be censured. Nevertheless the censure only occurs when it is a matter of the white, male, urban part of the exploited class. All censure or hesitation disappears at the moment when it is a question of the female part, or the immigrant part, or the neocolonized part in the relations of exploitation. Nature is nature, isn't it?

The obsession with the natural mark (proclaimed as the 'origin' of social relationships) operates today with great effectiveness. It does not do so with the same facility in all circumstances. But whatever the twists and turns of the line of argument, the natural mark is presumed to be the intrinsic *cause* of the place that a group occupies in social relationships. As such this 'natural' mark differs from the dress mark or the mark inscribed on the body known by pre-modern societies. For the old mark was recognized as *imposed* by social relationships, known as one of their consequences, while the natural mark is not presumed to be a mark but the very *origin* of these relationships. It is supposed to be the internal (therefore natural) 'capacities' that determine social facts. This is a throwback to the idea of endogenous determinism in human relation-ships, an idea characteristic of mechanistic scientific thought.

In short, the modern idea of a natural group is the fluid synthesis of two systems: (1) the traditional system of the mark, purely *functional*, in which there is no endogenous implication and which is no different from the marking of livestock; and (2) the archaeo-scientific deterministic system which sees in any object whatever a substance which secretes its own causes, which is *in itself its own cause*. What interests us here is the social group, and its practices are supposed to be the product of its specific nature.

For example: 'It is the nature of women to clean up the shit', a statement that (practically throughout the world) means: 'Women are women; it's a natural fact; women clean up the shit; it's their nature that makes them do it; and besides, since this is a specialization of genetic origin, it doesn't disgust them, which is itself proof that for them it's natural'. In the same way (in the United States), 'It's the nature of blacks not to work' means: 'It's a natural fact; blacks are unemployed; that's the way their nature makes them; and moreover they are lazy and don't want to do a stroke of work, which shows very well that for them it's natural to be out of work'. Notwithstanding that women don't 'like' shit more than men do (which is to say, not at all) and that blacks don't 'like' to do less work than whites do (which is to say, neither more nor less), what we have here is an intentionally purely subjective critique of their states of mind. On the other hand, that which refers to the effective experiences of the groups of 'women' and 'blacks' (cleaning up, unemployment), that which refers to the facts is correct: women do clean up the shit, and being black condemns one to unemployment – but *the relationship between the facts is false.*

The spontaneous idea of nature[10] introduces an erroneous relationship between the facts; it changes the very character of these facts. And it does this in a particular way: Nature proclaims the permanence of the effects of certain social relations on dominated groups. Not the perpetuation of these relations themselves (on which no one cares to fix their eyes, and that is understandable; they are like the sun, they burn), but the permanence of their effects – the permanence of shit and of unemployment. The crux of the question really is: A *social relationship*, here a relationship of domination, of power, of exploitation, which secretes the idea of nature, is regarded as the product of traits internal to the object which endures the relationship, traits which are expressed and revealed in specific practices. To speak of a specificity of races or of sexes, to speak of a natural specificity of social groups is to say in a sophisticated way that a particular 'nature' is *directly productive* of a social practice and to bypass the *social relationship* that this practice brings into being. In short, it is a pseudo-materialism.

The idea of the nature of the groups concerned precludes recognition of the real relationship by concentrating attention first (with the explanation to follow) on isolated, fragmented traits, presumed to be intrinsic and permanent, which are supposed to be the direct causes of a practice which is itself purely mechanical. It is thus that slavery becomes an attribute of skin colour, that non-payment for domestic work becomes an attribute of the shape of sexual organs. Or more exactly, *each* of the numerous obligations imposed by the precise relationships of race and sex is supposed to be a natural trait, with the multiplicity of these natural traits becoming merged to indicate the specific nature of the social group that suffers the relationship of domination. At this precise point the idea of a natural group is invented – of 'race', of 'sex' – which inverts the reasoning.

CURRENT FORM OF THE IDEA OF NATURE IN SOCIAL RELATIONSHIPS

Some ideas of race and sex can be said to be imaginary formulations, legally sanctioned and materially effective. Let us look at these three points one after the other.

Natural groups: imaginary formulations

It is certainly not an accident that the classic arguments about the non-pertinence of the idea of race (I would say, moreover, more aptly, of the idea of a natural group) have been made about natural categories that are not very 'distinguishable', and have been made in the case of those where the quality of the mark is rather ambiguous and even wholly evanescent. Both Jean-Paul Sartre in the past in his *Réflexions sur la question juive* and Jacques Ruffié today in his *De la biologie à la culture* use the same subject to support in an immediately convincing fashion the fact that races do not exist. Although their perspectives are different, both of them refer to a group, the Jews, who, whatever the time and place, are not physically distinguished from the dominant group.[11] Showing that belief in the natural characteristics of sociality is illusory, that this belief has been built up by a coercive history, is certainly much easier in the case where no fallacious distraction in terms of physical evidence or visibility is possible. The absence of visual criteria, which might support a counter-attack by supporters of the natural inscription of social characteristics, helps considerably in arguing a case that is in itself extremely difficult.

But, all things considered, is it such a good tactic? I do not believe that one can overcome preconceived ideas and commonplace beliefs – which go hand in hand with a unanimous and naïve belief in 'races' and other natural groups – by a rational argument making appeal to the suspension of judgement and to waiting for an examination of the facts. It seems to me that, on the contrary, it would be more logical to treat the problem by what is most 'evident' about it to the eyes of the believers in naturalness, and not by what seems at first view to support the argument of the ideological character of naturalness. What is 'least visible' is a trap in this field. For one is not operating within a classical framework of discussion where the terms of the debate are common and the definitions approximately shared. One is well and truly in a situation of conflict. The idea of the endo-determined nature of groups is precisely *the* form taken by the antagonism between the very social groups which are concerned. First let us try to start from scratch and take another approach that calls into question, at their level of highest visibility, the ideas of visual evidence themselves.

No, it is not a matter of fact that the idea of race, since its historical appearance, is found both in common sense and in the sciences.[12] Although physical traits, elsewhere and in the past, have certainly drawn attention, this was done without making distinctions and with a non-classifying attitude that has become difficult for us to understand. In short, such traits were noticed little more than baldness, eye colour, or size are today – interesting certainly, but not the basis for discrimination.[13] Today we are confronted with fierce realities, which it is not enough to say don't exist. We see them, we draw conclusions – (1) classifying conclusions, and (2) conclusions about *nature* – stages which are historically and analytically distinct, as we have seen by following the passage from the conventional mark to the natural mark, but which today are mingled, almost syncretically. Moreover, these classifying conclusions are not false, since people do belong to a group, a social group which is defined by its practices within one relationship (among many).[14] It is not by virtue of its (constructed) membership that the group is defined, despite the perception imposed on us by a naturalist apprehension that places the somatic nature of social actors as the origin of classifications and practices.

So there is both truth and falsehood in these classifications – truth (a group), falsehood (the 'somatic nature' of the group) – and the falsehood lives on the truth. Appearance (colour, sex) furnishes very good information about work (and even about the jobs within a line of work), about pay (or non-pay), and even, if there is one, about the wage level. In 1977 (and still today) in France, for example, if one encounters a woman, one surely encounters someone who does domestic work gratis and probably someone also who without pay, or sometimes for pay, physically cleans the youngest and oldest people in a family or in public or private establishments. And there is a very good chance one will encounter one of those workers at the minimum wage or below who are women. This is not nature; it is a social relationship. In France, if one encounters a Mediterranean man – and it is by design that I do not use a word indicating nationality, because nationality has nothing to do with it, while the region of the world is the determining factor – there is a very good chance that one will encounter one of those workers with a specific type of contract or even one who risks having none at all, and maybe not even a residence permit, someone who works longer hours than other workers, and does this in a construction trade, the mines or heavy industry. In short, he is one piece of the very structural 'labor cushion', which also includes the 46 per cent of women who have access to a paid job. If one encounters in France a Caribbean or West Indian man or woman, it is very likely that one encounters someone employed in the service sector – in hospitals, transport, communications – and precisely someone employed in the public sector. In France, if one encounters a Mediterranean woman, one will very likely encounter someone who also works in the service industries, but not in the public sector; she will be working in the private sector, for an individual employer or a collective employer (a company) – a cleaning woman, a *concierge*, a kitchen employee, etc. One will encounter someone who, for less than the minimum wage (as a woman) does domestic work (as a Mediterranean person), and who does family domestic work (as a woman) gratis.

So here we have these obvious 'natural' groups, whose activities, presumed to be 'natural' like those who do them, are only the actualization of a very social relationship. It is important to find out how these groups are reputed to be 'natural', and natural *first and foremost*. To find out how that is the 'logical consequence' of that nature to some people, who consider that one is born with a precise place and task in life, or how it is an 'abominable injustice' to others, who think it is cruel and unjustifiable to confine to the 'lower strata' or quasi-castes the members of these groups, who, poor things, can do nothing about where they naturally belong. Although the conception of what is wished for varies, the perception of reality is the same – there are natural groups. It is indisputable that nature, which serves us today as portable household god, is the ideological form of a certain type of social relationship. But, stratum or caste ('nature', no less!), it is also true that attention is focused on the subject in order to refuse to see the relationship that constituted it.

The idea of the somatic-physiological internal specificity of the social groups concerned is an imaginary formulation (in the sense that naturalness exists in the mind) associated to a social relationship. This relationship is identifiable through the criteria we have noted, which are completely material, historical, technological and economic. These traits are connected to a naturalist affirmation whose contradictions, logical silences, and affirmations (all the more confident because based on unclarified implications) demonstrate ambiguity and dubiousness. And the imaginary character of a term of the connection is invisible – thanks to Nature.

Imaginary formulation, legally sanctioned

Legally, and not, as has been claimed for a century, scientifically sanctioned. And the two terms – *legal* and *scientific* – form a pair in the social system. In the case of the natural, the legal plays the role of guarantee theoretically ascribed to scientific fact.

The *institutionalization*, the transformation of the idea of a natural group into a category sanctioned at the level of the state, was not done by the scientific community, despite all its efforts in that direction, but was in fact done by the legal system. Race became an effective legal category *as a category of nature* (that is, a category of non-divine, non-socio-human origin) at the end of the nineteenth century in the United States (the Jim Crow laws), in 1935 in Nazi Germany (the Nuremberg laws), and in 1948 in South Africa (the apartheid laws). These discriminatory, interdictory, segregating laws, which touch practically all areas of life (marriage, work, domicile, moving about, education, etc.), stipulate the interdictions as a function of racial criteria by *name*. It is not the fact of their being interdictions that is new – interdictions were not created yesterday – but the fact that they write into the law the 'natural' membership of citizens in a group. The failure to devise logical naturalist categories by scientific means was only a superficial episode in a process that could do without them. The law came to furnish the socio-governmental, institutional sanction which had not been produced by the channel from which it had at first been expected, even though the scientific field itself had not given up pursuing it.

The gigantic and grotesque enterprise of physical anthropology that Nazism launched in order to enunciate 'scientifically' its racial-legal 'truth' was not an enigmatic dysfunction, but the result of a logic of previous social relationships. This scientific justification, unceasingly proclaimed and actively researched in all possible directions, proved to be as elusive as it was foreseeable. And particularly elusive, since, aiming at a *functionality* of the idea of race, they tried, looking for a legitimation of a natural order, to create indicators that could coincide with a previous definition of 'Aryans' and 'Jews' according to the Nazi system. Frenzy by the dominant group about the racial or sexual 'nature' of the groups concerned bursts out in periods of open conflict or explicit antagonism. Witness the works on the various human 'races' in the post-slavery United States,[15] or the Jews in Nazi Germany, on the particularities of sexual chromosomes in the whole industrial world since the 1960s, and on the chemophysiological or genetic nature of deviance in the contemporary USSR. Whether it be in the United States, in colonizing France, in Nazi Germany, or in the transnational patriarchal system, it remains impossible to claim – despite the efforts in which considerable means and great energy were (and are) invested – that human heterogeneity is demonstrated or demonstrable.

So then it is a legal category and a *natural* category of the law. For it is not at all true that when one leaves the domain of the natural sciences in order to enter the realm of the law, one renounces the idea of nature. Quite the contrary. What is involved is the same nature and a guarantee directed at the same objective. The law more than science came to serve as witness of and assurance for the strong usable belief in the endo-determined character of groups in a given society. This transference shows that race is a category peculiar to social relationships, springing from them and in turn orienting them. The actual relationships come to be expressed in one of the two possible superstructural forms: legal institutions or science.

Imaginary formulation, legally sanctioned, materially effective

The social sciences themselves have a strangely ambiguous relationship, both reluctant and submissive, with the idea of a natural group. They are reluctant in that they do not accept the thesis that races are, in so far as they are a natural category, an effective, non-mediated cause of social relationships (the proponents of the naturalist thesis are found mostly among physicists, physical anthropologists or psychologists). They are submissive in that they nevertheless accept the idea of a natural category, but as something dissociated from social relationships and somehow able to have a pure existence. This results in an untenable position. A total abstention from the idea of naturalness would be an easier position to maintain. But the ideological implications of the idea of nature and of natural groups *cannot be passed over*, and therefore it occupies – even if one is loath to see it – a central place in almost all social relations. Ideologically hidden (if the ideology is hidden beneath the 'obviousness' of it, as I think), the 'natural' form, whether it be common knowledge or already institutionalized, is at the centre of the *technical means* used by the relationships of domination and power to impose themselves on dominated groups, and to go on using them.

As a technical/legal category, the proclamation of the existence of natural groups enters the order of material facts. The law is the expression of the ideological/*practical* techniques of the system of *domination*. One finds there the privileged guarantee of what is ideologically supposed not to need guarantee in social rules, since it is a fact of nature. Who can go against nature, the law of the world, the writing down of which can only be a nullity or a tautology? In affirming the specificity of groups, nature passes through legal inscription; it is affirmed as a social fact at the same time that it claims to be the origin of and the reason for human society. It is a sinister game of 'one is supposed to act as if . . .' and then, in fact, one does 'act as if'.

In fact, a natural characteristic (race, sex), being a legal category, intervenes in social relationships as a constraining and impelling trait. It inscribes the system of domination on the body of the individual, assigning to the individual his/her place as a dominated person: but it does not assign any place to the dominator.[16] Membership in the dominant group, on the contrary, is legally marked by a convenient lack of interdiction, by unlimited possibilities. Let me explain: Legally nothing prevents a member of the dominant group (which, moreover, is only a 'natural' group by negation; it is 'neither' this, 'nor' that) from taking up the activities of the dominated categories. Such a person can become a migrant farm worker, do home sewing, do the laundry gratis for a whole domestic group, be paid to do typing, not be paid to care for, wash and feed children. Outside of a low wage or none at all, this person would not encounter anything but sarcasm, contempt or indifference. In any case, there would be no barrier to doing it, but this person would not do it – it is just a theoretical possibility. For (1) while no one would prevent someone from doing it, (2) no one would require it. The two propositions are only meaningful in combination; each is important in itself *and when taken together*.

However, everything keeps the members of the dominated groups from (1) getting paid for jobs that are socially defined as being jobs performed without pay, and (2) becoming part of certain state or religious establishments. They are forbidden to them. And I am not even speaking here of the usual barriers so effective in barring access to high salaries, to personal independence, to freedom of movement. The dominated persons are in the symmetrical and inverse situation of the dominators, for (1) everything prohibits certain activities to them, and (2) on the contrary, everything requires them to do domestic work gratis, to be labourers, to work at (or below) the minimum wage level, etc. And this is done with an array of resources, including legal resources.

CONCLUSION

The invention of the idea of nature cannot be separated from domination and the appropriation of human beings. It unfolded within this precise type of relationship. But appropriation which treats human beings as things, and from that draws diverse ideological variations, is not enough in itself to lead to the modern idea of natural groups. Aristotle after all talked about the nature of slaves, but it was not with the meaning that we give today to this word. The word 'nature', applied to any object, fixed its purpose in the world order, an order which at the time was regulated by theology. In order for the modern meanings of the word to come into being there had to be another element, a factor internal to the object. Endogenous determinism, which ushers in scientific development, will come, by attaching itself to the 'purpose', to form this new idea of the 'natural group'. For beginning with the eighteenth century, rather than appealing to God to explain material phenomena, people turned to analysing mechanical causes in the study of phenomena, first physical phenomena, and then living phenomena. The stake, moreover, was the conception of Man, and the first materialism was to be mechanistic during this same century (see *L'Homme machine* by Julien Offray de La Mettrie).

If what is expressed by the term 'natural' is the pure materiality of the implicated objects, then there is nothing less natural than the groups in question, which precisely are constituted *by* a precise type of relationship: the relationship of power, a relationship which makes them into things (both destined to be things and mechanically oriented to be such), but which *makes* them, since they *only* exist as things within this relationship. This is the social relations in which they are involved (slavery, marriage, migrant labor) and which makes them such at every moment. Outside of these relations they don't exist; *they cannot even be imagined*. They are not givens of nature, but naturalized givens of social relationships.

NOTES

1 For a critical presentation of this position, see the collective work *Discours biologique et ordre social*, ed. Pierre Achard *et al.* (Paris: Seuil, 1977), which endeavours to demonstrate this fascination and constant reference at work.
2 In fact, the same problem arises in classical physical anthropology, for the 'natural' position is practically untenable. But it is with the social sciences that the present discussion is concerned.

3 At the time that the present article was written, an evening newspaper, in a review of recent books in French on South Africa, used the term *métis* (half-breed) to refer to the 'coloured' group. Correct in the logical sense, this is false in the social sense, the South African particularly. The word 'coloured' exists precisely in order to censor the word 'half-breed'. Everybody knows that half-breed is what is referred to – that is not the question – but *nobody wants to know it*.

4 But it would be pointless to keep resorting (as is the case) to reaffirmations of morphosomatic evidence if – as is often said (even among social scientists) – the somatic traits were 'striking' and 'obvious' and were, because of that, the cause of racial prejudice, conflicts and power relations between groups.

5 On the process that separated the two strands of the recruitment of forced labor, the European and the African, see Eric Williams, *Capitalism and Slavery* (Chapel Hill: University of North Carolina Press, 1944).

6 I mean here the idea of 'nature' in the present scientific sense. The theological societies gave to this word the meaning of 'internal order', a meaning always present within the contemporary idea, but until the nineteenth century it *did not include* an endogenous determinism, which is a fundamental characteristic today.

7 An allusion to this practice can be found in Tallemant des Réaux (a leading member of a bourgeois banking family) in the seventeenth century: 'She called him over to a corner of the room to ask him if he didn't find that black suited me well. At that time young people didn't wear black so early in the day as one does now'.

8 I distinguish here between dependence and belonging. Belonging – 'being' in a social station, in a religion – is supposed to be both permanent *and* subject to change. One could be ennobled or change one's religion in certain circumstances. Dependence implies a direct relationship, either contractual or coercive: The 'indentured' servant, the cleric bound by his vows, and the appropriated slave were considered to be in an irreversible situation for a specific term of time (which could be limited but which also could be for an entire lifetime).

9 Carl von Linné, the first great taxonomist of the human species, had, as in his vegetable classifications (which it may be noted in passing were, all the same, his essential preoccupation), a conception of method that did not place him at all within an empiricist perspective. His system is a set of statements of principle. He would probably have been very surprised if one had connected him to some endo-determinism, which today necessarily accompanies the idea of nature.

10 'Spontaneous idea': that is, an idea which is tightly associated with – or indissociable from – a specific historical relationship, and which is always present at the heart of this relationship.

11 Even supposing that one accepts this kind of argument, one can also point out that the 'obvious distinction' between a Tunisian and a Dutch person is completely invisible to someone who is neither North African nor European, as I have been able to note on numerous occasions. In any case these distinctions are less than those that distinguish between social classes or the sexes, where weight, height, etc. are differentiated.

12 I take the liberty of referring to some of my own previous works: Colette

Guillaumin, *L'Idéologie raciste. Genèse et langage actuel* (Paris: Mouton, 1972); and Chapters 1 and 2 of the present book, which originally appeared as 'Caractères spécifiques de l'idéologie raciste', *Cahiers internationaux de sociologie* (vol. LIII, 1972), and 'The Idea of Race and its Elevation to Autonomous Scientific and Legal Status', in *Sociological Theories: Race and Colonialism* (Paris: UNESCO, 1980).

13 One can only ask oneself why it is so frequently argued (and by important scholars) that the somatic – so-called racial – mark (in face, skin colour) is supposed to be so much more relevant than eye colour or hair colour and that it is supposed to have so much more value as a discriminating factor than the latter, which (I quote) 'can differ from parent to child'. It is forgotten curiously quickly that, as a matter of fact, racial characteristics such as skin colour can be *different between parents and children* (in the United States and the West Indies, for example, a white parent can have a black child). And this difference is more important than the shade of eye colour or hair colour not because it is more visible, but because it is socially proclaimed to be racial and assumes the characteristic of constraining violence. Here we have again an example of the lack of reality in the propositions that are presented as evidence of simple common sense.

14 For – let me repeat it – if there was not a *social* group, the physical trait (whatever it might be) would not be discriminating.

15 See, for example: John S. Haller, *Outcasts from Evolution: Scientific Attitudes of Racial Inferiority 1859–1900* (Urbana: University of Illinois Press, 1971); and Marvin Harris, *The Rise of Anthropological Theory* (New York: Crowell, 1968).

16 And it is at this precise point where we find the break with the traditional system of marks, which conventionally applied to all opposing groups. The groups of slaves, of deported prostitutes, of condemned criminals are in an intermediate classification, between those based on the conventional mark and the natural mark, in which the mark on the body was imposed only on the dominated persons.

Chapter 7

Women and theories about society

The effects on theory of the anger of the oppressed

IS THERE A DISTINCTION BETWEEN 'THEORY' AND 'POLITICS'?

Is theory a fortress? Or is it a private preserve? Or, rather, what is theory? In any society minorities – and here I mean not those who are perforce the least numerous but rather those who have the *least power*, whether economic, legal or political – are in a peculiar position as regards products of the intellect. Most often they hate theory, recognizing it for what it is: the sacred verbiage of those who dominate them; that which emerges from the head and mouth of those who dispose of power (tools, weapons, the police, the army) and nourishment (wages, lands, goods etc.). Since in the majority/minority relationship, the power, goods and individual freedom which flow from this relationship are the distinctive features of the dominators, the institutionalized expression of *their* consciousness and *their* view of the situation is the only one to be transmitted, diffused and expounded. This then is what is called theory. And rightly so. Whether the theorists bore the name of Malthus or Hegel, Comte or Gobineau, or whether in an earlier period they were theologians, they produced what for the minorities is a nightmare. The latter, who do not even know the theoretical details of the matter, merely know every day *in practice*, under duress, by the contempt with which they are treated, and through their hunger, what place they must always occupy – a sometimes life-threatening place of silence, of inferiority, of widespread menace – menace that at certain times is frightfully explicit in beatings and murder. And always at every moment there is work to be done, the necessity of being present, attention that must never flag. So they can only speak in tones of bitterness and fury; the thoughts which they express are never called theory. Theirs is the language of invective, of sarcasm, of controlled passion, of irony and blasphemy, or even of despair. 'I have often been utterly astonished since I came to the north, to find persons who could speak of the singing of the slaves as evidence of their contentment and happiness.'[1]

All that can be called 'theories of society' in the sense that we understand today have been – and are – the intellectual form of well-defined social relationships. In other words, to speak of 'politics' as the driving force of theory is a tautology. The concern with exposing the causes and mechanisms of human relations developed historically as the aftermath of political upheaval at a time which can broadly be labelled the eighteenth century. As long as the aristocracy, even though its economic power was replaced by that of the manufacturing and commercial bourgeoisie, remained politically and institutionally the class in power, the first theories of society were limited to legal commentaries on social forms, whether in terms of classical law or natural law. It was not yet the time of hypotheses about the actual causes and conditions of how things worked. Montesquieu is a good example of this state of affairs. He cited both natural law and legal institutions when he described the relationship of women to power: 'It is contrary to reason and nature that women should reign in families, as was customary among the Egyptians; but not that they govern an empire.'[2]

When political power and domination of the state were in the hands of that same bourgeoisie, the nature of how things were regarded and *analysed* changed. Saint-Simon can be considered as one of the first to formulate a *use theory*, the genre that was going to dominate the social sciences right up to today. Gobineau, at the same time as Marx, embarked upon an *investigation of causality*, which is the other dominant concern. Both of them, and their contemporaries, were adherents of theory which focuses on social effectiveness as much as on 'knowledge'. One recalls the famous remark by Marx on effectiveness ('The philosophers have only *interpreted* the world, in various ways; the point, however, is to *change* it)[3] as well as the concrete projects of Saint-Simon. It may seem surprising to choose these three notables as examples of the production of theory, for, although two of them have an unquestioned place in it, it is not customary to give Gobineau such a place. Politically disgraced by having his theory of social relations claimed by political regimes not so much 'totalitarian' (there were some of this type who renounced him!) as racist (legally or practically racist), Gobineau has not kept his position as a producer of theory. Nevertheless his later fate reveals even more plainly and bluntly that such usually appears to be the concrete and political nature of the theoretical. Even if he himself didn't know it.[4] In fact, he conceptualized what he called (in the *Essai sur l'inégalité*) social philosophy as the revelation of a prime cause (or series of causes), the driving force of history and of the variation in social forms.

The production of theories about the causes and functioning of social systems thus appears associated with a political transformation and clearly oriented within a practical political perspective. This perspective, which became less visible at the end of the nineteenth century, did none the less persist, and, whether it is a question of Comte, Tarde, Durkheim, or Weber (and other names could be mentioned), it sustained and fed their analyses. It would thus be completely inaccurate to claim that there has been a recent irruption of politics into the social sciences, which is supposed to be embodied in the works of minority groups who have succeeded in speaking out (but not only in speaking) in the last few decades – an opinion regularly advanced about texts by minorities, colonized peoples, Afro-Americans, feminists, etc. In short, there is no irruption, and 'politics' in practice is the correlative of 'social science'. The latter came out of 'politics,' and its existence is (at the very least) tightly tied to it, or rather dependent on it in practice.

The fact that certain analyses could pass for neutral and purely objective is a result of domination. But it doesn't last long, and this apparent neutrality is shattered under the critique of social groups (or members of social groups) who are *affected by* these theories or who are affected by those mental constructs which are more amorphous than changes in opinion. For example, ethology, the study of animal behaviour (but is it animal behaviour that is being studied?),[5] and functionalism (among others) are not highly regarded by women. And one can understand why. All socially dominated groups have this same legitimate distrust. The practical utility of these theories, which without excessive hypocrisy aim at maintaining the status quo in their ideas about relations between the sexes, does not at all escape the notice of those (women) who are the object of these works, even if that objective is neither explicit nor exclusive. In fact, one of them – ethology – claims (clearly) that it finds the laws of nature to be by definition absolutely binding. The other one – functionalism – claims (implicitly) to put forward the laws of social relations.

The remarks which follow are not an inventory of the changes that actual social movements have introduced into the way of looking at reality any more than they are a demonstration of their impact. Their aim is rather to be a stimulus to thinking about theoretical changes in terms of how they occur in an actual society as the result and expression of particular experiences of sociality. In the area that concerns us here, that of the relationship between theory and minorities (precisely, women – an area in which we have every reason to focus our particular attention on the facts and also every reason not to know these facts too well), conceptual perceptions are not distinguishable from social relationships; they are themselves a social relationship. It is not that these notions, ideas, concepts and theories are 'reflections'; to regard them that way would be simply to repress the problem of the origin of mental phenomena – of 'ideology.' But they are rather the *mental face* of concrete relationships.

This poses the question of consciousness in the modification or overturning of social relationships – and this is only a passing remark, because, although fundamental, it is not the subject of this chapter. It is not so obvious as is commonly claimed that before starting an action, one 'thinks out' beforehand a transformation of social relationships and that one clearly apprehends intellectually this transformation before undertaking it. However, whatever the modalities, whatever the place occupied by its producers, what in the final analysis theory is, or will be, is first of all consciousness – precisely that of the place that one occupies.

THE POLITICS, OR THE THEORY, OF 'SEX'

The entry of minorities into the field of theory does not lead, strictly speaking, to a 'refinement' or 'diversification' of knowledge. These certainly could be produced, but they are not the essential point. The essential point is the overturning of perspectives; it is the subversion that is introduced. Moreover, let us note that the first theoretical texts of minority groups are always without exception discounted as theory at the time of their appearance and presented as *'political'* products. This is obviously the case (but it is also true of all the theoretical texts in social science). Or they are discounted by being treated as pamphlets (which is sometimes the case) or as jokes (which is never the case), or finally as *terrorist* positions.

It is true that in practice it is impossible to make a serious distinction between a 'theoretical' text and a 'militant' text. The passage of time sometimes reveals the theoretical pertinence and substance of an analysis whose militant strength was the only thing that was appreciated at the time it came out. It is not without value to re-read today the *Scum Manifesto* of Valerie Solanas or the *Discourse on Colonialism* of Aimé Césaire. And although in certain texts the theoretical form is intentional and unquestionable, most of them are explicitly, clearly and unambiguously political, and bring theory to bear only where it is the sole possible course for the dominated. This fact is verified by the dis-approval and disrepute which greet original texts, and the censorship which in the eighteenth century, for example, made it necessary to have the key texts of social philosophy and critical philosophy published in Holland.

These intolerable texts ended up by producing integration in theory. The well-known fate of books like Fanon's *The Wretched of the Earth* and Marx's *The Eighteenth Brumaire of Louis Napoleon* illustrate this fact. Feminist texts are numerous and take many forms, and the success of Kate Millett's *Sexual Politics* is more as a symbol than as theory, although it is not unimportant that this text is an analysis of verbal works, which is also true of the *Discourse on Colonialism*. This is a method which had and continues to have a very important place in the understanding that minorities, and especially women, have of the social world in which they act.[6]

The Second Sex by Simone de Beauvoir has followed a similar course, and it may be recalled that this classic work was received with great savagery and contempt, including commentaries on the vagina of the author. I never hear that X (and insert here the male name that you please), writing on Man (with a capital M), reads a lot of commentaries on his penis in the review of his books, even if it is absolutely explicit that he is speaking of the male of the species while making him into humanity in general. In short, these minority texts, whose publication is even now not easy, are considered at the time of their appearance to be both lightweight and dangerous, a joke in more or less good taste, and a threat. *But, afterwards, it will never again be possible to view the problems in the same way as before.*

Our view of the academic milieu in the social sciences has been so changed in ten years that we can no longer clearly remember (and sometimes if we do remember, we cannot believe our memory) the way in which the 'sex' variable used to be envisaged in sociology, psy-chology, even ethnology, etc. Rather, it would be more correct to say: the way in which it was not envisaged. In one decade the face of social science has been transformed, and even if today we are still far from being in a satisfactory situation, nothing can bring back the theoretical low points of the 1950s and the beginning of the 1960s.

A certain number of articles – some of them first-rate and hard-hitting – have shown that the striking absence of an analysis of what is called *sex* covers up weighty and unavoidable theoretical questions, and that *this absence itself is one of the effects (the intellectual form) of social sex relationships.* They have shown that women and men are not harmonious partners in the maintenance and perpetuation of the social community, but rather that they are social actors belonging to well-defined groups in an antagonistic relationship. These theoretical questions are questions of life and death in a great number of cases, such as those which concern the free use of one's body and exposure to illness, access to nourishment, the possession and use of tools and weapons. Between pamphlets and systematic descriptions, between analyses and political projects, these texts have modified the perception of what is called sex. And we are not talking here, as you know, about sexology. In ten years the volume of work done has stirred up a theoretical debate in what used to be a desert. Yet a large part of this enormous amount of work, doubtless the most important part, was written in flimsy, transient forms, with limited distribution, and destined for a more or less rapid disappearance. These are the tracts, the working papers for conferences, the mimeographed sheets, etc. And the more lasting ones, which took the form of articles, reports or books, represent only a very small part of the critical explosion of the 1960s and 1970s, of all that was done and thought then (or thought and done), of the articulation and expression of women's consciousness of being a social group and of being able to change the relationships in which that group is involved.

These analyses had certain results in the domain of theory, some visible today, but others which will doubtless only be revealed later.

1   They brought a *radical critique* to the interpretation of facts which before were considered to be natural and thus 'unquestionable': the sexual division of labour, unequal access to resources, whether material (technical, alimentary, spatial, temporal) or economic (wages and monetary and financial matters). From then on, one saw a 'problem' where before one used to see nothing – nothing but the emptiness of infinite space, or rather natural harmony.

2   And if there was a 'question', from then on it was *subverted*. It is useful to recall some known examples of this mechanism, because they are so well entrenched in sociological customs that they are no longer noticed. There was a time when even in the social sciences one spoke of the 'black' *problem* or of the 'Jewish' *question*. (And many, who would no longer speak about the 'workers' condition', still speak about the 'female condition'.) This was the period when the effect of domination on theory (the fact that theory was the theory of the dominators) implied that the dominated ones – an incomprehensible thorn – were those who were the problem. In some way poorly adapted to a situation, they were presented as deviant figures. The revolts, sudden or regular, of groups or

persons were seen as expressions of functional maladaptation of individuals or groups of individuals; these revolts proved their natural unfitness or even their malevolence. At best they were regarded as a response to a situation which it was impossible to believe that they would not adjust to. This was a very widespread belief with regard to women. And one sought (seeks) the reasons for this lack of adaptation to the social order and, finally, to the order of things. So the United States was aware of a 'black problem', as Nazism was aware of a 'Jewish problem', which required a 'solution' – as the patriarchal states today are aware of a 'women's problem.'

One way of tearing out this thorn was adopting the reassuring proposition that in all cases these were marginal groups – a small but fraudulent displacement. In a way the 'real' central society, full of coherence, and also of contradictions, but nevertheless presenting a functional homogeneity, would tolerate along its edges such of the survivors or parasites of various human groups which had not succeeded in being integrated and were a burden on society. They are strangely regarded as being off to the side, floating in an intersocial space, manpower reserves, economic and sometimes legal 'misfits'; in short, having 'fallen out of' the normal society, they are supposed not to be part of society. 'The white man's burden' is an expression that brings ironic and bitter memories to mind, and today all we have to do is to remove the word 'white' from the expression to restore its aptness. Society thus designates as a threat and views as an incomprehensible bother those who are nevertheless its components and its foundation. Women put in more hours of non-paid work than are put in in the paid sector. Doesn't the expression 'the periphery,' used today in analyses of imperialism, show the same bias – the peculiar effect of the blindness of the dominators to their own practice, their own place, their own society? Is that which is dominated and exploited 'marginal', 'peripheral' in a society? And is it lack of consciousness or rather hypocrisy to speak in this way?

Thus the *relationships* of domination and the actors involved in these relationships are so seldom *thought about* that the discovery of the existence of the dominated actors, so surprising in itself, cannot for a certain period of time be integrated into their thinking.

3   These analyses finally result in (and produce) *theoretical tools* which permit the examination of such data.

This process has not all at once nor throughout the field of the social sciences transformed the view of social relationships. Tight little islands of ignorance and rejection still persist. One such is the notion of the 'domestic unit', although numerous studies have shown that there is no such unit at all, and that this innocent-appearing notion masks a fundamental social relationship – that of the sexes. And it does this as much from the point of view of the production of this unit (and its 'value') as from the point of view of the consumption of the individuals who compose it. This 'domestic unit' is not a homogeneous ensemble (it is as little that as it is possible to be), and it is not at all a social 'atom' as has been hypothetically posited:

> Unpaid work by women is institutionalized not only in practice but also in government bookkeeping . . . and in the demands of opposition political parties: the M.O.D.E.F. (French Communist Party organization concerned with agriculture) demands that each *family* farm be assured of having an income equivalent to *one* wage. The implication is that the wife's work, incorporated into household production, does not merit a wage; or, rather, that since the wife's production is exchanged by the husband as his own, the wife's work belongs to her husband. [Emphasis in original.][7]

The first step in this process, which still today constitutes most of the research being done, was the setting up of the group of women as a fragmented object of study, with each of its many characteristics being studied separately. But through the characteristics studied in isolation, little by little and despite the intent, what is revealed is a unity which produces and clarifies each of these characteristics – that is, a recognizable social relationship.

The non-payment of women's work and the wage gap between men and women (even when they are paid), for example, can only be understood and explained when linked to other aspects also studied in a fragmented way. One of these for women is the non-ownership of their bodily autonomy, which, although recognized, was given very little attention up to the time of the renaissance of feminism in the 1960s and 1970s. As far back as 1970, a 'militant' article brought the two factors together in the same analysis:

> There remains in modern law, alongside the clauses and contracts which regulate labor between management and workers, an implicit survival of feudal law which makes it possible that a whole category of individuals must, because of their sex, work without pay: us . . . And the children that we bear, we bear for our masters. And if we ever dare have children for ourselves, they are ostracized – 'bastard', 'illegitimate child' are some of the worst insults in our society. Men

can speak with impunity like masters: 'I take you, I possess you, you give yourself to me.'[8]

In the social process of reproduction a woman does not decide if she wants a child or not, since marriage in its contractual sense is silent on this point. In other words, the usage of a woman's body is not, *first of all*, at *her own* disposition. This is shown as clearly by non-free abortion (subject to outside evaluation by husband, psychiatrist, doctor, social services, etc.) as, reciprocally and mainly, it is shown by the constant potential presence of rape. The abolition of slavery led people (and doubtless many women) to believe that there were no longer any human beings socially deprived of ownership of themselves. The domination exercised over women had to be very deep-seated for it to be invisible for such a long time and relegated to 'fate' – even though there is no known society where in fact begetting children is not socially manipulated, and even though the rules and the material facilities for enforcing them are fixed and controlled by these societies.

Things have gone so far that the social sciences have hypocritically turned a blind eye to this aspect of social sex relationships:

This very general refusal to reflect upon the sociological meaning of *nonmaternity* (hence upon maternity as a social decision) doubtless derives from the fact that in most of the Western societies which have produced scientific accounts (accounts which are mostly masculine), abortion had been thrust into darkness and ignorance by the *ideology* and practiced in silence and solitude by individual women – until the feminist movements threw light on its importance. But in reality the *demographic* regulation of our societies functions, and has functioned, largely on abortion and infanticide . . . However, the existence of such social intervention in procreation is denied when a caricature of 'maternity' is presented – as an 'immediate given' of femininity. [Emphasis in original.][9]

It is the same situation with respect to the bodily servicing owed by women to males as well as to children, the sick and the disabled. And when one speaks of bodily servicing *owed*, this means that it is carried out – and to be carried out – without any wage consideration (without monetary evaluation), whether within the institution of marriage or within a religious institution (and in these cases it is done in exchange for the simple 'support' of the woman) or within a larger family institution – these acts being dressed up with the honour of 'duty', 'devotion' or religious sentiments in place of a wage. And the situation is the same with respect to the prohibition against freely moving about; women are neither allowed to travel great distances nor to be absent from the home except in rare circumstances; they are not permitted to go to all neighbourhoods (nor all places), just as night hours are totally forbidden to them, under threat of severe penalty if they infringe such a prohibition.

As in children's number drawings where the numbers to be connected transform a vague nebula into an identifiable form, making a sailing ship or a clown emerge from the page, so this inventory – and empirically speaking it is an inventory – gives shape step by step to the form of a specific and more and more explicit social relationship – a relationship of appropriation.[10] Nevertheless many still hesitate to recognize this form and prefer to regard each point of the design as being isolated.

MENTAL ATTITUDES? REALLY?

Some people explain these detailed difficulties by talking about backward *mental attitudes* (about what, in fact?), or about the poor *psychological disposition* of men toward women, or even simply about their thoughtless *habits*. Thus each aspect of the relationship is isolated and reduced to being an exception or an aberration. Looked at this way, all these things could be corrected by education. Better informed and better educated, men certainly could take care of children, wash them, dress them, feed them, and even perhaps go so far as taking over continuous care of them, as women do. They could turn these same children over to the care of their neighbour while they go every day to look after their aged ill father, and use the midday work break to do the shopping for dinner, which they will prepare after rushing home from work. To be sure! It is just a question of education and mental attitude, one seems to think. So it appears that, using this kind of logic, we ought to continue the excellent line of reasoning we are pursuing and think about undertaking the education of bosses and managers so that they can take their turn in doing factory or secretarial jobs, or even teaching landowners joyously to pull up beets alongside their seasonal immigrant workers. And thus through the reform of mental attitudes we would have a society where everyone smiles. However, no one would dream of making such a proposal for matters that concern the 'division' of labor in industry or on the land. In 1840 Flora Tristan turned livid with anger on hearing workers declare that their boss 'gave' them work:

> I wanted to speak to all those I met and to make them understand what it was that made up the working class – the right to work, etc. . . . . All

of them answered me in a rough manner: Well, there have to be rich people to give poor people work; otherwise how are the poor going to live? – It is clear that their priests continually repeated that to them. There have to be rich people and poor people; the former make it possible for the latter to live.[11]

In more recent times I have heard with my own ears remarks along this line, and I have heard men praised for 'being willing to marry such a woman.'

The modification in the terminology used to designate the phenomena studied is without doubt the most visible of the changes which have come in the apprehension and comprehension of social phenomena. Modifying the words shows clearly that the *perception of a fact has changed*. For a long time colonization was analysed with a wealth of psychological terms which today have almost completely disappeared from the vocabulary used in the analysis of imperialism. But we are not so distant from the time when the colonial relationship was explained as a 'predisposition' of the colonized to be colonized. 'The Madagascan . . . desires neither personal autonomy nor free responsibility.'[12] Or else: 'One feature of this dependent psychology would seem to be that, since no one can serve two masters, one of the two should be *sacrificed* to the other' (emphasis in original).[13] In some way the colonized ask for what happens to them, just as women ask for dependence and rape. The arsenal of words that underlies this brilliant theory, which has practically disappeared in the one case, persists in matters that concern sex relationships: in this domain a whole constellation of words floats around 'desire' and 'difference.' But if it is a question of psychology, I am astonished that so many individuals would choose to do the cooking, push the broom, wipe the children's bottoms, and in addition take care of them during all their non-school hours (and today they are talking about abolishing schools, which oppress children so much, in order to offer them an enriching and creative life at the side of their mothers, who have so much free time and who will thus run still less risk of vanishing into the spaces forbidden to them – so what will they think of next?). The other choice, never made by some (for good reason) but always made by the others (also for good reason), is – in addition to not doing the preceding – to earn their living properly (as well as, or as poorly as – take your choice – a man), to bestow their precious presence at fixed times (and especially not indefinitely), and to move about freely (supposedly for carrying out the heavy burden of responsibility).

If it is a question of psychology, I am astonished at how rape is institutionalized:

In theory and in the letter of the law (except for the laws on marriage) NOTHING is specifically forbidden to women. But in real life and judicial practice, society has instituted a 'risk of rape', which increases with autonomy of behaviour. The fact that this 'risk' is socially established and graduated is not accidental. It is part of a whole set of rewards and punishments which form a system: the system of the social control of women, which ensures that they stay in their women's place in the patriarchal order. Violent sexual assault represents the outer limit of the continuum of punishments, the penal sanction (physical and violent) *par excellence*. The social control of women thus includes a PENALTY OF RAPE.[14]

If it is a question of psychology, I am astonished that the tools of male domination could be so materially 'apprehendable':

> . . . the solid rock upon which male domination is founded: the impossibility for women to make weapons for themselves, their dependence upon men for almost all instruments of production. Men's control of the production and use of tools and weapons is confirmed as the necessary condition of their power, based upon violence (the male monopoly of weapons) and upon the underequipment of women (the male monopoly of tools).[15]

But this constellation, even though it has survived a long time, is just a leftover. Now people talk about social sex relationships; they have stopped thinking that the social sciences should be content with psychology, mental attitudes, natural division as the whole story in this domain.

Terms such as the 'female condition' or 'Woman' have had a long run as compared to the simple expression 'women'. And the almost total abandonment of the term 'condition' now seems assured. (As far as workers are concerned, the last traces of the expression 'workers' condition' can be found in right-wing regimes and religious hearts.) Traditional French usage equates the word 'condition' to patriarchal dependence. In the first half of our century 'to be in condition' meant in French to be 'in domestic service' in a house; one used to speak of the 'servile condition' with regard to slavery and serfdom. *But 'condition' signified a 'state' and not a relationship.* It was a way of describing personal dependence, but without analysing it – by taking it as a factual given. It is a perspective comparable to that of essences in philosophy, grace in theology or jurisdictions in law. Dependence was a well-known fact, and it was discussed, but the reality was masked and did not appear as a *relationship* (with men).

One of the effects of this was the focusing of understanding and analysis *on* women. And only on women. Only they were seen, and not men. The latter word was moreover practically non-existent for designating anything but an abstract and general entity: 'humanity' held sway for long years under the expression 'men', according to an interchangeability of terms which in fact excluded 'women' from humanity. The idea that women are a natural group existing in and of itself tends to make it less exclusive. It begins to be seen that one cannot speak abstractly about women – and about them alone – and it becomes advisable to look at the (social) relationship which creates 'women', to examine what (social) system makes up this relationship and how it functions. And it is seen that this must involve the use of the term 'men' and the use of it in the precise meaning of: group of social males. This stage has not really been reached yet. And the following analysis of the state of sociology in 1970 remains true:

> The state of sociological knowledge concerning sex categories might be summed up in the following formulae:
>
> 1 As a specified sociological category the category man does not exist. Not that it never serves as a reference in descriptive studies of the most varied phenomena, or in general theories, quite the reverse. But this functioning of thought remains unconscious. One thinks one is speaking in general when in fact one is speaking in the masculine gender.
> 2 The category woman:
> – either women do not exist, as a result of the preceding system of thought; this is a real obliteration, not a hidden presence as in the case of men;
> – or women appear as an appendage of the main discourse, emerging from the back of the house, discreet, unknown, enigmatic and silent, to disturb for a moment the reflection of man on man;
> – or they exist alone, isolated.
>
> We have seen that the first two types of discourse are statistically due rather to men and the last almost entirely to women.[16]

The last statement – that women do studies about women – was the consequence of a fact that was new at that time. In 1970 these studies in fact began to grow in number, as one of the effects of the women's liberation movement and the interest that it aroused. One of the first academic studies to appear in French, *La Condition de la Française aujourd'hui* (The Condition of the Frenchwoman Today), by Andrée Michel and Geneviève Texier, came out in 1964.

WOMEN – OBJECT OF RESEARCH

To regard 'women' as the *object of research* can in one sense be regarded as one of the new ideas in the social sciences during these recent decades. It is nevertheless somewhat ironic to be rejoicing about something which is, if you think about it, one of the aspects of the actual social situation of this group – being the *object* in social relationships, the *object* in theoretical discourse, etc.

None-the-less it is a real change after women's long absence from social science studies, even though it is a paradoxical advance. It is an advance because at last there has been introduced into intellectual thought, into consciousness – whether it be deviant, false, objectifying or stammering consciousness (but we have seen that it has also been quite another thing) – *that which up until now has not existed* because it has been covered by a mask, a veil (like those often worn by women) – the mask of naturalness, of spontaneous reality, that which literally is not thought about, because it is pre-thought, regarded as the preliminary to any society and to any form of consciousness. *Thus becoming an* object *in theory was the inevitable result of becoming a* subject *in history.*

It is a process which, like many others we have touched on here, is not specific to social sex relationships. It occurs in all the instances where a dominated group, whether a people, a class, a nation or a culture, rises up against the domination to which it is subjected. And this refers to actions which go beyond explosions of revolt. This happens each time that an idea, a political view, unites a group and informs its actions. Whether it be the working class, women or colonized peoples, the process is comparable. The political uprising of women, the development of their own consciousness of their social existence shatters the compactness of the ideas which the dominant society has about them. And at one go it makes the group of women into a sociological reality, which then enters into theory as an object of interest and so of study. Whether empirical or speculative, Marxist or liberal, the social sciences previously did not make provision for that which would gradually appear (beyond the description of women as a single group) as a fundamental social relationship, that of the sexes.

This discovery – and the progressive ramifications of the social factors implied in it – occurred with such force that I can think of only one comparable scientific event, and that is the emancipation of the natural sciences from theology. In this instance there is not just a simple adding on of individual pieces of knowledge, but a restructuring of the apprehension of social relationships. It is a theoretical revolution which leads to the reconsideration of knowledge about societies, to going beyond the evidence of the reputed 'natural' 'division' of the sexes in order to arrive at social sex relationships. Carried forward by the partisan analysis which perceived and pointed out the relationship of power and appropriation which socially defines 'women' and 'men', the job of empirical description leads toward this same revolution, even if it is sometimes hesitant and locked into a step-by-step process which rejects (and sometimes is denied to have) *meaning*.

In its theoretical leading edge – that of explicit 'political' texts – this revolution has two major characteristics. The first is that it is the *direct expression* of the group concerned (without mediation by anyone else). It is women, individuals belonging to the group of women (and not an individual from another group setting himself up as the mediator and interpreter of a group to which he himself does not belong), who have produced this reversal and are continuing to develop its consequences. The second characteristic is that it is not the work of one particular person. Rather than being *the* unique and signed work of one particular person, which is the way theory is ordinarily produced, it is the work of a vast ensemble of individuals doing a variety of political jobs, ranging from direct action to writing tracts, from writing articles to legal projects, from consciousness-raising to writing books – in fact, *truly collective* work. The fact that this is taking place within and against a relationship of domination results in the process being sorely shaken by divisions and contradictions and scarcely having the look of a linear – or harmonious – development.

Analyses of specific oppressions have many features in common: exposing and analysing the exploitation, describing the legal ideas and practice, and finally detecting the power relationships behind the façade of 'organic' sociality (the 'complementarity' of the groups). Although the particular incarnations, the forms of each type of oppression and exploitation, of each social relationship of domination, are specific, there is all the same a *structural analogy* which makes each one an example of a phenomenon at one certain unique level – that of power relationships. One must be aware that oppressed peoples have a common consciousness (if not common interests) because it is in struggling for other oppressed peoples that women have discovered that they must struggle for themselves – the entry of minorities into the field of theory also reflects their solidarity. And the social sciences have gained from this the knowledge that social groups are the *results* of relationships and not just the 'elements' of those relationships. Oppressed peoples by speaking out opened up a theoretical debate which overturned a conception of the world which had remained very deeply theological even throughout the atheism of nineteenth-century science. From oppressed peoples comes the radical contention that the world can be thought of in terms of essences. From them comes the knowledge that nothing happens that is not historical, that nothing is ever impervious to change, that no one is the bearer (or expression) of a 'being' or of an eternal fate, and, ultimately, that practice makes this history.

THE INTERRELATEDNESS OF LEVELS OF SOCIAL REALITY

Perhaps the major accomplishment of feminism from a theoretical point of view – that is, what it has introduced into the social sciences – is the concrete and systematically clarified knowledge of the interrelatedness of levels of social reality. The homogeneity of levels of social reality – or their interrelatedness – has been better demonstrated by the ground-swell which brought sex relationships to the forefront of the analysis of social systems than by the attention given to the facts of class (in the popular sense) or to imperialism. The difficulty of envisioning a situation in its totality (even though the will to do so is present) has been overcome in the analyses produced by and around the movement which mobilized women during the last fifteen years. Abortion, housework, sexual harassment both public and private, and all the other issues involve the most complex legal systems as well as the direct concrete fact of compulsion for each individual; they involve collective dependence as well as individual dependence; the concrete and the ideological are shown most clearly in this relationship as the two faces of the same coin.

It was in those analyses that a class system was revealed, a system so perfect that it had long remained *invisible*. It is an invisibility that the oppressed themselves have only with difficulty destroyed; an ambiguous invisibility, since at the same time the real situation of compulsion is perfectly well known by all women, for it is not possible to live as a woman without knowing it (just as it is not possible to live as a member of a minority without *knowing* it). Nevertheless it is an undeniable invisibility, anchored in a commonplace fact: the fact that if things are thus, they are naturally thus and fated to remain so; therefore there is nothing particularly unusual about it, it cannot be analysed, and there is nothing there to be discovered or understood, since the only reason for analysing something is to change it, to interfere with it. (Thinking already means changing. *Thinking about a fact already means changing that fact*.) It is obvious that the long-standing blindness of theory, whether psychological or sociological theory, simply resulted in attesting to belief in the natural ineluctability of these relationships. The fact that there was compulsion and exploitation was obvious to women although it was a matter of indifference to men, but it was devoid of *meaning*; it fell into the category of unquestioned facts. In physics or mechanics, in biology or medicine, however, *it is precisely the category of natural facts that is questioned*. Sex relationships was one of the fields to gain by calling into question accepted ideas. And the story of the investigation and discovery of the social logic hidden behind these sex relationships is the story of a synthesis between revolt, activism, analysis, and consciousness.

NOTES

1 Frederick Douglass, *Narrative of the Life of Frederick Douglass, An American Slave* (Cambridge, Mass.: Belknap Press of Harvard University Press, 1960; originally published in 1845).
2 Montesquieu, *The Spirit of the Laws* (New York: Hafner, 1949), 1: 108.
3 Karl Marx, 'Theses on Feuerbach', Thesis XI, in Karl Marx and Frederick Engels, *Selected Works* (New York: International Publishers, 1980): 30.
4 Which I doubt, because his aim was clearly to counter the budding nationalisms. Ironically for him who would find himself 'the' theoretician of racist nationalism, he regarded the young nationalisms as the expression of the common people, that 'hideous' unit of societies, the 'racial sweepings' which filled him with disgust, and he regarded himself as the bard of the aristocracy (the Aryans, he said), itself, of course, being transnational.
5 See Chapter 12 of the present book, previously published as 'Herrings and Tigers: Animal Behavior and Human Society', *Feminist Issues* 3(1), 1983 (originally published in French in 1978).
6 A rigorous demonstration of the sexist implications of language, using ethnological texts, has been made by Claire Michard-Marchal and Claudine Ribery in their book *Sexisme et sciences humaines, pratique linguistique du rapport de sexage* (Lille: Presses Universitaires de Lille, 1982).
7 Christine Delphy, 'The Main Enemy', *Feminist Issues* 1(1), 1980: 23–40. (Original publication in French in 1970.)
8 Monique Wittig, Gille Wittig, Marcia Rothenburg, Margaret Stephenson, 'Combat pour la libération de la femme', *L'Idiot international*, May 1970.
9 Nicole-Claude Mathieu, 'Biological Paternity, Social Maternity', *Feminist Issues* 4(1), 1984. (Original publication in French in 1977.)
10 See Chapters 9 and 10 of the present book, previously published as 'The Practice of Power and Belief in Nature', *Feminist Issues* 1(2 and 3), 1981 (originally published in French in 1978.)

11 Flora Tristan, *Le Tour de France, journal 1843–1844*, vol. 1 (Paris: Maspero, 1980).
12 Quoted by Aimé Cesaire in his *Discourse on Colonialism* (New York: Monthly Review Press, 1972): 41. Cesaire is quoting from O. Mannoni, *Prospero and Caliban, The Psychology of Colonization* (New York: Praeger, 1956).
13 Ibid.: 42.
14 Text of the Féministes révolutionnaires, 'Justice patriarcale et peine de viol', published in *Alternatives* 1, 1977.
15 Paola Tabet, 'Hands, Tools, Weapons,' *Feminist Issues* 2(2), 1982: 3–62. (Original publication in French in 1979.)
16 Nicole-Claude Mathieu, 'Notes towards a Sociological Definition of Sex Categories', *The Human Context* 6(2), 1974: 345–61. (Original publication in French in 1971.)

Chapter 8

Sexism, a right-wing constant of any discourse
A theoretical note

When we attempt to analyse the Right we tend to focus on its theoretical output. Our interest is drawn to editorials, electoral speeches, posters, founding texts, in other words, to the utterances of constituted parties or movements known to have a blueprint for society and who wish to play a role in the public arena. However, research on sexism and the Right conceives political discourse as being much broader. It is part of a totally different problematic than that which only knows and only recognizes right-wing discourse as a self-explicit, political act. Obviously, an analysis of sexism and the Right in no way excludes this kind of explicit discourse, but the mundane street statement, ordinary conversation, news or everyday comment also fall within its scope and receive particular attention.

The data analysed within this perspective is not simply the object of research: the data constitutes the field itself. In other words, the main purpose is not so much to identify the content of a political discourse – or to reveal the structure – but rather to identify the political project that is being constructed, to identify and grasp an ideology in its very process of articulation, in a way that is to some extent pre-theoretical and in the process of enunciation, and which has not yet taken the form of a blueprint for society.

This technical 'position' is derived from a postulate which also has the status of an empirical observation, and this is that the Right is an ideological form peculiar to relations of domination. All *productions of sense* bear their stamp as soon as they emerge in that type of relation. This hypothesis is based on a wide familiarity with all types of discourse, oral and written. It is clear that the Right cannot be reduced merely to a political programme or to a corpus of ethical proposals. These are part of it, but they do not define it.

The explicit dimension of the political which is identifiable in articulated discourse, and relates to such immediately recognizable subjects as blueprints for society, or civic values – and hence is labelled as 'political' – is the emergent and more visible part of a whole, the ideology proper, in other words, the mental configurations of a society. In the case we are considering, it is a society of domination, a society of order and one which tends toward order. We therefore come across the expressions of the conventional, acknowledged Right. But these are also produced by left-wing parties and movements whenever certain social facts are seen as impenetrable to critical scrutiny. These are facts which are widely considered as non-political and non-social and are seen as belonging to the *natural order*.

Societies are 'thought' by their actors, both majority (in the sense of possessing power) and minority. They are 'thought' while at the same time acted upon. Every society is both a concrete entity (in that it involves material social relations) and a 'symbolic' entity (the interpretations of these relations and the systems of value), and where a relation of power exists between the social groups. When this relationship is hierarchical or exploitative – they are generally found together – these relations constitute the order of that society. Right-wing discourse, and speech, which present 'facts as they stand', claim, therefore, that these facts are correct, that they must be maintained and/or improved, according to their own logic and in conformity to their nature. Relations of domination, exploitation, inequality are held as socially necessary and, furthermore, they are sometimes dressed up in terms of 'complementarity'.

At this point, we need to make a further observation. In general terms, analysts can agree on these premises, even if they express some reservations. To speak of relations of domination and exploitation in general is sufficiently vague as not to be contentious, hence their existence is unlikely to be denied. The fact is that even if the designation of certain social relations in terms of domination and exploitation irritate certain researchers, they are perfectly well aware that many relations, relations of class, of 'race', and colonial and imperialist relations, amongst others, are inegalitarian. Even if they propose another analysis and, consequently, other designations, this does not contest the facts.

However, one of these relations of domination and exploitation which is to be found at the centre of social systems as we know them occupies the same place as the stolen letter in the story by Edgar Allan Poe. Its place is both obvious and invisible. And it follows that this relation is not considered worthy of criticism and analysis in terms of a 'political' issue. Yet the Right gives a great deal of importance to this social relation which is presented as a *natural relation*. The reader will have understood that we are referring to the relation between the sexes which is seen as the foundation and crux of any society. Both the classical, conservative right, through the family, and the cynical right, through the channel of reproduction, treat this relation between the sexes as a fundamental and incontrovertible datum. The arguments may be put forward in a natalist framework, or in the associated framework which prohibits women's physical autonomy; or, alternatively, as part of a eugenics discourse, which includes sterilization and abortion. In any event, the directed and mandatory reproduction for human females in conformity with the chosen model, including elimination for those who do not conform, exhibits a constant feature: *the confinement of women to reproductive materiality*. This is the prerequisite of a right-wing position, but which may not always be labelled as such.

If, therefore, the classical analyses of political discourse do not usually show any spark of interest in sexual politics (and we are not referring to what is generally called 'sexuality' here, but to relations between social sex groups), if there is no analysis of natural evidence and of the prescriptions which derive from them, then it is because this political dimension is not supposed to be perceived as political. It escapes notice and, therefore, knowledge as a political fact because it is not considered as being part of an analysis of trends and motivations that are conventionally held to be political.

As members of the dominated social sex group, we can only be struck by the ubiquity of the discourse in respect of the places assigned to women and men by Nature (in fact to the first, rather than to the second), and by the 'natural' character of the social relation of gender. Their dominant ideological trait is precisely not to be recognizable as political. In this respect gender relations do not occupy the same space in everyday talk and in political discourse as that occupied by *culture, immigration, nation*, and so on, which are immediately recognized as being essentially political.

Furthermore, the discourse concerning gender relations does not follow the usual Left/Right divisions. In fact, there is simply no division. If parties and movements are classified as being to the Right or the Left according to their options in the areas defined as 'political', the general consensus is that it is convenient for the clarity of their debates that the question of the sexes is left undefined somewhere in the middle. For it is a fact that the so-called 'natural' politics of the sexes is equally to be found in what passes for the Left. The Left does not call this category into question any more than does the Right.

Right-wing discourse is an element of a relation of fact, and those belonging to the minority (the social actors of minor status, with no access to power) are familiar with the Right as a state of fact, and a crystallization of a body of practices and values. If right-wing discourse as an element of an existing current relation is the mental side of a relation of domination, left-wing discourse may only be seen as a critical intervention, that is, as an attempt to deconstruct these practices. One is part of the existing order, the other is no more than a projection into a problematic future. Any critique constantly needs reformulation and revision; and as an unsubordinated, non-legitimized perception of reality, it exists as an attempt to transform the order of fact. The Right, on the other hand, is the ideology of an actual order: it is both a *statement of fact* (that of the order that exists, however imperfectly) and a *prescription* (this order must be perpetuated, be supported or be restored).

The term 'revolution' is equally favored by the extreme right and the Left. And there is no quarrel on the grounds of semantic purity. 'Revolution' also has a political boomerang effect, and may signal a return to an original order. The use of violence does not imply that the revolutionary movement is creating anything new. On the contrary, when it calls upon its devotees to display even greater energy and brutality, we can be confident that it does so in order to restore an even greater measure of conformity. In this way, the foundations are strengthened so that what already exists takes on a more heightened form; and this must remain intact: it must not be 'tampered with', 'perverted', 'altered', 'buried', 'degraded' or 'spoiled'. And in these very terms which denote the values and the choices of the Right, we recognize the obsession of the founding and primary order.

It is easy to understand that where there is no critical intervention, ideology, whether implicit or openly expressed, is indistinguishable from statements of facts. In this respect, the Left, which may consist of parties or individuals, is capable of producing a discourse of the Right, and of allowing practices of the Right to remain intact. While this may be doctrinal homogeneity and right-wing practice, this is not the case on the Left where numerous traces of the 'order of things' subsist, hence 'the dominant ideology' is not a meaningless expression. There is no dichotomy between Right and Left: the parting of the waters is not made on the basis of a line which cuts through the middle of opposing ethical options so that an individual 'of the Left' is the same as an individual 'of the Right', immersed in an altogether comparable homogeneous apprehension of the world. To think 'Right' is to think cynically, that is, in conformity with the order of things; and a right-wing thinker may even protest against the 'perversions' inflicted on the 'order of things'. To think 'Left' is to attempt to focus one's mind to counter the weight of facts and constraints. In concrete reality such critical interventions are rare, so that large areas of conformity remain unchallenged, and this always includes generalized sexism. It follows that the ideology of the Right is not the exclusive property of a movement, or of a party of the Right, or of the extreme right. It is invariably present in all relations of domination.

Chapter 9

The practice of power and belief in Nature

Part I The appropriation of women

APOLOGUE

This morning in the Avenue Général Leclerc in Paris I saw what popular opinion calls a madman behaving in a way that psychiatrists call psychotic. He was making large gestures with his arms and was leaping from one side of the pavement to the other. He talked and talked and scared the passers-by with great gyrations of his arms, apparently enjoying this immensely, since he burst out laughing each time he managed to induce a fearful movement.

So he frightened the passers-by. The passers-by? Well, yes, if you like, though in fact this man in his sixties grabbed at women with these enveloping gestures. At old and young women, but not at men. They were indeed enveloping gestures; he even tried to grab hold of the genitals of one young woman. He laughed even more at this.

Now people only publicly take what belongs to them; even the most unrestrained kleptomaniacs are covert when they try to take something which does not belong to them. Where women are concerned, though, there is no need to be covert. They are common property, and if truth comes from wine and from the mouths of babes and madmen, this truth is told us plainly very often. The very publicness of this seizing, the very fact that in many people's view, and anyway in that of men as a whole, it assumes such a 'natural' character and seems almost a 'matter of course', is one of the daily violent expressions of the materiality of the appropriation of the class of women by the class of men. Theft, swindling and embezzlement are done covertly, and to appropriate male men a war is necessary. But not to appropriate female men, that is, women – they are already property. And when we are spoken to concerning the exchange of women, here or elsewhere, this truth is shown to us, for what 'is exchanged' is *already* possessed; women are already the property, before the exchange, of whoever exchanges them. When a male baby is born, he is born a future subject, who will have his own labour power to sell, but not his own materiality, his own individuality. What is more, as proprietor of himself, he will also be able to acquire the material individuality of a female. And on top of that, he will also dispose of the labour power of that same female, which he will use in whatever way suits him, including showing that he is not using it.

If you are not afraid of bitter exercises, watch how young lovers and sweethearts hold hands in the street. Who takes whose hand, and walks ahead – oh, ever so slightly? Watch how the men hold 'their' woman by the neck (like a bicycle by the handlebars) or how they pull her by the arm (like the wagon of their childhood). It varies according to age and income, but the physical interactions shout out this appropriation in each movement, word and look. And I end up by asking myself seriously if this supposedly gallant masculine gesture (which, however, is tending to disappear) of allowing a woman to pass first (that is, to make her go in front) was not simply the way of making sure that she was not out of sight for a second – you never know, even in very high heels, it is possible to run and escape.

Habits of speech tell us the same story. The appropriation of women is explicit in the very banal semantic habit of referring to female social actors by their sex as a matter of priority ('women', the women), a habit which irritates us very much and which obviously has many meanings, but whose real import, as a matter of fact, has passed unnoticed. In any context whatever, be it professional, political, etc., all appellations in these domains are omitted or refused to actors of the female sex, while, of course, these same applications designate only the other (male) actors. The following phrases, for example, were collected in the last forty-eight hours: 'A *pupil* has been punished with compulsory detention of one month; a *young girl* has been reprimanded' (report of disciplinary action at the École Polytechnique); 'a company director, a lathe-operator, a croupier, and a woman . . .' (about a group meeting to give their opinion on some matter); 'They killed tens of thousands of workers, students and women' (Castro on the subject of the Batista regime). These phrases, whose imprecision (as we believe) is so exasperating to us about job, status and situation as soon as it is a question of women, cannot be faulted for omitting information. On the contrary, they are factually correct; they are photographs of social relationships. What is said, and said only about female human beings, is their effective position in class relations: that of being primarily and fundamentally women. That is their social existence; the rest is additional and – we are made to understand – does not count. Corresponding to an employer, there is a 'woman'; corresponding to a polytechnic student, there is a 'woman'; corresponding to a worker, there is a 'woman'. 'Women' we are, and this is not one descriptive term among others; it is our social definition. We are fools if we think that it is only a physical trait, a 'difference', and that starting from this 'given', there will be multiple possibilities open to us. Well, it is not a 'given'; it is a 'fabricated', which we are ceaselessly made to stand for. It is not the beginning of a process (a 'start', as we think); it is the end, a termination.

This is extended even to the point of trying to squeeze us out of a piece of news where we might have been able to slip in under a fraudulent name, of taking us out in order to return us to our true place (to put us in our place); 'Three communist agents, of whom one is a woman . . .' (about spying in West Germany). There we are! A woman is never anything but a woman, an interchangeable object with no other characteristic than her femininity, whose fundamental characteristic is belonging to the class of women.

From popular wisdom to the vulgarities of the corner bar, from sophisticated anthropological theory to legal systems, we are ceaselessly being told that we are appropriated. At best there is rage on our part; in most cases there is apathy. But it would doubtless be a political fault to reject without examination such a set purpose which, coming from the antagonistic class, ought, on the contrary, to arouse amongst us the keenest interest and the most careful analysis. After all, in order to know, it is enough to listen, without shrinking, to the daily banal discourse which reveals *the specific nature of the oppression of women*: appropriation.

Various intellectuals and anthropologists effect a classic projection, attributing to exotic or archaic societies the reality of women's reduction to the state of an appropriated object which has become a medium of exchange. For it is only with reference to these societies that they speak of the *exchange* of women in the strict sense; that is, of the absolute degree of appropriation, where the object is not only 'taken in hand', but also *becomes the equivalent of any other object whatever* – the stage where the object passes from the status of *livestock* (Latin *pecus* in its first meaning) to the status of *money* (*pecus* in its derivative meaning).

'Exchange of women', 'appropriation of women', etc. – what do intellectuals and anthropologists know about it, we ask? They certainly know something about what is going on somewhere, but, whatever they pretend, it is perhaps not ancient or exotic societies that they are talking about. Perhaps it is not societies where goods and women are exchanged on the same level, even though, they also say, one can question the status of women as objects, for, after all, they do speak. Yes, indeed, we speak; and let us see whether under the guise of 'elsewhere' and 'times past' they are not talking of the here and now.

INTRODUCTION

Two facts dominate the account which follows – a material fact and an ideological fact. The first is a *power relation* (yes, I say a 'power relation' and not just 'power'): the power play which is the appropriation of the class of women by the class of men. The other is an *ideological effect*: the idea of 'nature', that 'nature' which is supposed to account for what women are supposed to be.

The ideological effect is not at all an autonomous empirical category; it is the mental form which certain determined social relationships take. The fact and the ideological effect are the two sides of the same phenomenon. The first is a social relationship in which the actors are reduced to the state of appropriated material units (and not simply to bearers of labour power). The other, the ideological-discursive side, is the mental construction which turns these same actors into elements of nature – 'things' even in the realm of thought.

In this chapter, 'The appropriation of women', we will see the concrete appropriation, the reduction of women to the state of material objects. In Chapter 10, 'The naturalist discourse', we will see the ideological form that this social relationship takes, that is, the predication that women are 'more natural' than men.

Everyone – or almost everyone – acknowledges that women are exploited, that when they sell their labour power in the labour market, its price is much lower than that of men, since on an average the wages of women are only two-thirds of those earned by men. Everyone – or almost everyone – agrees that the housework performed by all women, whether or not they are otherwise employed, is unpaid work.

The exploitation of women is the basis of all thinking about the relations between sex classes, whatever its theoretical orientation.

When the exploitation of women is analysed and described, the idea of 'labour power' occupies a central position. But, strangely enough, it is used in the perspective of a social relationship which is precisely that in which women, as a class, are absent. Labour power in this perspective is presented as 'the only thing that the worker has to sell, his ability to work'.[1] This, which is correct for the man worker today, is not true of the woman worker or of any other woman today. This meaning of labour power as being the ultimate thing which can be used to earn a living is inadequate for the whole class of women.

This reminds us of the time when the unbridled imagination of researchers went so far as to make the prodigious effort of envisaging that the greatest possible closeness between two individuals of different races was marriage (or sexual relations). Thus they brilliantly demonstrated to what extent they themselves were blinded by racist structures, not to see that this greatest possible closeness is quite simply blood kinship, the fact of being parent and child (mother and daughter, father and son, etc.). An extremely common and banal situation, but one that is completely ignored intellectually, literally denied.

It is exactly the same situation with regard to labour power in sex classes. A whole class, which makes up about half of the population – that is, women – does not suffer just the monopoly of its labour power, but also a relationship of direct, physical appropriation. To be sure, this type of relationship is not unique to the relationship between the sexes. In recent history it characterized plantation slavery, which disappeared from the industrial world scarcely a century ago (United States in 1865, Brazil in 1890), although this does not mean that slavery disappeared completely. Another form of physical appropriation, serfdom, which characterized the feudal landed estate, disappeared at the end of the eighteenth century in France (the last serfs were emancipated around 1770, and serfdom was abolished in 1789), but persisted for more than a century longer in certain European countries. The relation of direct physical appropriation is, therefore, not a form which is characteristic of relations based on sex alone.

Physical appropriation in relations based on sex – which I will try to describe in this chapter – includes the pre-emption of labour power, and it is through the form that this pre-emption takes that we can detect that it is a material appropriation of the body. However, it has a certain number of distinct characteristics, of which the essential one (as in slavery) is the fact that *in this relationship there exists no form of measurement of the pre-emption of the labour power*. This labour power, contained within the limits of the individual material body, is taken as a whole, without evaluation. The body is a reservoir of labour power, and it is as such that it is appropriated. It is not labour power distinct from its supporter/producer, in that it can be measured in 'quantities' (of time, money, tasks), which is appropriated, but its origin – the labour-power-machine.

If relations of appropriation do indeed generally imply the monopoly of labour power, they are prior logically, and they are also prior from the historical point of view. It is the result of a long and difficult process that it has become possible to sell only one's labour power without being appropriated oneself. Physical appropriation appeared in most known forms of slavery: for example, in that of Rome (where, besides, the totality of the slaves of one master was called his *familia*), and in that of the eighteenth and nineteenth centuries in North America and the West Indies. On the other hand, certain forms of slavery, in which the duration was limited (to a certain number of years of service, as in Hebrew society, in the Athenian city-state with certain reservations, or in seventeenth-century America), and certain forms of serfdom which fixed limits on the usage of the serf (the number of days per week, for example) are the transitional forms between physical appropriation and the monopoly of labour power. What will concern us here is *physical appropriation itself, the relation in which it is the producing material unit of labour power which is appropriated and not just labour power.* Called 'slavery' and 'serfdom' (in the feudal economy), this type of relation can be designated by the term *sexage*[2] in the case of the modern domestic economy when it concerns the relations between sex classes.

THE CONCRETE EXPRESSION OF APPROPRIATION

The utilization of one group by another, its transformation into an instrument, manipulated and used for the purpose of increasing the assets (and therefore also the freedom and prestige) of the dominant group, or even (as usually happens) simply of allowing this group to live in better conditions than it would be able to achieve by itself, can take various forms. In the relations of sexage the particular expression of this relation of appropriation (that of the whole group of women, and that of the individual material body of each woman) are:

(a) the appropriation of time;
(b) the appropriation of the products of the body;
(c) the sexual obligation;
(d) the physical charge of disabled members of the group (disabled by age – babies, children, old people – or illness and infirmity), as well as the *healthy members of the group of the male sex.*

The appropriation of time

Time is *explicitly* appropriated in the marriage 'contract', in so far as there is no measurement of time and no limit placed on its use. It is expressed neither in an hourly form, as is the case in standard work contracts, whether or not they are for wages (contracts for hire or in exchange for maintenance specify time of work and time of freedom – holidays, days off, etc.); nor is it expressed in the form of a money measure: no monetary evaluation of the wife's work is envisaged.

What is more, this appropriation of time *does not concern just the wife, but also members of the group of women in general*, since, in fact, mothers, sisters, grandmothers, daughters, aunts, etc. who have made no individual contract with the husband, the 'head of the family', contribute to the maintenance and upkeep of his property (living or inanimate). The laundry, the care of children, the preparation of meals, etc., are some-times taken charge of by one of the mothers or sisters of the spouses, by their daughter or daughters, etc. This is not by virtue of a direct contract of appropriation as in the case of the wife (whose naked appropriation is demonstrated in the legal obligation – first and foremost – of sexual service), but as a function of the general appropriation of the class of women, which implies that *their time* (their work) may be disposed of without contractual compensation, and may be generally and indis-criminately disposed of. *It is as if the wife is actually owned by the husband, and each man has the enjoyment of the class of women, and particularly each man who has acquired the private use of one of them.*

At all times and in all places, in the most 'familial' as in the most 'public' circumstances, women (the woman, the women) are expected to do the cleaning and arranging, to look after and feed the children, to sweep or to serve the tea, to do the dishes or to answer the telephone, to sew on the button or to listen to the metaphysical and professional ramblings of men, etc.

The appropriation of the products of the body

'It wasn't the hair of *our* Burgundian women which we sold, but their milk.' These words, which were heard straight from the mouth of an old male writer (on television, 16 December 1977), say clearly enough that, contrary to what many of us believe, neither our hair nor our milk belong to us, for if they are sold, it is by their lawful owners. These owners, moreover, evoking their own fathers (cargo shippers), referred to some wet nurses as follows: 'They made a shipment of women to Paris' (quoted from the same spokesman).

But the still present proof of the appropriation of the products of the body is that in marriage *the number of children is not the subject of contract*, is not fixed or subjected to the wife's approval. The absence for most women of the real possibility of contraception and abortion is the result of this. The wife must and will bear all the children that her husband wants to impose on her. And if the husband exceeds what is convenient for him, he will put all the responsibility on the wife, who must give him everything that he wants, but only what he wants. The status of abortion, clandestine for such a long time, existing without existing, confirmed this relationship, abortion being *the recourse of women whose husbands did not want the child*, as much as the recourse of women who did not want the child themselves.[3]

We know that children belong to the father, and in France until a short time ago, for a mother to be able to take her child out of the country, she had to get the authorization of the father. The converse was not the case. It is not that today and in rich countries the ownership of children is advantageous economically.[4] Children, on the other hand, remain a very important instrument of blackmail in case of marital disagreement: it is the ownership of them that men demand, but not the material burden of them, which they hasten to confide to another woman (mother, servant, wife or companion), according to the rule which requires that the possessions of the dominant group be materially taken care of by one (or some) of the possessions of the same. The ownership of children, a 'production' of women, in the last resort is juridically in the hands of men. Children continue to belong to the father, even when their mother has the material charge of them in the case of separation.[5] Besides, doesn't a wife 'give' her husband children, whereas the converse is not true?

The individual material body of a woman belongs, in what it produces (children) as in its divisible parts (hair, milk), to someone other than herself – as was the case in plantation slavery.[6]

The sexual obligation

It is not so easy to give a name to this relationship. 'Sexual service'? Like compulsory military service? Not bad. 'Sexual duty'? As in household duties or Duty? That is not bad either. 'Laying', as those on the good side of the relationship call it? 'Droit du seigneur', 'laying rights', is one more of those terms that we have thrown in our faces. It at least has the merit of saying outright what is being talked about: a *right*, and a right exercised over us without the least importance being given to our opinion on the subject,[7] but this has the serious defect of being the term used by those who enjoy the right. As for us, we fulfil the duty. We have always been taught that to all rights there are corresponding duties, but what was not specified to us is that some people's rights correspond to other people's duties. In this case it is clear.

When you are a woman and after a certain time you meet an ex-lover, his main preoccupation seems to be to sleep with you again. Just like that, it seems. For after all I do not see that physical passion has much to do with this attempt. Obviously not. It is a clear way of showing that the essential thing in the relationship between a man and a woman is *physical usage*. Physical usage expressed here in its most reduced, most succinct form – sexual usage. It is the only physical usage possible when the encounter happens by chance and there are no stable social ties. It is not sexuality which is in question here, not 'sex'; it is simply usage. It is not 'desire'; it is simply control, as in rape. If the relationship is re-established, even in an ephemeral way, it must be once again through the usage of the woman's body.

There are two main forms which this *physical sexual usage* takes: that in which there is a non-monetary contract – marriage; and that which is directly paid for in cash – prostitution. Superficially these are opposed to each other, but it actually seems, on the contrary, that they confirm each other in their expression of the appropriation of the class of women. The apparent opposition is based on the intervention or non-intervention of payment, that is, of a *measure* of this physical usage. Prostitution consists in the fact, on the one hand, that the practice of sex is remunerated by payment of a specified sum, and, on the other hand, that this remuneration corresponds to a determined length of time (which can vary from a few minutes to a few days) and to codified acts. The main characteristic of prostitution is that the physical usage purchased is sexual, and sexual only (even if it sometimes takes forms which seem remote from what is strictly sexual relations and shows common characteristics with prestige-giving behaviour, maternal conduct, etc.). *Sale* limits the physical usage to sexual usage.

Marriage, on the contrary, extends physical usage to all possible forms of this usage, with the sexual relationship in the central position, but encompassing other forms. It is obligatory in the marriage contract, and, moreover, its non-exercise is a peremptory reason for annulment (not 'divorce', but 'annulment'). It is thus the main expression of the relationship which is established between two particular individuals in the form of marriage – and also in the form of cohabitation, which is common-law marriage.

The practice of this physical usage outside marriage – in other words, for a woman to accept or seek being taken in hand by another man, even if limited to sexual relations – is grounds for divorce. One can say, a woman must not forget that she is appropriated, and that, as the husband's property, she obviously cannot do what she wants with her own body. The husband may equally be the cause of divorce if he is himself an 'adulterer', but, for him, it is not enough that he sexually use another woman; he must *appropriate* this other woman. How? Adultery is only established for a man in the case of a liaison, that is, in the attempt to shatter the monogamy which is the conventional form of the conjugal appropriation of women here and now.[8] (In other places and at other times it could be polygamy.) But a man's recourse to prostitution is not adultery and is in no way grounds for divorce. It is thus that when a man has a sexual relationship, his body is not considered 'taken in hand'; rather he keeps the ownership and subsequent freedom of use of it. He can use it freely, sexually or in any other way, outside of the link that he has established with a particular person, 'his wife'.

So it is only when he establishes a customary relationship of appropriation of another specified woman (and not a transitory relationship with a woman held in common), and when he infringes the rules of the group of men (and not at all because he would 'offend' his wife!) that he can find himself facing the sanction of divorce, and find himself deprived of the extended physical usage (including the task of the maintenance of his own person) of a specific woman, as was assured to him by marriage.[9]

The same word, 'adultery', for the woman, on the contrary, implies, means that her body does not belong to her personally, but to her husband, and that she does not have the free use of it. And this is doubtless the true reason for the absence (despite the exceptions that some people make great exertions to find) of male prostitution for the use of women – and not the 'physiological unavailability' of men, which is constantly evoked in this regard.[10] This is what is suggested by the non-existence of prostitution *for* women, as opposed to prostitution *for* men. There can be no prostitution *for* those who do not own their own bodies.

Possessions

'The body' – many of us are very concerned about this question and attach a lot of importance to it. Recently on a 'cultural' radio programme a man, who was usually more moderate, got himself all worked up explaining that all these women writers (I quote approximately) 'speak insistently of the realities of the body, about the inner organs, saying things that no one usually says, with a sort of insistent complacency'. He did not use the word 'morbid', but it is the sort of thing that was implied; in any case, in his view all this was disgusting.

I asked myself what was going on here, since one should always pay close attention to what the antagonistic class is saying. A man was expressing his anger at those of us who keep returning to the body and who do so for our own reasons: our bodies have been denied for so long, let us discover them! Our bodies have been despised for so long, let us rediscover our pride, etc.!

In the disgust and contempt expressed by this journalist, in his irritation, I heard an uncertain echo, which was familiar to me, but which I could not succeed in identifying. His remarks obviously seemed to be an idealist commentary about *something else* (some kind of super-structural commentary). I definitely felt that there was something – but what? All that reminded me of – but yes! It reminded me of what people who have money say about it (money stinks), and what they say about material goods (property is contemptible, etc.). Money stinks, like women; property is contemptible, like women. It is thus that goods, women and money are identical in some way. Which way? They are possessions, *material possessions*.

In so far as they are possessions, all remarks about them are only acceptable from the mouth of the proprietor. He may speak of them as it suits him, and when it suits him. Moreover, since these goods are at his disposition, he can be contemptuous about them from the elevated viewpoint which sometimes characterizes well-to-do people who (thank God!) are not attached to worldly goods, neither to their livestock, nor to their money – at least when their possession of it is assured.

Better still, they can divest themselves of it symbolically: of their female possessions, for example, through literary and cinematic porno-sadism, which is a widespread and well-established activity of their class.[11] But it is not a question of these possessions gambolling around in any direction they choose and making the mistake of believing themselves the owners of anything at all, and mainly not of them-selves.[12]

All this, therefore, is only secondarily a matter of contempt, and not at all a matter of denial. Contempt and denial are what we hear and suffer, but they are only the surface of a relationship. The contempt and the disgust at women's demands for their own bodies only derive from the possession of these bodies by men. As for denial, we are not exactly denied. Moreover, they would not so much go for us ('after us' would be more correct) if we did not exist materially. It is as subjects that we do not exist.[13] Materially we exist only too much: we are properties. All this is a banal affair of fixing boundaries between properties. It is because we are taken in hand as a whole class that we are 'dispossessed' of ourselves.

Individual mental rejuvenation and yoga may help for a time, but it is important that we regain (and not just with our minds) the possession of our *materiality*. To regain the ownership of ourselves implies that our entire class regain the ownership of itself, socially and materially.

The physical burden of members of the group

The relations of sex classes and the 'ordinary' relations of classes bring into play different instrumentalities. If slavery and serfdom imply being reduced to the state of a thing, of a tool whose instrumentality is applied (or applicable) to other things (agriculture, machinery, animals), sexage, like house-slavery, concerns reduction to the state of a tool whose instrumentality is applied *in addition* and fundamentally to other human beings. In addition and fundamentally, because women, like all dominated people, of course, carry out some tasks which do not imply a direct and personalized relationship with other human beings; but *always* they (and only they nowadays in western countries) are dedicated to assuring, outside the wage system, the bodily, material, eventually the emotional, maintenance of the totality of social actors. It is a matter of services which are (a) required (unpaid, as we know), *and* (b) given in the framework of a lasting personalized relationship.

In the two cases of extensive physical service and sexual service, the relationship of appropriation is shown in the banal and everyday fact that the appropriated person is assigned to the material service of the body of the dominator and to the bodies which belong to or are dependent on this dominator. The fact of being taken in hand as a thing by this dominator is demonstrated by the physical availability which is dedicated to the material care of other physical individuals. And this takes place in a relationship which is not evaluated in terms either of time or of money.

To be sure, these tasks of physical maintenance *also* exist in the monetary work sphere and are *sometimes* carried out professionally for a wage (but it is not by chance that even under those conditions, here and now, it is almost exclusively women who do these jobs). But if we compare the number of paid and unpaid hours dedicated to these tasks, the overwhelming majority of them are carried out outside the sphere of paid work.

Socially, *these tasks are carried out in the context of a direct physical appropriation*. For example, religious institutions absorb women whom they assign 'free of charge' to this work in hospices, orphanages, and various asylums and homes. As in the context of marriage (besides, they are married to God), it is in exchange for their upkeep and not in exchange for a wage that the women called *sisters* or *nuns* do this work. And certainly it is not a question of religious 'charity', since when it is men who are grouped together in these sacred institutions, they undertake none of the tasks of the maintenance of humans at all. It is a matter of a fraction of *the class of women* who, having been brought together, carried out socially, without pay, the tasks of the physical care of the sick, the young and the unattached elderly.

They are the height of femininity, just as prostitutes are (and perhaps even more so), the latter being another version of the specific relationship of sexage, although apparently different because they are 'paid'.[14] Moreover, abominable common sense (that deep well of conformist hypocrisy) agrees with this view, since it only pictures the nun or the prostitute as women. They are the allegorical figures in an everyday relationship which unites the two. The physical burden and the sexual burden, which are the subject here, are actually at the centre of the relations between the sexes.

Effects of appropriation on individuality

To speak of the physical maintenance of bodies is to say little; there are misleading appearances here that we think we know about. In fact, what does *physical material maintenance* mean? First of all, it means a constant presence. No clocking-in here, but a life whose entire time is absorbed, devoured, by face-to-face interaction with the babies, the children, the husband, and also the elderly or sick people.[15] Face-to-face, because their gestures, their actions hold the mother-wife-daughter-daughter-in-law directly within their domain. Each gesture of these individuals is full of meaning for her and modifies her own life at every moment: a need for something, a fall, a request, some acrobatics, a departure, a pain obliges her change what she is doing, to intervene, to worry about what has to be done immediately, about what will have to be done in a few minutes, at such and such a time, this evening, before such and such a time, before leaving, before X arrives, etc. Each second of her time – and without hope of seeing this absorption end at a fixed hour, even at night – she is *absorbed into other individualities*, diverted from the activity which is going on to other activities.[16]

The constraint lies not only in the persistence of this presence and this attention, but also in the material physical care of the *body* itself. The washing of the dead is the task of the group of women, and that is not negligible. Nor is the washing of the bodies of the very ill.[17] Furthermore, the material attachment to physical individualities is also a *mental* reality. There is no abstraction: every concrete gesture has an aspect that is full of meaning, a 'psychological' reality. Although they relentlessly try to coerce us into not thinking, this attachment cannot be lived mechanically and indifferently. Individuality rightly is a precarious conquest, often denied to a whole class, whose individuality is forced to become diluted, materially and actually, into other individualities. A central constraint in the relations of sex classes, this deprivation of individuality, is the sequel or the hidden face of the material appropriation of individuality. For it is not obvious that human beings so easily distinguish themselves one from another, and constant proximity/physical burden is a powerful hindrance to independence and autonomy. It is the source of an inability to discern and *a fortiori* to put into practice one's own choices and actions.

Surely it is no accident that the members of the dominant sex class are 'disgusted' by the children's shit, and as a result 'cannot' change them. No one would even dream of thinking that a man could change the clothes of old or sick people, could wash them or do their laundry. But women do it, and 'must' do it. They are the social tool assigned to those tasks. And it is not only hard and obligatory work (there is other hard work which does not depend on the social-sexual division of labour); it is also work which in the social relations in which it is done destroys individuality and autonomy. Performed outside the wage system, in the context of the appropriation of her own person, attaching the woman to determined physical individuals, 'familiars' (in the literal sense of the word), with whom the ties are strong (whatever the love–hate nature of them), it dislocates the fragile emergence of the subject.

The panic into which many women are plunged when they have new-born children – whatever they call it, nervous depression or post-partum depression – what is it but the realization that one is disappearing, that one is devoured, not only physically, but also mentally – physically and therefore mentally; that one is wavering on a tightrope and one does not know if it will throw one permanently into the fog of quasi-physical absorption in others. Or if it will allow you to cross this unmeasurable and unmeasured time without losing yourself definitely. Or if it will allow you to emerge at the other end of the tunnel at some indeterminable time.

The confrontation with material appropriation is the very dispossession of one's own mental autonomy. It is made more bluntly clear in the physical charge of other dependent beings than in any other social form that appropriation takes. When one is materially appropriated, one is mentally dispossessed of oneself.

THE MATERIAL APPROPRIATION OF BODILY INDIVIDUALITY

Appropriation of the physical individuality and of labour power in sexage

Like any dominated group, we embody labour power. However, the fact of embodying labour power is not in itself material appropriation. The coming into being of a proletariat along with industrial development broke the syncretic link between appropriation and labour power that used to exist in slave or feudal societies (let us say, in an agricultural landed society).

Today this non-equivalence, this distinction, is expressed in the *selling* of labour power; this introduces a *measuring* of labour power which is more clear-cut than had been the time limitation put on the utilization of labour power under serfdom. The selling of labour power is a particular form of its usage: it is an evaluation both monetary and temporal, even if there is a tendency to confuse this evaluation with its maximum usage. The person who sells is selling so many hours, and he/she will be paid for these hours, in a monetary form or some other form. In any case there is always evaluation. However the labour power is employed, whatever the tasks done, the sale involves two elements of measure – time and wages. Even if the price is fixed by the buyer (as in the case of times of unemployment), the seller, *as a material individual*, disposes of *his or her* own labour power (it is not a question here of concluding whether it gets him or her very far or not) and thus distinguishes his or her individuality from the usage of that individuality.

Unlike other dominated groups with labour power, we women are, in the relations between the sexes, non-sellers of our labour power, and our appropriation evinces itself precisely in this fact. We are distinct from those oppressed people who can bargain *beginning with* the disposition of their labour power – that is, to exchange it or sell it.

There is great suggestive power for practical and tactical reasons in evaluating in terms of money the amount of work performed within marriage, and this has been done.[18] But we can ask ourselves if this does not contribute to hiding the fact that this work has as one of its specific characteristics the fact of not being paid. It would, moreover, be more correct to say that its intrinsic character is the fact of being *non-paid*.[19]

If it is non-paid, it is because it is not 'payable'. If it cannot be measured or converted into money (measurement and money being doublets), this means that it is acquired in another way. And this other way implies that it is acquired in aggregate, once and for all, and that it no longer has to be evaluated in terms of money or timetables or by the job – evaluations which generally accompany the ceding of labour power. And it is precisely these evaluations which do not take place in this case.

When evaluations take place in a relationship, they establish a contractual-style relationship: so much X in exchange for so much Y, so many hours for so much money, etc. Not all social relationships are translatable into contractual terms, and a contract is the expression of a specific relationship. Its presence or absence (which is highly relevant to the collective relationship of sexage) is the mark of a particular relationship. It cannot be considered as a secondary arrangement of relationships which could equally well be translatable into contractual terms. For example, the paid labour force is *within* the contractual universe; slavery is *outside* it. The generalized sexed relationship (which is ideo- logically interpreted as a guaranteed relationship outside the contractual universe and founded in Nature) is not translated, and *is not trans- latable*, into contractual terms. This is habitually obscured by the fact that the *individualized* form of this relationship is itself considered to be a contract: marriage.

This individualized form contributes through its banal appearance of being contractual to hiding the real relationship which exists between sex classes as much as it reveals it. The reason for this is that the contractual universe confirms AND assumes, *before all other things*, the quality of proprietorship in the parties to the contract. Minors, the insane, those under guardianship, i.e. those who are still the property of their father and who do not have possession of their subjectivity (which means in fact that they cannot have property of their own, as it is expressed in the Civil Code), do not have the power to make a contract. In order to make a contract, the ownership of material goods (land and funds put into play in the contract) and possibly the ownership of living things (animals, slaves, women, children) seems superficially to be the determining factor. But what in fact is the determining factor is *self-proprietorship*, which, in default of any 'property of one's own', is expressed in the possibility of selling one's own labour power. This is the minimum condition for any contract. But the fact for the individual of being the material property of someone else excludes that person from the universe of contracts; it is not possible for anyone to be at one and the same time self-owned and the material property of someone else. The nature of such social relationships as sexage or slavery is in a certain way invisible, because those who are involved in them as the dominated ones do not have a degree of reality very different from that of an animal or an object – however precious these animals or objects may be.

The sale or exchange of goods, and *especially of that which emanates from one's own body, which is what labour power is*, constitutes the proof of self-proprietorship; I can only sell that which belongs to me.

In the statute which codifies the marriage relation, there is no legal pronouncement about self-ownership either. Just as in the contract for sale of labour power, where the hidden meaning is self-proprietorship, in the marriage 'contract' the hidden meaning is the non-ownership of oneself, expressed in a specific relationship. Women *do not cede labour power* in this contract; we have already noted that no time measurement nor agreement on remuneration are involved. Only the guarantee of being 'kept' in working order according to the means of the owner (alive, 'well maintained', as a machine is well maintained or not) is given in exchange for ceding. Ceding what, in fact? What kind of a cession can it be which gives unlimited time and the whole bodily space to the taker? *The fact that there is no limit put on work, no measure of time, no notion of rape*[20] *(this is of primary importance) shows that this ceding is done* en bloc *and without limits*. And in consequence what is ceded is not labour power, but indeed the material unit which forms the individual herself.

If we compare the relationship in sexage with the classic sale of labour power on the market, we are confronted with the notion of exchange. However, there is no exchange in the relationship of sexage, since in fact there is no ledger entry for anything which could be the material of the exchange. If nothing is evaluated or entered into the accounts, if EVERYTHING is owned and if everything is property (time, labour power, children, everything, without limits) the relationship of sexage is not a market relationship. How could we express the terms of a transaction, how open negotiations? What exactly is to be negotiated here? Is it possible to negotiate what is already appropriated and already belongs? One can only exchange that which one owns. And we own neither our labour power nor our reproductive capacity. Being the bearers of labour power like any other dominated group, we are, however, in contrast to the other dominated groups of the contemporary industrial society, not in a position to negotiate or sell this labour power, *precisely as a result of the fact that it is derived from the physical body and that this body is already appropriated.*

It was not due to some incomprehensible aberration that during the nineteenth century the earnings of women and children went to the husband-father and belonged to him. Only since 1907 (in France) have women had the right to draw their own wage (but still without having the personal right to work; the husband had the right to decide this and thus kept the ownership of her labour power until 1965). This legal fact is made even more interesting by the situation that in practice women themselves drew their own wages since the husband was for most of the time notable for his absence in the class where women worked for wages (there was little marital stability). But this wage which they drew did not belong to them legally; it belonged to the owner of the woman-work-tool.[21]

Sexage

The reduction to the state of a thing, more or less admitted or known about in relations of *slavery* or *serfdom*, exists today in industrialized urban centres, under our very eyes, dissimulated/exposed in marriage, an institutionalized social relationship, if ever there was one. But the idea that a class is *used* (literally: manipulated like a tool), that is, treated like a cow or a reaper, is in the very progressive minds of our contemporaries supposed to be ascribable to past ages or to despotisms as oriental as they are primitive, or at best to be the expression of a provocative cynicism. We do not see what we have before our eyes – even when we belong to the enslaved class.

For all that, marriage is only the institutional (contractual) surface of a generalized relationship: the appropriation of one sex class by the other. It is a relationship which concerns the entirety of the two classes and not a part of each of them, as the consideration of the marriage contract alone might lead one to believe. The marriage contract is only the individualized expression – in that it establishes an everyday and specific relationship between *two* particular individuals[22] – of a general class relationship where the whole of one class is at the disposition of the other. And if, in fact, the individualization of this relationship almost always happens (around 90 per cent of women and men are married at one time or another of their lives), marriage is none the less only the restrictive expression of a relationship – it is not in itself this relationship. It legalizes and confirms a relationship which exists *before* it and *outside* of it: the material appropriation of the class of women by the class of men – sexage.

However, marriage also contradicts this relationship. If it expresses and limits sexage by restricting the collective use of a woman and by giving this usage to a single individual, it also deprives other individuals of his class of the usage of this particular woman, who would, without this act, remain common property. This is only ideally speaking, because in practice the *enjoyment* of the common right belongs either to God (nuns), to the father (daughters, in which state one remains until one becomes a wife, according to the Civil Code), or to the pimp (women who are officially 'common property').

This contradiction at the centre of social appropriation itself operates between collective appropriation and private appropriation. A second contradiction takes place between the appropriation of women, whether it be collective or private, and their *re-appropriation by themselves*, their objective existence as social subjects – in other words, the possibility of their selling *on their own authority* their labour power on the classical open market. This contradiction is also revealed by marriage. In France it is only since 1965 (Article 322 of the Civil Code) that a wife has been able to make the decision herself to work; in other words, that she has been able to do without her husband's authorization. However, the abolition of this authorization by the husband was not accompanied by any modification of Article 214, which codifies the relations between spouses and ratifies the type of appropriation characteristic of marriage. In the stating of the respective contributions of the husband and the wife to the responsibilities of the marriage, this article brings out that the contribution of the wife is different in essence from that of the husband. The husband is supposed to bring in the cash, that is, in most cases to sell his labour power. The contribution of the wife, on the other hand, is based either on her dowry and inheritance ('pre-existing' money), or – and it is this which is the main thing – on 'her activity in the home or her collaboration in her husband's occupation'. This is to say that the wife is not supposed *to sell* her labour power in order to support the conjugal commonalty, nor even to furnish a *specific quantity* of this labour power to the commonalty, but 'to pay with her own person', as the popular saying so correctly puts it, and *to give her individuality directly to her husband without the mediation of either monetary or quantitative considerations.*

The shadow of this specific relationship between spouses lurks behind all the discourses which, from the Right to the reddest Left, regard as a theological fact the existence of a 'woman's work', that is, the physical maintenance of her husband, his dependants and the house – a relation which, if they were honest, they would do better to call the appropriation of the woman. These discourses are generally replete with considerations, sentimental or not, about the exhausting (but intangible) 'double workday'.

Social appropriation (the fact for individuals of one class of being material properties) is a specific form of social relations. It exists *today and here* only *between sex classes* and runs up against the solid incredulity which usually greets facts too 'obvious' not to be *invisible* (as was housework before feminism). This type of social relation can only find acceptance if it is 'in the past' (slavery or serfdom) or 'elsewhere' (so-called primitives of various kinds).

On the invisibility of appropriation

The appropriation of women, the fact that it is their materiality *en bloc* that is acquired, is accepted at so deep a level that it is not seen. From the ideological point of view, that is, from the point of view of the mental consequences (or the mental aspect) of a material fact, the attachment of serfs to the land and the attachment of women to men are in part comparable. The dependence of serfs on the land appeared at the time to be just as 'inevitable', just as 'natural', and must have been just as little called into question as the present-day dependence of women on men. And the popular movement, which, at the time of the birth of the communes, detached certain individuals from the feudal land-owning chain (or which used those who had already 'dropped out' of this chain by fleeing),[23] is perhaps comparable to that which today lets a small but increasing number of women escape from the patriarchal and sexist institutions (from marriage, from the father, from religion, which are the obligations of the sex class).[24] But there is this difference: the serfs were the movable goods of the land, and it was land (*and not directly them*) that was appropriated by the feudal landholders, while women are directly – as was the land itself – appropriated by men. The plantation slaves of the eighteenth and nineteenth centuries were, like women, objects of direct appropriation; they were independent of the land and belonged to the master.

No one in these cases questions the naturalness of it; in the case of the serf's belonging to the land, the degree of reality felt must have been that of the obviousness of hot and cold, of day and night, of a fact, as it were. Slaves' belonging to their master, women's belonging to the group of men (and to one man), as tools, are facts of the same kind. Their status as a tool used for maintenance is so deeply rooted in everyday life, in facts, and therefore in people's mentality, that there is no wondering, much less any questioning, and no unease whatever when faced with the fact that women keep in material working order their possessor and the other properties and dependants of this possessor (and moroeever all the social marginals: the sick, the elderly, the infirm and orphans) either in the framework of private appropriation (marriage) or in the framework of collective appropriation (family, religious life, prostitution).

THE MEANS OF APPROPRIATION

What are the means by which the appropriation of the class of women is carried out?

(a) The labour market.
(b) Spacial confinement.
(c) Show of force.
(d) Sexual constraint.
(e) The arsenal of the law and customary rights.

The labour market

The labour market does not allow women to sell their labour power in exchange for the minimum necessary for existence – their own existence and that of the children which they inevitably will have. They are thus *constrained* by this market, which grants them in France on average only two-thirds of a man's wage.[25] (Until the beginning of the twentieth century women's wages in France were only half those of men.[26]) Above all, this labour market imposes on them an unemployment rate considerably higher than that of men: at the beginning of 1977 the French Ministry of Labour announced that *82 per cent of those under 25 years of age seeking employment were women*. This figure, moreover, only concerned those women who were already on the labour market, and at least 52 per cent do not appear in the labour statistics. In this way women are forced to find employment as a wife, that is, to sell THEMSELVES and not to sell just their labour power, in order to live and let their children live.

Spacial confinement

The place of residence for a married couple is still today fixed by the husband ('mutual agreement' only means acceptance by the wife, since in case of disagreement it is the husband who decides, unless the wife takes him to court). The general principle is thus fixed: the wife must not be anywhere except in her husband's home. For property which can move but not speak (pigs, cows, etc.) enclosures made of stakes, metal, rope or electric fencing (consult manufacturers' catalogues) were invented. For property which moves *and speaks* (thinks, is conscious, what more can I say?) a comparable thing has been tried – female property belongs in the gynaeceum, the harem, the house (in both its meanings) – but, in addition, because of their character as speaking property, their confinement has been embellished with internalization – the perfect example of an internal fence, whose efficiency can hardly be improved upon.

The internalization of this enclosure is effected by positive training and also by negative training. The first kind goes thus: 'Your place is here, you are the queen of the house, the magician in the bed, the irreplaceable mother. Your[27] children will become autistic, psychotic, idiots, homosexual, failures, if you don't stay at home, if you are not there when they come home, if you don't breastfeed them until they are three months, six months, three years old, etc.'. In brief, you are the only one who can do all this; you are irreplaceable (most of all, by a male). The second kind of training goes something like this: 'If you go out, other guys like me will pursue you until you give in, will threaten you, will make your life impossible and exhausting in a thousand ways. You have permission (it is an order) to go to the grocery, the school, the market, the town hall, and down the main street where the shops are. And you may go there between seven o'clock in the morning and seven o'clock in the evening. That's all. If you do anything else, you'll be punished in one way or another, and in any case I forbid it for *your* safety and *my* peace of mind'. This sort of thinking has even entered the labour laws: 'If you are of the female sex, you will only have the right to work at night in those places where you are 'irreplaceable' (we are definitely not replaced, in fact) – in hospitals, for example'. The bitter inventory of the times and places which are closed to us, the spaces which are forbidden, and the emotional training through gratifications and threats is a list which is beginning to be drawn up today.

Show of force (physical violence)

Physical violence exercised against women, which also was in a sense *invisible*, in that it was considered as an individual, psychological or circumstantial 'failing' (like the 'mistakes' of the police) is more and more being revealed for what it is. It is first of all quantitatively not an exception, and above all it is socially significant of a relationship:[28] it is a socialized sanction of the right which men arrogate to themselves over women – this man over that woman, and also over all other women who 'do not walk the straight and narrow'. This is related to spacial confinement and sexual constraint.

Sexual constraint

Nowadays we are largely in agreement about the fact that sexual constraint in the form of rape, provocation, cruising, harassment, etc. is, first of all, one of the means of coercion used by the class of men to subdue and frighten the class of women, at the same time that it is the expression of their property rights over this same class.[29]

Every woman who has not been officially appropriated by a contract which restricts use of her to a single man, in other words, every woman who is not married or who acts alone (travelling about alone, eating alone, etc.), is the object of a competition which reveals the collective nature of the appropriation of women. This is the meaning of brawls over women, and I have always been distressed to see that most women accepted this monstrosity and did not even perceive that they were being treated like a seat at a rugby match or a piece of cheese, that in fact they accepted the 'value' which was immanent in them – that of *an object* which can be disposed of. To gain the maximum benefit from their common property right, men will bring into play among themselves their prerogatives of class and prestige, as well as their physical strength. This does not necessarily take an apocalyptic form with bruises and black eyes, but the competition between individuals of the dominant sex class to take (or recover, or benefit from) every 'available' woman, that is, *automatically* every woman whose material individuality is not officially or officiously fenced in, expresses the fact that the *totality of men* have the use of *each woman*, since it is a matter of negotiation or struggle between them to decide who will *carry off the piece*, according to the most exact way of expressing it.

The more or less violent insults and threats that are traditionally thrown at all women who do not accept the terms of this relationship, of this game, are intended to proclaim publicly that males (men) keep the initiative, that they do not agree that a woman should state anything whatever on her own authority, or make a decision. In brief, that they do not allow women to take the place of a subject.

So-called 'sexual' aggression is as little sexual as it is possible to be. Moreover, it is not by chance that literary symbolization of masculine sexuality is derived from the police (confessions, torture, gaolers, etc.), sadism and the miliary (strongholds, brutality, laying siege, conquest, etc.); nor is it by chance that, reciprocally, relations of force have a sexual vocabulary (to screw, to fuck over, etc.).

It is difficult to distinguish between constraint by pure physical force and sexual constraint, and in fact they do not seem to be very clearly distinguished in the minds and actions of those who use them. If the legislator distinguishes them, it is only in terms of the *ownership of children*, who can always arrive unexpectedly. This is why in the legal sense rape only occurs through penile-vaginal coitus, and only outside marriage.[30] Sexual violence towards a woman is only considered to be rape if she is liable to produce children for *a man without his consent* – yes, I do say *for a man without his consent*. It is only rape if the owner of the woman (husband or father), thus of her children, risks finding himself landed with children who are obviously not his own – as the Civil Code would say.

The arsenal of the law and customary rights

The arsenal of the law determines the modalities of the private appropriation of women, if not the collective appropriation itself, unspoken and uncontractualized as we have seen it to be. In one sense it determines the limits in so far as it only intervenes in marriage – the restrictive form of the collective appropriation of women. But if the appropriation of women is evident through the diverse arrangements that marriage includes (labour power, parent–child relationships and rights over children, place of domicile, etc.), women's non-existence as subjects extends far wider than the network of laws relating to it. If laws which refer to the possession of property and its disposition, to children, to decisions of all kinds are explicitly male (and where this is not made explicit it is still the case in practice),[31] a more 'general' notion, such as citizenship, is just as sexed. The law in the French Code which treats the question of a *name* is particularly meaningful in this regard and expresses the non-proprietorship of oneself for women. One of the very first laws of the Code, which forbids every citizen on pain of punishment to adopt another name than that which appears on the birth certificate, is visibly not applied to women, since in marriage customary law imposes the name of their husband upon them.[32] They are, therefore, called exactly what they are – appropriations of their husband and non-existent as subjects before the law. I do not think that the fact of taking another name than that given at birth (which does not conform to the law, at least for *a citizen, a subject*) has ever led to the prosecution of any woman when it was a question of her *married name*. Better still, the law itself confirms the customary law, since it specifies that at the time of divorce (the ending of appropriation) 'each spouse' is obliged to take back his or her name. What appears from the Code as a whole, and which is particularly marked in this example, is that women are not fundamentally legal subjects; they are not subjects before the law. What are they then, when we know that the Civil Code is only the codification of property rights, and principally of what stems from the ownership of goods – the ownership of oneself?[33] The absence of women, or, more exactly, the sole presence of men as such, expresses the simple fact that women as such do not have the ownership of themselves.[34] This is confirmed besides by the private marriage contract, where the availability of women is guaranteed to be complete, physically and through time, in exchange for the simple maintenance in working order of the transactional object – that is, the women themselves.

CONCLUSION

What are the effects of this appropriation? Socially the effect is the production of a discourse of nature with which women are saddled (to be discussed in Chapter 10). Individually and psychologically it produces a tragic phantasm, that of autonomy and individuality. A crazy feat of imagination makes us rise above the fact of our appropriation with a panoply of phantasms which sustain the dream of our independence – the phantasm of 'morally dominating the situation', the phantasm of 'personally escaping', the phantasm of 'it's the others who are the real women, the little old ladies and the dolly birds'. Perhaps even the great phantasm of being 'a man', that is, an autonomous individual, a sort of human being, if you like. No, I don't say 'free'; human beings, be they men or women, are not as naïve as that! But what about the phantasm of not being, oneself, materially, individually appropriated ('had')? Constrained? Certainly. Exploited? Unquestionably. Not free? Obviously. But not an appropriated material object, not a 'thing', definitely not that! This is the great phantasm which we display in the cinema of our unconscious. Nevertheless, in the relationships of sex classes that is exactly what we are – cows, chairs, objects. Not metaphorically, as we try to suggest and to believe (when we speak of the exchange of women or of the re-appropriation of our bodies), but in a quite banal way.

And to help us to cultivate this phantasm and to make us swallow this relationship without reacting against it, to make it disappear without pain, and to try to prevent us from seeing clearly what is going on, all means are good. Even tales, from passion to tenderness, from prudent silence to the obvious lie, and flowers and ornaments, always available to crown the foreheads of cattle on holidays or at the fair. And if this is not enough (and indeed it is not enough), there are still other ways of trying to stop us from interfering, which range from physical violence to the law.

SUMMARY

1. *The material appropriation of the bodies of women*, of their physical individuality, has a legalized expression: the contractual relationship of marriage. This appropriation is concrete and material; it is not a question of some metaphoric or symbolic 'figure'; it is not a question either of an appropriation which only concerns ancient or exotic societies.

It is manifested by the object of the contract: (1) the *unpaid* character of the wife's *work*; and (2) *reproduction*: the children belong to the husband, and their number is not specified.

It is manifested by the *material, physical taking of possession*, physical usage, which is sanctioned in case of 'disagreement' by physical constraint and violence.

Unlimited physical usage, the utilization of the body, and the non-payment for work – that is, the fact that there is no measure of the labour power that comes from the body – express the fact that the individual material body of a woman belongs to her husband, who has the contractual right to make unlimited use of it, with the exception of murder (since rape does not exist in marriage, violence must be 'severe and repeated' to give her the right to escape).

Some tens of years ago the appropriation was also manifested by the possibility that the husband had of selling, for wages, the labour power of his wife, since in fact her wage belonged to him and came as a matter of right to the owner of the wife.

2. This ownership is also expressed by the *nature of certain of the tasks performed*. We know that certain tasks are empirically *associated with the relationship of bodily appropriation*, with the fact that those dominated are material property. This can be historically established for the pariah castes in India and for the household slaves in the United States (in the eighteenth and nineteenth centuries). These tasks of material maintenance of bodies (the bodies of the dominant group, of each of the owners in slavery and marriage, but *also and at the same time* the bodies

of the other properties of these same owners) include feeding, care, cleaning, rearing, sexual maintenance, physical-emotional maintenance, etc.

When the sale for money of the labour power of those appropriated is possible, this labour power, for a still undetermined time and now for wages, remains practically the only one assigned to these tasks. Those appropriated do indeed perform all possible tasks, but they are the only ones to perform the tasks of physical material maintenance. Over 80 per cent of service personnel in France are women; in the United States service personnel are Afro-American men and women; in India they are men and women of the pariah castes. Here today in France practically all daily household helps are women; almost all nurses are women, as well as social workers and prostitutes; three-quarters of all schoolteachers are women, etc.

If labour power becomes subject to contract, saleable, this does not mean *ipso facto* that physical appropriation, the ceding of bodily individuality, does not persist – elsewhere in another relationship.

3. The contradictions.

(1) The class of men in its entirety appropriates the class of women in its entirety and in the individuality of each woman, AND, on the other hand, each woman is the object of private appropriation by an individual of the class of men. The form of this private appropriation is marriage, which introduces a certain type of contracting into the relations between the sexes.

The social appropriation of women thus includes *at the same time* a collective appropriation and a private appropriation, and there is a contradiction between the two.

(2) A second contradiction exists between physical appropriation and the sale of labour power. The class of women is materially appropriated in its concrete individuality (the concrete individuality of each of its members), therefore not free to dispose of its labour power; and at the same time it sells this labour power on the wage market. In France changes in the law have marked the stages of the presence of women as sellers of labour power on the labour market (this class has been on the labour market for a long time, but as appropriated persons and not as sellers; its members were hired out by their owners to a boss). The first stage was the right to one's own wage (ownership of her wage for a woman in 1907); and the second was the right *to work without the husband's permission* (1965).

This second contradiction thus bears on the simultaneity of the relationship of sexage (concrete material appropriation of her bodily individuality) AND the classic work relationship where she is simply the seller of her labour power.

These two contradictions govern all analysis of the relations of sex classes, or, if you prefer, the relations of sexage. Collective appropriation of women (the one that is the most 'invisible' today) is manifested by and through private appropriation (marriage), which contradicts it. Social appropriation (collective and private) is manifested through the free sale (only recently) of labour power, which contradicts it.

4. Physical appropriation is a *relation between owner and object* (not to be confused with a relation between two 'subjects'). It is not symbolic; it is concrete, as the material rights of one over the other remind us. The *appropriated* individuals *being,* IN THIS RELATIONSHIP, *things,* the ideological-discursive face of this appropriation will be a discourse asserting that the appropriated dominated individuals are natural objects. This *discourse of nature* will make plain that they are set in motion by natural mechanical laws, or possibly by mystical-natural laws, but in no case by social, historical, dialectical or intellectual laws, and even less by political ones.

NOTES

1 This is Selma Jones's formulation in her analysis of capitalist social relations in *The Power of Women and the Subversion of the Community* (Bristol, England: Falling Wall Press, 1975). (Done in collaboration with Mariarosa Dalla Costa.)

2 T.n: The author coins a word, *sexage,* on the model of *esclavage* (slavery) and *servage* (serfdom), and subsequently uses it throughout Chapters 9 and 10.

3 The fall in the birth rate in Europe in the eighteenth and nineteenth centuries shows that birth control is not necessarily related to *female contraception* and that it can occur without this. This drop in the birth rate is known to depend largely on *male control* (in terms of coitus interruptus, terms which include, for us, *political control* of women by men). The violence of the resistance to contraception (or to abortion) being actually accessible to women, and to all women, shows clearly that what it is all about is a conflict of power. On the other hand, in certain forms of marriage, not providing the husband with children, or the desired children (i.e. sons) is grounds for annulment of the marriage.

4 The owner of social welfare payments remains the husband–father (and as it also sometimes happens that he is not present, his dear children may have the greatest trouble in obtaining allowances theoretically intended to render their 'maintenance' less difficult). On the other hand, the administrator of the potential property belonging to the children and to the family com-

munity remains the father; this is not without interest in the middle and upper-middle classes.

5 The custody decision is in any case never final and may be called into question. Custom and judgements confirm that the smaller the children (which means the greater the burden) the more likely are mothers to have exclusive material charge of them, whereas at adolescence, when the children are already raised, the links with the father are strengthened. On all these questions see: Christine Delphy, 'Continuities and Discontinuties in Marriage and Divorce', in D. L. Barker and S. Allen (eds) *Sexual Divisions and Society: Process and Change* (London: Tavistock, 1976); and Emmanuèle de Lesseps, 'Le Divorce comme révélateur et garant d'une fonction économique de la famille' (mémoire de maîtrise, Université de Vincennes).

6 In the diverse forms of slavery known historically, a few (in the ancient world, for example) did not include their children, or, more exactly, their children did not belong to their master, whereas in modern plantation slavery the master was able to keep the children on the plantation or in his house, or to sell them to another master. The materiality of the slaves' bodies could be manipulated at the mercy of the master, and they could be treated as beasts of combat – as happened in Rome. Serfdom and certain historical or non-occidental forms of marriage do not imply such extended rights either.

7 This feudal right has left in popular French culture a memory whose evocation is usually accompanied by a virile joviality which contrasts with the reality. For after all, in theory, the feudal lord exercised this right *over the husband*, and this might have led to a sadder reaction. But all that remains is the true meaning of this right – that of the appropriation of women by men, of their character as physically manipulable objects usable for all purposes: work, reproduction and pleasure. The 'droit du seigneur' is only the institutionalized expression of the competition among men, discussed below in relation to the means of appropriation (cf. sexual constraint), who try to gain personal usage of a communal object.

8 Today the Spanish law still requires the installing of the woman in the conjugal home as a condition of adultery for men, as was the case in French law in former times. And the asymmetry of the law concerning legal sanctions for adultery, according to whether men or women are concerned, has struck even those jurists who could least be suspected of a fondness for women.

9 We can ask, with some plausibility, whether the demand for a divorce does not represent two different situations, according to whether it is *initiated* by a man or a woman. We can ask whether, when a woman initiates the proceedings, it is not an attempt to break a tie (to become free of him at last), whereas, when a man files the suit, whether it could not actually be the ratification of a new link (a woman is already 'taking care' of him).

10 Moreover, if this physiological unavailability of men did exist, it would show once again to what point sexual functioning is never anything but what one has in one's mind, in other words, the image of what happens in relations in actual fact. In fact, it would be inadmissible for a man to appear to be *available for use*, since socially he is not an object, and this is

precisely what distinguishes him from the woman who, belonging to men, is by definition always available.

11 This type of literature, just like murderous after-shave lotions (e.g. 'Brut'), is elegant and conventional among executives and intellectuals; these images soar into the zones of 'sexual misery', which is so touching – when it is a question of males. And in fact sexual misery is never spoken of for women; this is logical since sexual misery is the fact of being impeded in, or deprived of, the exercise over women of those rights which other men exercise. Who speaks about sexuality?

12 With still stronger reasons, there is no question of a woman behaving like a proprietor of other human bodies and doing her own personal little porno number; you only have to see the reception recently given to the latest film of Liliana Cavani, *Au-delà du bien et du mal* [Beyond Good and Evil]. At the most, they can praise *masochistic* pornography (or what is presumed to be such) on the part of a woman film-maker. The ecstatic quaverings about *Histoire d'O* were significant in this respect, as was the success of Cavani's preceding film, *The Night Porter*; the few critical voices that were raised in the national press were about the possible racist implications, but not about its sexist implications.

13 The snag, moreover, is that these particular properties, material as they are, move and talk, which complicates things considerably. Artists try to put this right: they often deprive us of head, legs, arms. The Cnidian Venus (the one in the Louvre), decapitated, legless and armless, remains a reference for a feminine ideal. The best is 'dead but still warm', as the male culture of *bons mots* and spectators of westerns do not let us forget.

14 Perhaps it is not so obvious that they are paid, because finally it is the pimps who are paid – and this is 'normal': they are renting out their property. In a certain way we can say of prostitutes' services that they are indeed *sold* (they give rise to a monetary exchange), but the prostitutes are not paid.

15 The transition from the 'extended family' to the nuclear family is supposed to have profoundly altered family ties and the duties that they imply. However, if the members of the same 'family' no longer live together, this does not imply that the material duties which fall on the women have disappeared. It may be less frequent, but even in Paris women continue to move around the city, taking meals to sick or aged relatives, doing the house-cleaning and shopping, and visiting them once or several times a day, depending on how far away they live. The tasks which are supposed to have disappeared (one asks why this idea is so widespread) remain very current.

16 On this point the abundance of writing, from de Beauvoir to the most anonymous of us, is so great that almost all feminist literature is relevant.

17 A little familiarity with this universe seems to provide decisive immunization against the poetic lectures which suggest to us that the good old days, with their great ritual devotion, carried with them heart-warming values. On the ritual tasks of the group of women, see Yvonne Verdier, 'La femme-qui-aide et la laveuse', *L'Homme* XVI(2–3), 1976.

18 See articles and bibliography in *Les Cahiers du Grif* 2, 1974.

19 *Not to be paid* simply means that work is completed without a determined quantity of money or upkeep being provided to confirm its completion, while being *non-paid* for a job means that it is part of its character *not to*

have any relation with any quantitative measure whatever, of money or of upkeep.

20 Ed.: There have been some recent changes in this situation. For example, in the United States six states (New Jersey, Nebraska, Oregon, California, Minnesota and Iowa) now have laws which allow prosecution for rape in marriage in most or all circumstances.

21 We can say quite logically (and not everyone thinks it funny!) that the woman was 'kept' by her husband with the money that she brought in to him (with the price for which she was 'knocked down', as they say in auctions).

22 Two individuals: this dual relationship is specific to the relations of the present-day European sex classes, in contrast with other relations of appropriation: for instance, slavery, where the relationship is actualized between a *number* of specific individuals (the slaves/the master); similarly for serfdom and for polygynous marriage. Each woman has a personal boss who has only her as a *private* domestic (from *domus*, meaning 'house') worker.

23 Fugitive serfs and artisans were, in the urban regroupings of the Middle Ages, at the origin of the *commune* (free town) movement, which developed an anti-feudal solidarity, necessary to resist the attempts by the feudal lords to recapture or seize the individuals who were trying to take their freedom. There was a contradictory situation between the charters granted to communes in their capacity of profitable economic units, and the pursuit of the private individuals who composed these communes. Also a time of *de facto* emancipation was fixed: a year and a day of residence.

24 In fact, they escape the *institutions* which are an actualization of sexage, and only the institutions. The relation of social appropriation of the whole class by the other class remains dominant, and collective appropriation is not overcome even if private appropriation does not take place.

25 Ed.: In the United States women earn only 59 per cent of what men earn.

26 See Evelyne Sullerot, *Histoire et sociologie du travail feminin* (Paris: Gonthier, 1968).

27 Always 'your' children, when it comes to keeping an eye on them, feeding them, or being responsible for their faults and inadequacies.

28 Cf. Jalna Hanmer, 'Violence and the Social Control of Women', *Feminist Issues*, Winter 1981.

29 Cf. 'Justice patriarcale et peine de viol', *Alternatives* 1, *Face-à-femmes*, June 1977.

30 See note 20.

31 For the last few weeks bus shelters and underground station walls have been covered with a poster whose funny side is certainly not intentional. It says: 'Have "your" photograph put on "your" cheques to be sure that they won't be accepted by shop assistants unless you present them yourself (and not a thief)'. The argument for this is security, and to illustrate the point the photograph of a 50-year-old man appears on the cheque next to the name and address of the owner of the bank account. And then, and then – one reads the name of the owner of this account. It is Mr *and Mrs* So-and-So. But no photograph of Mrs So-and-So. After all, this is normal according to what we know of the relations of sex classes – but in these conditions, for

security! Could any woman whatever (and it is quite true that we are a large mass) then use this cheque-book without hindrance? Or could none of us use it, not even Mrs So-and-So?

32   Cf. Anne Boigeol, 'A propos du nom', *Actes* 16, *Femmes, droit et justice*, 1977.

33   Cf. Colette Capitan-Peter, 'A propos de l'idéologie bourgeoise: Note sur les décrets révolutionnaires instituant l'argent marchandise', *L'Homme et la Société* 41–42, 1976.

34   Today the possession of property, as of labour power, seems to guarantee to a woman a certain legal autonomy, a space where she can be a 'subject'. But it was not so long ago that a woman's own property was legally at the disposition of the husband (like the wife herself), since he managed their common property AND the wife's own property. Today things are far from clear in this sphere in France, and the legal texts still contain contradictions of such a kind that the rights remain fundamentally with the husband when economic matters are concerned.

Part III

The practice of power and belief in Nature

Part II The naturalist discourse

INTRODUCTION

Part I of this article (see Chapter 9) described the social relationship in
which the class of women, and each individual woman, is appropriated,
treated as an object. In this second part we are going to look at what the
consequences of this can be in the realm of ideas and beliefs. 'The
naturalist discourse' hopes to create an awareness of how the fact of
being materially treated like a thing ensures that you are also considered
as a thing in the mental realm. Furthermore, a very utilitarian conception
is associated with appropriation (a conception which considers only the
tool in you): an object is always in its rightful place, and what it is used
for, it will always be used for. That is its 'nature'. This kind of finality
accompanies power relations in human societies. It can be further perfected, as it is today in science; that is, the idea of nature is no longer
reduced to a simple finality about the place that objects should have, but
it further claims that each of them, like the whole group of them, is
internally organized to do what it does, to be where it is. This is still its
'nature', but it has become ideologically even more constraining. This
naturalism can be called racism, it can be called sexism. It always comes
back to saying that Nature, that newcomer which has taken the place of
gods, establishes social rules and goes as far as organizing special
genetic programmes for those who are socially dominated. We shall also
see that, as a corollary, the socially dominant see themselves as
dominating Nature itself. In their view this is obviously not the case for
those who are dominated, who, precisely, are only the pre-programmed
elements of this Nature.

FROM APPROPRIATION TO 'NATURAL DIFFERENCE'

Things within thought itself

In the social relationship of appropriation *the physical material individuality, which is the object of this relationship*, is at the centre of the preoccupations which accompany it. This relationship of power, perhaps the most absolute which can exist (physical ownership – direct in the same way that products are appropriated), entails the belief that a corporeal substratum motivates, and in some way 'causes', this relationship, which is itself a material-corporeal relationship. The material taking possession of the human individual leads to a *reification* of the appropriated object. The material appropriation of the body causes a 'material' interpretation of conduct.[1]

(a) The ideological-discursive face of the relationship turns appropriated material units into *things within the realm of thought itself*; the object is expelled 'out' of social relationships and inscribed in a pure materiality.[2]
(b) As a corollary, the *physical* characteristics of those who are *physically appropriated* are assumed to be the *causes* of the domination which they undergo.

The owner class builds a statement about *natural constraint* and *somatic evidence* onto the practices imposed on the appropriated class, onto the place this class occupies in the relationship of appropriation, and onto the appropriated class itself. 'A woman is a woman because she is a female' is a statement whose corollary, without which it would have no social meaning, is 'a man is a man because he is a human being'. Aristotle already said: 'It is then part of nature's intention to make the bodies of free men to differ from those of slaves, the latter strong enough for the necessary menial tasks, the former erect and useless for that kind of work' (*Politics* I:5:25).

In the relations of sex classes, the fact that those who are dominated are things in the realm of thought is explicit in a certain number of traits which are supposed to connote their specificity. It is found in the discourse on women's *sexuality*, in that on their *intelligence* (its absence or the particular form that it is supposed to take among women), and in that on what is called their *intuition*. In these three domains it is especially clear that we are considered as things, that we are seen in exactly the same way as we are actually treated every day in all spheres of existence and at every moment.

Take sexuality, for example. Either the dominant group assigns a fraction of the class of women to sexual use – supposed to be the only ones to embody 'sexuality' (and sexuality alone), as are prostitutes in urban society, 'widows' in certain rural societies, 'coloured mistresses' in societies based on colonization, etc., and the women imprisoned in this fraction of the class are *objectified as sex*. Or, on the other hand, the dominant group is ignorant of women's sexuality, and they boast about this ignorance, as do psychoanalysts, both orthodox and heterodox. Or, in a third mode, women's sexuality is quite simply thought not to exist; woman is without desire, without carnal impulses, as the classic virtuous versions of sexuality explain to us, from the Victorian middle class, which called it 'modesty' (i.e. absence of interest in it),[3] to the working class, who believe that women submit to men's sexuality without having any themselves (unless they are fast, a characteristic which is not highly thought of and not found very frequently). This is also, when all is said and done, what is implicit in the diverse Christian ecclesiastical versions, where woman is more temptress than tempted. Besides, we ask ourselves how she can be a temptress without having any reason to be so; it is true that, for a woman having no more brains or resolution than sexuality, this would undoubtedly be the work of the devil.

The absence (of desire, of initiative, etc.) reverts to the fact that ideologically woman ARE sex – wholly sex and used as such. And toward sex they have, of course, no personal appreciation, nor any impulses of their own: a chair is never anything but a chair, a sexual organ is never anything but a sexual organ. Sex is woman, but she does not possess a sexual organ; a sexual organ does not possess itself. Men *are not* sex, but they possess a sexual organ; besides, they possess it so well that they regard it as a weapon and effectively give it the social attribution of a weapon in situations of male bravado, as well as in rape. Ideologically men have the free use of their sexual organ, and practically women do not have the use of themselves – they are directly objects; ideologically therefore they are a sexual organ, without mediation or autonomy, just as they are any other object according to the context. The class relationship which makes them objects includes even their anatomical-physiological sex, without their being able to have any decision in, or even any simple autonomous actions in, this matter.

The version which makes women into 'devouring sexual organs' is only the obverse ideological face of the same social relationship. If the least autonomy appears in sexual functioning itself (in the most reduced and most genital meaning of the term), this autonomy itself is seen as a devouring machine, a threat, a rock crusher. Nor are women human beings having, among other characteristics, a sexual organ: they *are* always and directly a *sexual organ*. The universe of object relationships, the grim denial that women could be anything but a sexual organ is a denial that they could have a sexual organ, that they could be sexed.

Sexuality is the domain in which the objectification of women is the most visible, even to those not predisposed to notice it. The woman-object is a leitmotiv of protests against certain forms of literature, advertising, cinema, etc., where she is conceived of as a sex object – 'woman-object' means, in fact, 'woman-as-sex-object'. And if indeed this is the only domain where the status of women as objects is socially well known, even there it remains widely regarded as metaphoric – although it is well known, it is not recognized.

The same applies in the realm of intelligence: their 'specific' intelligence is the intelligence of a thing. Supposed to be naturally alien to intellectual speculation, they do not create with their brains; nor are they supposed to have deductive ability, logic. Considered even to be the incarnation of illogicality, they can get by, if worse comes to worst. But to achieve this, they stick to practical reality. Their mind does-not-have-the-impetus-or-power-necessary-to-tear-itself-away-from-the-concrete-world – from the world of material things to which they are attached by an affinity of thing to thing. In any case, their intelligence is supposed to be caught in the world of things and operative in that realm alone – in short, they are supposed to have a 'practical' intelligence.

On the whole, this intelligence would cease to be operative when, for example, things are submitted to the action of thought, for the ordering of things is the reflection of intellectual activity and logical operations. Thus, technology, engines and motors are subjects about which the stupidity of women is well known. The universe of women is supposed, rather, to be that of clothes, potatoes, floors, dishes, typewriting and other chores. And the forms of technical organization implied in these domains are *ipso facto* found unworthy and relegated to the world of zero technology, if not to non-existence pure and simple.

And *intuition* (so specifically 'feminine') classes women as the expression of fluctuations of pure matter. According to this notion women know what they know *without reasons*. Women do not have to understand, because they know. And what they know comes to them without their understanding it and without their using reason: in them this knowledge is a direct property of the matter of which they are made.

That which is called 'intuition' is very indicative of the objective position of oppressed people. In fact, they are reduced to making very close analyses (contrary to what is claimed), using the tiniest and most tenuous elements of the data that can reach them from the outside world, for *access* to this world, as well as *action* in it, is *prohibited* to them. Now this mental exercise of putting fragmented details in place is glorified and called deductive intelligence when done by members of the dominant group (and it is developed at great length in detective fiction), but it loses all its intellectual character as soon as it is manifested in women, where it is systematically deprived of comprehensive meaning and takes on a metaphysical character. The operation of denial [*dénégation*] is truly stupefying in the fact of particularly brilliant intellectual exercises which use heterogeneous elements to construct a coherent whole and propositions applicable to reality. Here again the strength of social relationships permits the relegation of (the existence of) the appropriated persons to the realm of pure reified matter. And it permits calling intelligence or logic by the name of 'intuition', just as violence is called 'order' or despair 'caprice'.

Being in a dominant position leads one to see those who are appropriated as matter, and as a kind of matter which has diverse *spontaneous* characteristics. Only those dominated can know that they *do* what they do and that what they do does not spontaneously spring from their bodies. Working is tiring. And working requires thinking. And thinking is tiring. When one is appropriated, or dominated, thinking means going against the vision of (and against) the social relationships imposed by the dominators. It does not mean ceasing to know what the relationships of appropriation harshly teach you.

The ideological aspect of the practical conflict between dominators and those they dominate, and between appropriators and those they appropriate precisely concerns *consciousness*. The dominators generally deny a consciousness to them precisely because they take them to be things. Furthermore, they incessantly try to make them swallow their own consciousness, because it is a threat to the status quo, while the dominated individuals eagerly defend and develop it by all possible means, scheming and contriving subtly and indirectly (women are 'liars', blacks are 'childish', Arabs are 'hypocrites') to protect and expand it.

'Natural' things – or how the idea of nature and the notion of thing are fused

The current idea of nature and that of former times are not exactly the same. The one we know today took form approximately in the eighteenth century.

The old idea of nature, which we can call Aristotelian for purposes of simplification, expressed a finalistic conception of social phenomena: a slave was made in order to do what she/he did, a woman was made in order to obey and to be submissive, etc. The idea of the nature of a thing scarcely meant anything other than the place in actual fact that a thing had in the world; it was almost completely identical with the idea of *function*. (We have, besides, retained this meaning when we speak of the nature of an object or of a phenomenon. Modern functionalism is not far from this position, and this is the pertinent critique that Kate Millett made of it in *Sexual Politics*.) The modern idea of nature – closely tied to and dependent on that of Nature[4] – has developed concurrently with the sciences, the physical and natural sciences, as they are called. The latter, while preserving a common meaning – that of the *intended purpose* of the thing under consideration – changed the configuration of the 'natural' by modifying it in major ways.

What modifications have taken place in the configuration of the 'natural'? What has been 'added' to the status of 'things-intended-to-be-things' of certain human groups? What has been 'added' is principally the idea of (a) *determinism*, and (b) determinism internal to the object itself. Determinism? Yes, indeed, in so far as belief in a mechanical action was introduced into a configuration which until then was relatively static. The finalistic aim of the first naturalism became in our naturalism a proclamation of a scientific aspect. The place occupied by a dominated group (slaves on the plantations, women in houses) became effectively *prescriptive*, from the point of view of socially proclaimed scientific rationality. Not only (a) being in their place within such social relationships must the appropriated persons remain there (the finalism of the first idea of nature), but also (b) they were thenceforth considered to be *physiologically organized* (and no longer only anatomically organized) for this place and prepared for it *as a group* (prescription of determinism). And (c) they were no longer in such a place in social relationships as the result of divine decision or mystical-magical mechanisms exterior to the perceptible world, but precisely as the result of an organization internal to themselves, which expresses in each of these individuals the essence of the group in its totality. This internal programming is in itself its own justification, depending on the very belief in a personified and technological Nature. From the eighteenth century until today, this new type of naturalism has taken on ever more complex features, and if in the last century the origin of the programme was sought in physiological functioning, today they track it down in the genetic code. Molecular biology is taking over from experimental physiology.

In the naturalist ideology developed today about the dominated groups, three elements can thus be distinguished. The first is the *status of thing*, which expresses the actual social relationships; the appropriated individuals, being material possessions, are *materialized* elements *within thought itself.* The second element corresponds to what can be called a *design of order*, a finalistic and teleological system which can be summarized thus: things being what they are (that is, the appropriation by certain groups, or one group, of others, or one other) is what makes the world function properly. Therefore, it is fitting that this situation should remain as it is, and this will avoid disorder and the overturning of true values and eternal priorities. (In the fragile minds of the dominators, the slightest sigh of impatience by a dominated person triggers visions of the most apocalytic turmoil – from castration to the end of the earth's rotation.)

The third element specific to modern thought since the eighteenth century, 'naturalism', proclaims that the status of a human group, like the order of the world which has made it the way it is, is *programmed from within the living matter.* The idea of endogenous determinism came to be superimposed on that of finality, to be associated with it, and not to abolish it, as is sometimes too quickly believed. The end of theocentrism did not mean the disappearance of metaphysical finality. Thus there is still a discourse of finality, but about an internally programmed 'natural' instinct, blood, chemistry, the body, etc., not of a single individual, but of a class in its totality, each member of which is only a fragment of the whole. This is the *strange* idea that the actions of a human *group*, of a *class*, are 'natural'; that they are *independent of social relationships, that they pre-exist all history and all determined concrete conditions.*

From the 'natural' to the 'genetic'

The idea that a human being is internally programmed to be enslaved, to be dominated, and to work for the profit of other human beings seems to be strictly dependent on the *interchangeability of individuals* of the appropriated class. The 'internal programming' of domination in the dominated individuals happens to the individuals belonging to a class which has been appropriated as a class. That is, it takes place when collective appropriation precedes private appropriation. For sex classes, for example, the appropriation of the class of women is not reducible solely to marriage, which certainly expresses it, but not completely, as we saw in Chapter 9. In other words, *the genetic idea is associated with and dependent on the relationship of class appropriation.* It is a non-random appropriation, which is not the result of chance for the appropriated individual, but of a social relationship which is the foundation of the society. And thus it implies the existence of classes born of this relationship, classes that would not exist without it.

This ideological fact comes into play when all women belong to a *group which is appropriated as a group* (sexage)[5] and when the private appropriation of women (marriage) stems from it. If this were not the case, we would find ourselves confronted with a random power relationship – acquisition by simple coercion, such as enslavement by wartime capture or military raids, and (if it exists, which is dubious) by marriage by abduction.[6]

For the appropriation of *an individual* who does not already belong to a statutorily appropriated class (within which the private appropriation of each particular individual can freely be carried out) takes place through open conflict and recognized relationships of power and constraint. To take a slave from a neighbouring people or from a free class, war or abduction are necessary. It is in this way that slaves were recruited in the ancient city-states; and this is how the first white and black servants and slaves were recruited for the European colonies in America in the seventeenth century, while to acquire a slave 'normally' *within an already existing slave class* it is enough just *to buy her/him.* To acquire a woman in a society where *there is an existing class of women*, it is enough to *'ask for'* her or *buy* her.

In the first case the appropriation is the result of a power relationship – power which comes into play as the *means* of acquiring *material individualities which were not previously explicitly and institutionally destined for appropriation.* It does not seem that in this case the appropriation is accompanied by a developed and precise idea of 'nature'; it remains embryonic. By contrast, when an appropriated class is set up and logically ordered – and then characterized by a constant symbolic sign[7] – the idea of nature is developed and made precise, accompanying the class as a whole and each of its individuals from birth to death. Power is then not involved except as a *means of controlling those who are already appropriated.* The idea of nature does not seem to have been present in the ancient Roman and Hebrew societies which practised slavery as the result of war or debt, while modern industrial society, with plantation slavery, the proletarianization of peasants in the nineteenth century, and sexage, has developed a complex and scientized belief in a specific 'nature' of dominated and appropriated individuals.

Furthermore, the idea of nature becomes progressively more refined.

This is because the ideological interpretations of the forms of material appropriation are nourished by scientific developments, as they also affect the meaning and choice of these developments. If the idea of a specific nature of those who are dominated or appropriated ('racized', 'sexized') has 'benefited' from the development of the natural sciences, for the last fifty years the attainments of genetics and then of molecular biology are coming to be swallowed up by that bottomless well which is the ideological universe of appropriation, the real instigator of this research.

The idea of a *genetic* determination of appropriation and belief in its 'programmed' character (Darwin had begun to speak of the 'marvellous instinct of slavery') are thus the product both, on the one hand, of a particular type of appropriation (where one entire class is institutionally appropriated on a stable basis and considered as the reservoir of *exchangeable material* individualities), AND, on the other hand, of the development of modern science. This juncture is scarcely ever found except in the relationships of sexage[8] and those of eighteenth and nineteenth century slavery in the first industrial states.

All this partially explains the fact that, ever since an interest has been shown in the question, a comparison has often been made in the relationships existing between the sexes, in the caste system, and in the institution of slavery. And, indeed, the caste system shows the apparent extraordinary *stability* which the institution of sexage also shows. In our society this stability supports a geneticist formulation; in Indian society a hereditarianist one.[9] The affinity between the institution of slavery and sexage resides in the *unlimited appropriation* of labour power, that is, of the material individuality itself. Thus there really is a juncture or convergence of sexage with these two social forms, but sex classes are specific classes, created by specific social relationships. We cannot then merely define them by their affinity with other social forms and establish analogies between institutions which express particular relationships of appropriation. But we have no doubt long been blinded by the illusion that ours was a 'natural relationship', where we could not recognize a particular social form.

All human beings are natural but some are more natural than others

The simultaneous occurrence of subjection, material servitude and oppression on the one hand, and of the highly intellectual discourse of Nature, that great organizer and regulator of human relationships, on the other hand, is today principally 'embodied' in the class of women. They are seen as the favoured location of natural impulses and constraints. If in the past this burden has weighed on other social groups (for example, the group of Afro-American slaves, that of the first industrial proletariat, or the peoples colonized by the industrial metropolises), here today, in these same metropolises, the imputation of naturalism is focused on the group of women. It is with respect to them that the belief in a 'natural group' is the most constraining – the most unquestioned. If the accusation of having a specific nature still today affects formerly colonized people, like former slaves, the social relationship which succeeded colonization or slavery is no longer a relationship of direct material appropriation. Sexage is still a relationship of the appropriation of bodily material individuality of the entire class. As a result, if there is a *controversy* about the question of the supposed 'nature' of former colonized people and former slaves, about that of women there is *no controversy*. Women are considered by everybody to have a particular nature; they are supposed to be 'naturally specific', and not *socially*. And if the scientific world begins to seethe with excitement as soon as genetic hereditarianism in the social sphere resurfaces (examples: workers are a particular race composed of those who are genetically incapable of succeeding; or blacks are intellectually inferior and morally weak; these two ideas are expressed in forms which are more and more oblique, but always identical in their essential features), we are, by contrast, very far from seeing the least agitation about the 'natural difference' between the sexes. There the greatest calm prevails. And if the pronouncements about the appropriated class (in this case, women; and they are pronouncements which always without exception affirm the 'particular nature' of women) may at times be eulogistic or even rhapsodic (as is also the case with the other 'naturalized' groups), they do not lack imputations of natural specificity.

In all cases the imputation of a natural character is made about the *appropriated* and dominated inviduals; only those who are in the dominated group of the relationship of domination are natural. Nature is absent from spontaneous definitions of dominant social groups. Strangely absent from the natural world, the latter have disappeared from the universe of definitions. Thus a bizarre world takes shape, where only those appropriated float in a universe of eternal essences which completely encircles them, from which they do not know how to escape, and where, enclosed in their 'being', they fulfil duties that only nature assigns to them, since nothing in sight, absolutely nothing, could make one think that another group is also involved.

Appropriation is a relationship

'Difference' is the result of . . .

This burden which weighs on us, the imputation of being 'natural', the imputation that everything – our life, our death, our acts – is imposed on us by our Mother Nature in person (and for good measure, she also is a woman), is expressed in a discourse of noble simplicity. If women are dominated, it is because they are 'not the same'. They are different, delicate, pretty, intuitive, unreasonable, maternal, without muscles, lacking an organizing character, a little futile, and unable to see beyond the end of their nose. And all this happens because they obviously have a smaller brain, slower nervous reactions, different hormones which behave irregularly; because they weigh less, have less uric acid and more fat, run more slowly and sleep more. It is because they have two X chromosomes instead, stupid creatures, of having an X and a Y – which is the satisfactory way of having chromosomes. It is because they are 'incomplete men', OR because they are 'the future of man', because they are 'a mosaic', OR because they are 'the basic sex', because they are 'stronger and more resistant' than men, OR because they are 'the weaker sex'. In short, they are different.

How are they different? In what way? In what way are they different? Being different all by oneself, if one thinks of it grammatically or logically, is an impossibility, just as is a 40-foot ant with a hat on. Being different is not like being curly-haired; it is being different FROM – different from something. But of course, you will say, women are different from men; we know perfectly well from whom women are different. Yet if women are different from men, men themselves are not different. If women are different from men, men themselves are men. For instance, we say: men in this region have an average height of 5 feet 4 inches and (throughout the world) are carnivorous, walk at a rate of two and a half miles per hour, can carry 66 pounds for such and such a distance, etc. But it is certain that women, who are different from men, do not have an average height of 5 feet 4 inches, do not always eat meat (because it is reserved for men in most cultures and poor classes). And yet, different from men, delicate and lacking strong muscles, they still carry heavy loads. But when it comes to work done here and now by women, all eyes are virtuously lowered. I am not talking about road-making in the eastern bloc, but about the 20- to 30-pound bags of groceries carried every day plus a child in the arms – groceries and child being carried in a horizontal direction for several hundred yards and in a vertical direction up one to six flights of stairs. And I'm not talking about terrace-builders in India, but about the loads handled in France in the isolation of farms or behind the walls of factories, such as the child picked up and put down and picked up again to waist and face level an incalculable number of times in a movement little resembling weight-lifting, because that allows (outside of the satisfaction of its uselessness) regularity, calm, the use of both arms, and the docile immobility of the weight being lifted, advantages which the strong personality of a human being a few months or years old does not offer.

Well, sure enough, women are different from men, who themselves are not different; men differ from nothing. At most, a highly subversive mind might go so far as to think that men and women differ among themselves. But this audacity is lost in the ocean of the real difference, that solid and powerful characteristic which marks a certain number of groups. Blacks are different (whites simply *are*); Chinese are different (Europeans *are*); women are different (men *are*). We are different – it is a fundamental characteristic. We are different, as one can 'be retarded' or 'have blue eyes'. We succeed in the grammatical and logical feat of being different all by ourselves. Our nature is difference.

We are always 'more' or 'less'. And we are never the term of reference. The height of men is never measured relative to ours, whereas our height is measured relative to that of men (we are 'smaller'), which is only measured relative to itself. It is said that our wage is a third less than that of men, but it is not said that men's wage is half again as much as ours. It represents just itself. (Yet we should say it none the less, for to say only that women earn a third less than men hides the fact that *in practice* men earn half again as much as women. For example: a woman's wage of 1,000 francs, a man's wage of 1,500.) We say of blacks that they are black relative to whites, but whites are just white. Moreoever, it is not even certain that whites have any colour. It is no more certain that men are sexed beings; they *have* a sexual organ, which is different. It is we who *are* sex, wholly sex.

Moreover, there isn't really such a thing as masculine (there is no grammatical *male gender*). One says 'masculine' because men have kept the general for themselves. In fact, there is a general and a feminine, a human and a female. I look for the masculine, and I do not find it. And I do not find it because there is no such thing – the general takes care of men. They are not so very insistent on identifying themselves as a gender (males) while they are a dominant class. They are not eager to find themselves denoted by an anatomical characteristic – they who are *men*. 'Man' does not mean 'male'; it means human species. We say 'men' the way we say 'sparrows', 'bees', etc. Why in the world would they want, like *women*, to be only a portion of the species? They prefer to be the whole, which is easy to understand. Are there perhaps languages where there is a grammatical masculine gender?

As for us women, what I am saying is that we are not even a portion of the species, for if 'women' designates the female gender, this in no way means 'human being', that is, the species. We are not a portion of the species, but a species – the female. We are not an element of a whole, one of two elements of a sexed species, for example. No, all by ourselves we are a species (a natural division of the living), and all by themselves men are men. Thus there is the human species, composed of human beings, who can be divided into males. And then also there are women. And they are not in the human species, and therefore do not divide it up.

The dominant group, as the great Standard, could not ask for anything better than that we should be different. What the dominant group cannot stand, on the contrary, is similarity, *our* similarity. They cannot stand that we have, that we want, the same right to food, to independence, to autonomy, to life, and that we take these rights or try to take them. They cannot stand that we have the same right as they have to breathe, the same right as they have to live, the same right as they have to speak, the same right as they have to laugh and the right to make decisions. It is our similarity to them that they repress in the most decisive way. All they ask is that we be different. They even do all that they can to see to it that we are paid no wage, or a lesser wage; that we have no food, or less;[10] that we have no right to decision-making, but only to be consulted; and that we love our very chains.[11] They want this 'difference' – they love it. They never stop telling us how much it pleases them. They impose it with their actions and their threats, and then with their beatings.

But this difference – in rights, food, wages, independence – is never spoken of in this form, its real form. No. It is a 'difference', an exquisite internal characteristic with no relation to all those sordid material questions. It is elating, like the bird-that-sings-at-dawn or the river-that-flows; it is the rhythm-of-the-body; it is difference – and that's that. It makes women tender and warm as the soil is fertile; it makes blacks fuck well as the rain falls, etc. The technicolour of the soul and the eternal values are the real location of difference. Let us be different, let us differ, and then we won't bother anyone. Indeed we won't. Instead of materially analysing difference in daily social relationships, we slide straight into mysticism.

Women, like blacks and Asians, and also like demonstrators and alcoholics, are thus 'different'. And, we are told, they are different 'in nature'. We can immediately find the obvious reasons for the oppression of blacks and women, and for the exploitation which crushes and suffocates them. It is skin pigment for the former, and the anatomical form of their reproductive organs for the latter. The reason for the 'difference' of alcoholics and demonstrators is just now on the verge of being found. It also is natural. It is that they do not have the same genetic code, that they have a different DNA. It is more hidden, but it comes to the same thing.[12]

... is the result of appropriation

As soon as people want to legitimize the power that they exercise, they call on nature – on the nature of this difference. Oh, how I love our prominent politicians when they publicly express their wish that we should at last return to our true nature, which is to guard the fire, as we squat in the cave of the master.[13] How accommodating Nature is to confirm the necessary differences. And all the while they will decide our life for us – our lesser nourishment (our lower wages), the disposition of our material individuality, and the rights that we will not have.

What they do not want to hear about is called 'obvious'; they are thus freed from thinking about it, and that allows them not to see anything of the situation. 'Yes, yes, yes, I know' means 'I do not want to know about it'. This is one of the reasons for the new inflation of the term 'appropriation', which has been very frequently used in the last two or three years. The re-appropriation of the body is much talked about, and doubtless not by chance. But in using this term one expresses a truth so crude and violent, so difficult to accept, that at the same time its meaning is distorted, which happens when the literal meaning has been ignored. 'Appropriation', turned into an image or a 'symbolic reality', both expresses and dresses up a brutal and concrete reality. So this term is used in a timid way, which claims that, in order to take back the ownership of our physical materiality, all we have to do is dance. This is a way of speaking the truth in order not to have to face it. So appropriation is admitted, but *as if it were abstract*, in thin air, coming from nowhere, some sort of quality, like difference. We are appropriated. Period. By nothing, we are expected to believe. One word or ten makes it seem as though what is said is not really true. A characteristic defusing tends to make *a fact* disappear into a metaphoric form. Is this the effect of censorship (often self-censorship) when faced with growing consciousness of the fact that the relationship of sex classes is actually *a relationship* of appropriation? We act as if appropriation were one of the characteristics of our anatomy, in the same way as eye colour, or (putting things in the worst light) in the same way as a bad case of flu. We consent to being 'appropriated' on the condition that it remain vague and abstract. Above all, let there be no accusations.

To reappropriate one's body! This body is either 'one's own', or it is not; it is possessed or it is not, by oneself or by someone else. In order to grasp the exact meaning of appropriation and the hypocrisy of this metaphorical game, here is a suggestion: 'Appropriate for yourself' the funds of the establishment where you go to re-appropriate your body. Now the meaning of the term appears very quickly in all its crudity. *The physical violence exercised against women* (blows given them by men themselves) conveys in the same way the message that women do not have the right to decide their own actions. It denies their right to decision, whether it be in the sexual or sentimental sphere ('simple' flirtations and friendships with other women are controlled just as strictly as sexuality *sensu stricto*), or in the realm of domestic work, which is customarily (and legally) recognized as giving men the right to violence and reprisals if it is not done satisfactorily. The owner of the woman tries to prevent her from acting as she wants. And that is his right. 'Satisfaction guaranteed or your money back' could be a good slogan for male divorce.[14] Women cannot make decisions for themselves, because they do not belong to themselves. No one can decide what will be the allocation of objects as long as they have an owner. Basically we do not want to see that we are *actually* taken as objects in a well-defined relationship, that *appropriation is a relationship*, and that it requires at least two people.

In other words, we accept in some way – and alas, we even insist upon it sometimes – that we might be naturally 'women', that each and every one of us is the expression (exquisite or formidable, according to differing opinions) of a particular species – the species *woman*, defined by her anatomy, her physiology. One of the traits of this species, like breasts or relative hairlessness, is said to be a strange characteristic that 'quite naturally' makes our companions pinch our bottoms and our children order us around. All in all, the posters, the pinching and the orders are supposed to stem directly from our anatomy and our physiology – but never from social relationships themselves.

And if we are ever oppressed or exploited, it is the result of our nature. Or better still, our nature is such that we are oppressed, exploited, appropriated. These three terms express in ascending order our social situation.[15]

WOMEN IN NATURE AND NATURE IN WOMEN

Dissymmetry of 'nature' according to sex

The idea that there exists a natural finality in social relations is not uniformly applied. Naturalism does not apply indifferently to all groups involved in social relations, or, more exactly, if it concerns all of them, it does not apply to them in the same way or at the same level. The imputation of a specific nature is made to the full against those who are dominated, and particularly against those who are appropriated. The latter are supposed to be explainable *totally and uniquely* by Nature, by their nature – 'totally', because nothing in them is outside the natural, and nothing escapes it; 'uniquely', because no other possible explanation of their position is even envisaged. From the ideological point of view, they are absolutely immersed in the 'natural'.

The nature of some . . .

By contrast, dominant groups do not, in the first stage, attribute a nature to themselves. They may, with considerable detours and political quibbling, acknowledge, as we shall see, that they have some link with nature – some link but nothing more, and certainly not an immersion in it. Their group, or rather their world (for they hardly conceive of themselves in limited terms), is understood as resistance to Nature, conquest of Nature, the location of the sacred and of culture – of philosophy, of politics, of planned action, of 'praxis' – but, whatever be the term, it is certainly the location of *distancing* through consciousness or creative activity.

The first move of dominant groups is to define themselves in relation to the system which is ideologically decreed to be the foundation of the society. Obviously this varies according to the type of society. In this way the dominant group can consider itself as defined by the sacred (the brahmins in India, the Catholic Church of the Middle Ages), by culture (the élite), by property (the bourgeoisie), by knowledge (the mandarins, the scribes), by their action on the real world (solidarity among hunters, accumulation of capital, conquest of territory), etc. In any case, they define themselves by mechanisms which create history, not by constraints which are repetitive, internal and mechanical, constraints which they reserve for the dominated groups. In this way *men claim to be identified by their actions, and they claim that women are identified by their bodies.* Furthermore, the relegation of women to 'Nature' and the affirmation of their clearly natural character tend to show the male of the species as *the* creator (in himself and by himself alone) of human society, of socio-human systems, and in the last analysis, of consciousness, as project or organization.

However, revolts, conflicts, historical upheavals and other reasons sometimes force dominant groups to enter into a problematic which they loathe for themselves just as strongly as they cling to it for those whom they exploit. They may then try to define their links with that very attentive Nature which furnishes them so conveniently and opportunely with living 'supplies'. At this stage, they can undertake to develop those 'scientific ethics' (triumphantly liberal as well as Nazi), which proclaim that certain groups have the right to domination by the excellence of their qualities and innate capacities of all sorts.[16]

None the less they do not abandon the feeling that they are not one with the elements of Nature. And they consider that their capacities, as it happens, give them (what luck!) the possibility of transcending internal determinations. For example, Nature gives them intelligence, which is innate, but which, as it happens, allows them to understand Nature, and thus to dominate it in a certain measure. Or else Nature gives them strength, which is innate, but which, as it happens, allows them to dominate the material elements of Nature (which includes other human beings, for example) – in other words, it allows them to be confronted in a practical way with the organization of the real and to enter into a constructive or dialectical relation with it.

In this vision, human culture (technology, prohibition of incest, etc., said to be the source of human society, but varying according to the writer) is the fruit of solidarity and co-operation between males of the species – solidarity and co-operation which derive either from hunting or war. In short, once rid of the burdensome females, the men, all on their own, like grown-ups, soared to the summits of science and technology. And apparently there they have remained, leaving the females of the species behind in Nature (out of the running) and immersed in contingency. And there they still are. This orientation is so totally androcentrist that we cannot even call it misogynist in the common meaning of the term, as the human race appears in it to be composed solely of males. The dialectical relationship to the environment, the 'transformation of Nature', are described in, and with regard to, the class of men (males) – leaving the rest in an obscurity that would be nonexistent if it were not that occasionally a ray of light was thrown on the female, a distant silhouette busy with natural activities, destined to remain in that situation and maintaining no dialectical relationship with Nature. This view is present in almost all social science works. In a still more sophisticated form, it takes the form of a conceptual dissymetry in the analysis, as Nicole-Claude Mathieu has shown – a dissymmetry which has each sex class described and analysed according to different theoretical assumptions.[17]

So Nature does enter into their discourse about themselves at a certain point, but at a place where they are assumed to have exteriorized links with Nature, albeit in very sophisticated forms of exteriority at times, such as appear in neo-Engels writers, for example.

The second stage of naturalist belief thus implies that the nature of some and the nature of others is subtly different and not comparable – in a word, that their nature is not the *same* nature. The nature of one group is supposed to be entirely natural, while the nature of the other is supposed to be 'social'. 'Basically', one could say, as an analyst ironically comments in a recent text, 'man is biologically cultural. Woman on the contrary is biologically natural'.[18] Law and architecture, strategy and technology, the machine and astronomy are supposed to be the creations that 'move' humanity out of Nature. And thus civilization and society, being the inventions of the group of men as well as the intrinsic and potential characteristics of each male, are supposed to be the dynamic expression of a *creation* which leads the male of the species to 'dominate', to 'use' the natural environment by virtue of a particular ability, of a quite specific orientation of natural behaviour.

Whereas, conversely, reproduction, child rearing, and food preparation are supposed to be the expression of stereotyped instincts, perhaps adaptive, but in any case, expressions of the *permanence* of the species – permanence carried by women. I definitely make the situation look better, moreover, by using this term, for indeed on the one hand females are content to be irreducibly natural, and when I speak of 'permanence' I interpret it with a care for balancing responsibilities and decorative symmetry. On the other hand, my mind wanders too freely when, in listing the instincts, I mention other things than reproduction. The latter is indeed quite sufficient to account completely for the theoretical specificity of females.

In brief, if there really is a nature peculiar to each of the groups, one of these natures tends toward nature, while the other tends toward culture (civilization, technology, thought, religion, etc. – use whichever term is indicated by your choice of theory, be it culturalist, Marxist, mystical, psychoanalytic, functionalist, etc.). Whatever it is, the term you choose is likely to imply that nature tends in THIS group (the group of men) to transcend itself, to distance itself, to transform itself or to dominate itself, etc. And another nature, the one which is basic, immobile, permanent (that of women and dominated groups in general), appears mainly in activities which are repetitive and capricious, permanent and explosive, cyclical, but which in no case have *dialectical and antagonistic relationships* with themselves or the exterior world – a pure nature which constantly renews itself.

. . . and the nature of others

This is exactly the nature attributed to us. Our periods and our intuition, our childbirths and our whims, our tenderness and our caprices, our endurance (in all trials) and our very special recipes, our fragility (unfathomable) and our old wives' remedies, our healing magic, the telluric permanence of the body of *women*. Well, that grates a little – permanence? In fact, our bodies are interchangeable, and even more than that, they must be changed (like sheets) because it is youth that is telluric in women. And it is about us as *species*, not as particular individuals.[19] We believe it for a moment, just as we believe we can say 'I', until reality explodes on us, telling us that it is nothing of the sort.

Each of our actions, each of the actions which we engage in in a specific social relationship (speaking, laundering, cooking, giving birth, taking care of others) *is attributed to a nature which is supposed to be internal* to us, even though that social relationship is *a class relationship imposed on us by the modalities and the form of our life.* And this nature – outside of all relationships – is supposed to push us to do all those things because we are supposed to be 'programmed' and 'made for that', and because we obviously are supposed to 'do it better' than anybody else. Besides, we are ready to believe this when we are confronted with the legendary resistance of the other class to performing such acts as cleaning, *really* taking care of children (and not just taking them out for a treat or having 'a really serious talk' with them), really taking charge of food (every day and in detail), not to mention the laundry, ironing, tidying-up, etc. (which a grown man has no qualms whatever about leaving to a child of ten, as long as the child is female) – all of these being areas in which the amount of co-operation known and observed is close to zero.

Certainly our 'nature' also has sides which are more fantasizing and joyful and superficially less utilitarian, but which all the same reinforce the idea that we are supposed to be made of special flesh which is suitable for certain things and not at all for others (like, for example, *making decisions*).[20] In short, 110 pounds of spontaneous but not serious-minded flesh, cunning but not logical, tender but not persevering, resistant but not strong – each one of us is a little piece of the female species, a great reservoir from which 'you' draw the fragment that suits you ('one lost, ten re-found'), that fragment which is esteemed according to the formula of Georges Brassens, 'all of it is good and nothing is to be thrown away'.

No, it is definitely not esteem that we lack. Thus it is not that we have to recover some lost value, as many of us shout ourselves hoarse proclaiming. We have lost no esteem and we are well appreciated for our value: that of being tools (for maintenance, reproduction, production, etc.). To cry out that we are honourable and that we are subjects is to make a statement about the future. If we are the subjects of history, it is the very history that we are making.

The idea that we are made of a particular flesh and that we have a specific nature can be dressed in charming colours. That is not the question. Whether couched in contemptuous or eulogistic language, the nature argument tries to make us into finite *closed beings*, who pursue a tenacious course, consisting of repetition, enclosure, immobility, and maintenance of the (dis)order of the world. And this is exactly what we are trying to resist when, described as 'unpredictable', capricious and perplexing, we then accept the idea of a feminine nature which, in this guise, seems to be the opposite of permanence. Deviations are willingly granted us, as long as it means that we are outside history, *outside actual social relations*, and that everything that we do comes only from the surging forth of some obscure genetic message buried deep in our cells. For thus we leave the dominant group all the benefits of being the inventors of society and the masters of the great unknown and the gamble of history, the latter being not the expression of a profound fatality, but, on the contrary, the fruit of invention and risk – 'taking chances' suits them better than seeing themselves as 'programmed'.

Two distinct species?

Rather than envisage the social process which determines the two 'genders', they prefer to consider either: (a) that there exist *two 'neutral' somatic groups*, which can be considered to be linked by organic ties of complementarity and functionalism or which can on the contrary be seen as opposing each other in a relation of 'natural antagonism'; or (b) that there are two groups, also anatomical and natural, but heterogeneous enough at the same time so that one group frees itself from nature, and the other remains immured in it. In no case do *class relations* occupy a central position in the discussion; in fact, they are not even envisaged. The real existence of these groups is hidden from view by describing them as anatomical-physiological realities onto which a few social ornaments such as 'roles' or 'rites' have come to be grafted. And in order to be able to consider them in this way and to maintain the affirmation of their natural specificity, one arrives at a division into two heterogeneous species with specific genetic messages and distinct practices rooted in these messages. Ultimately this interpretation can lead to theorizing the relations between the sexes as being ascribable to symbiotic groupings of instinctive exploitation, like ants and their little parasites.

These insinuations, which imply the existence of a male species *and* a female species, are unquestionably *the sign of the real relations* which exist between the two groups – that is, of the social relations of appropriation which are expressed by stating the existence of distinct species. But this is not an *analysis* of these relations, for what it is really about is the intraspecific social relations and not the species-to-species relations (interspecific).

The arrogance of these conceptions, enunciated with emphatic indifference, pervades daily life. Educated men – from paid-by-the-word journalists to secondary school teachers, from armchair philosophers to ivory-tower researchers – enunciate them with explanations, examples, variations and other rhetorical accompaniments. Professional intellectuals, when they start to think about the sexes, do not consider them as classes, but as natural categories dressed up in a bit of socio-ritual cheap finery. With perseverance and persistence, whatever be their discipline or their theoretical tendency, they shape this heterogeneity of 'the natural' according to whether it is men or women of whom they are talking.

The imputation of being natural groups is thus made about dominated groups in a very specific way. These dominated groups are stated to be, in everyday life just as in scientific analyses, submerged in Nature and internally programmed. And environment and history are said to have no influence in practice over this. Such a conception asserts itself even more forcefully as the domination exercised gets closer to naked physical appropriation. In this conception an appropriated individual will be considered as having to do with Nature *immediately*, while the dominators are one step removed from it. What is more, the protagonists occupy different positions in relation to Nature: the dominated are *within* Nature and subject to it, while the dominators emerge *out of* Nature and organize it.

Political consequences

The political consequences of this ideology are incalculable. Apart from the prescriptive aspect of such a discourse (the dominated are made to be dominated; women are made to be submissive, ordered around, protected, etc.), this naturalist discourse attributes all political action and all creative action – indeed, even all possibility of such action – to the dominant group alone. All political initiative on the part of the appropriated individuals will be rejected or severely repressed, using the classic repressive mechanism of total power over any challenge or any project which does not espouse the dominant view. But it will also be repressed as a *terrifying irruption of 'Nature'*. Struggle itself will appear as a natural process *without political meaning* and will be presented as *regression* toward the dark zones of instinctive life. And it will be discredited.

This would not be important if it only affected the opinions of the dominators (generally speaking, political conquests are not made with amenity, and we certainly cannot count on it). But an ideology characteristic of certain social relations is more or less accepted by all the actors concerned: the very ones who are subjected to the domination share it up to a certain point – usually uneasily, but sometimes with pride and insistence. Now the very fact of accepting some part of the ideology of the relationship of appropriation (we are natural things), deprives us of a large part of our means, and of some of our potential, for political thinking. *And this is indeed the aim of this ideology, since it is precisely the expression of our concrete reduction to powerlessness.* We ourselves more or less come to admit that our struggle is supposed to be 'natural', immemorial, a metaphysical 'struggle between the sexes' in a society forever divided by the laws of Nature – in short, nothing but submission to the spontaneous impulses that issue from the depths of life, etc.[21] Thus, presto, no more analysis of society, no more political plans, no more science, nor any attempts to think the unthinkable.[22]

Since men are naturally qualified for founding society and women are just natural, full stop, and qualified for nothing except to express this nature, the result is that as soon as women open their mouths, it can only be a threat from the depths of Nature. It can be nothing but a threat to the highly humane enterprise which is society, which belongs to the men who invented it and who manage it, by protecting it from all undertakings emanating from that threatening Nature, to which belongs that specific species, 'women'.[23]

CONCLUSION

Some aspects of practice and some aspects of theory

Let us summarize. As a result of the fact that women are actual material property, a naturalistic discourse is developed *about* them (and *against* them). They are credited with (as certain optimists believe) or accused of (as is, in fact, the case) being natural beings, immersed in Nature and set in motion by it – *living things*, in some sort of way.

And these living things are seen as such, because *in a determined social relationship – sexage –* they are things. We tend to deny it, to forget it, to refuse to take account of it. Or better still, we tend to dress it up as a 'metaphorical reality', even though this relationship is the source of our political and class consciousness.

Men, however, know this perfectly well, and for them this constitutes a set of clearly conscious habits on which they draw every day, *outside of* as well as *within* the legal ties of private appropriation. It is also a set of practical attitudes which range from harassment designed to obtain continuous physical services from women (clearing the table, giving men the right of way on the pavement by clinging to the wall or stepping down into the gutter, leaving them two-thirds of the seats on the underground or bus, passing the ashtray, the bread, the noodles, the tobacco, leaving them the meat, etc.) to the eventual exercise of *de facto* rights over our physical integrity and our lives.[24]

From these habits and attitudes they draw not only practical conclusions that have a constant utility, but also theoretical propositions. The latter aim to give a 'scientific' form to the status of appropriated individuals as things and to *affirm* in this way that this status as a thing *is not* the product of a human relationship. Leading the existence of a material, manipulable thing, the appropriated group is then *ideologically materialized*. From this comes the postulate that women are 'natural beings'. From this comes the absolutely normal conclusion that their place in the social system is entirely enclosed within this matter.

In this manner these conceptions eliminate the class relationship between the two sexes, the intrahuman relationship. They strengthen exploitation and seizure by presenting them as natural and irreversible. Women are things, therefore they are things – in essence.

The idea of nature is the absolutely everyday recording of an actual social relationship. In one sense it is a pronouncement; after all, the naturalist discourse never means quite simply that X (women, for example) are dominated and used. *But* it is a pronouncement of a particular type, a prescriptive pronouncement in all cases, whether it is Aristotle talking about the nature of slaves or the recent colloquium at Royaumont once more expounding the specificity of women's brains.[25] In both cases the pronouncement of the particular place occupied by those called slaves or those called women is associated with the implied obligation to remain in this place since they are 'made like that'. Both forms proclaim that social relations being what they are, they *cannot* be otherwise and *they must* remain the same. The modern naturalist discourse introduces a novelty into all this: internal programming of the appropriated individuals, which implies that they themselves work at their own appropriation and that all their actions tend in the last analysis to perfect it.

Species consciousness or class consciousness?

Everything keeps telling us that we are a natural species. Everybody strives to persuade us more and more that we, a natural species, are supposed to have instincts, patterns of behaviour, qualities and inadequacies characteristic of our nature. Within humanity we are supposed to be the privileged ones who bear witness of innate animality. And our behaviour and the social relationships in which we are involved are supposed to be explainable by Nature alone, *contrary to the other facts of society* – so much so that certain, if not all, scientific theoretical systems openly show their hand: women are the natural part of the human socius; they are only analysed *separately*, and in a naturalist perspective. The more that domination tends toward limitless, total appropriation, the more insistent and 'obvious' will be the idea of the 'nature' of the appropriated ones.

Today we are building up the consciousness of our class, *our class consciousness*, against spontaneous belief in ourselves as a natural species – consciousness as opposed to belief, analysis as opposed to spontaneous behaviour. We are waging a struggle against the truisms which are whispered to us to distract our attention from the fact that we are a class, not a 'species', that we are not outside time, that it is very concrete and very daily social relationships that form us and not a transcendental Nature (which we could only call on God to account for). Nor are we formed by an internal genetic mechanism which is supposed to have put us at the disposition of the dominators.

NOTES

1 A *material* interpretation, and not a *materialist* interpretation. There is a

logical leap involved in explaining *processes* (social processes in the case we are interested in, but they could be of another kind) *by* material elements which are fragmented and imbued with spontaneous symbolic qualities. If in practice this attitude is the line of traditional idealists more attached to the social order and to sound distinctions than to a materialism which they accuse their enemies of, it is sometimes presented as materialism on the pretext that in this perspective 'matter is cause'. This is not a materialist proposition, because the properties attributed to matter have a specific characteristic here: they arise *not as consequences* of the relations which the material form maintains with its universe and its history (that is, with other forms), but actually as *characteristics intrinsically symbolic of matter itself.* It is simply the idea of (metaphysical) finality decked out with a materialist mask (matter as the determining factor). We are far from abandoning a substantialism which is the direct *consequence* of a determined social relation.

2 The religious institutions of the theocentric societies, chiefly the Catholic Church, have been explicitly confronted with this question: first, with women during the Middle Ages, then later with slaves as early as the sixteenth century, but above all during the seventeenth and eighteenth centuries. Do women have a soul? Should slaves be baptized? In other words: are they not things? If they are things, it is out of the question to let them enter the universe of salvation. But do not they speak? In that case we must consider them as being part of the universe of redemption. What to do? Can objectification and salvation be reconciled?

3 The notions of the Victorian middle class are the best known on this subject, and are almost caricatures. Several generations of women were mutilated and crushed by them. But there are other forms. One of them is the morals of the American plantation society. There the wife of the master and the mistress of the master fulfilled opposite 'functions' as object, one devoted to reproduction and reputed to be devoid of all sexuality, and the other devoted to diversion and reputed to be unalloyed sexuality. The Fascist and Nazi societies professed an identical view. The common feature of these forms – which deny the existence of sexuality in women/wives – is the reduction of their genitality to reproduction. In these forms reproduction is considered as necessary to the maintenance of 'the line' in the aristocratic classes, or as indispensable to the constitution in the popular classes of a permanent and inexhaustible reserve of workers or soldiers. The very idea of sexuality is unimaginable in these perspectives.

4 While the older meaning of the term *nature* designated the usage and the purpose of *one* thing, of *one* phenomenon, and the configuration of its *particular* characteristics, we will here understand Nature to mean the joining in one single entity of the totality of characteristics in the perceptible world. This notion, which appeared in Europe in the eighteenth century, tends to *personify* this entity, as is shown by the use made of it by the intellectuals of the Enlightenment, and even more so by the Romantics. Nineteenth-century science took up the notion to designate the laws of inert and living matter *as a whole.* In this text the term *Nature* will be understood in the personified meaning which virtually always underlies it.

5 T.n.: The author coins a word, *sexage*, on the model of *esclavage* (slavery) and *servage* (serfdom) as in Chapter 9.

6 Since the expression *marriage by abduction* conveniently designates a certain type of marriage whose rules are completely institutionalized, in one sense then it is the opposite of a real 'abduction', which seems to be more related to ancient mythology and exoticism than to any actual practice.

7 By 'constant symbolic sign' we mean an arbitrary mark which replaces the individual and assigns each individual his or her position as a class member. This sign can have any somatic form whatever: it can be the shape of the genitals, it can be the colour of the skin, etc. Such a characteristic 'classifies' the bearer of it; a woman, who is the child of a man and a woman, will be relegated to the class of appropriated persons. This is a mechanism very close to that by which Jacob built his own flock from that of his father-in-law Laban (Gen. 30: 31–35): 'And he said, What shall I give thee? And Jacob said, Thou shall not give me any thing . . . I will pass through thy flock today, removing from thence all the speckled and spotted cattle, and all the brown cattle among the sheep, and the spotted and speckled among the goats; and *of such* shall be my hire . . . And Laban said, Behold I would it might be according to thy word. And he removed that day the he-goats that were ringstraked and spotted, and all the she-goats that were speckled and spotted, *and* every one that had *some* white in it, and all the brown among the sheep'. The determination of our class affiliation is made according to the conventional criterion of the shape of the reproductive organs. And thus *designated by the female genitals*, as were Jacob's sheep by the colour of their coats, we *become women*.

8 It is important to determine the *different social relationships* which make use of the anatomical difference between the sexes. In theory there is no reason why the sexes should necessarily be the occasion for a relationship of *sexage* (in the sense in which this term is used in Chapter 9 – that of generalized appropriation). And if in practice everyone considers that the dichotomy of sex in the human race is a primordial characteristic, to the extent that all known societies today, as Margaret Mead has pointed out since the 1930s, associate some sort of division of labour with the anatomical shape of the sex organs, it is nevertheless not an identical social relationship which always overlays the difference between the sexes.

9 Indeed, the recognized principle of caste society is the closed character and homogeneity of each of the castes, and as a result the status of member is acquired by *descent* – you belong to the caste which engenders you. This does not correspond to reality, but it is the theoretical version of the facts. (If we took account of the mother's caste, we would doubtless see that it is possible to be someone's descendant without that person's transmitting her caste to you; so it is a case of descent from the father.) This is therefore a typical form of hereditary transmission of class, while in the case of the sexes, the transmission is not hereditary but aleatory. Naturalism thus takes a directly genetic form – the natural specificity of the sexes.

10 Cf. Christine Delphy, 'Sharing the Same Table: Consumption and the Family', in *The Sociology of the Family*, eds C. C. Harris *et al.* (London: Sociological Review Monograph, Keele, 1979).

11 *Work*: 'A man worthy of the name keeps his wife at home.' 'But why do you want to bore yourself working; it's enough for one of us to do it.' 'And besides it doesn't bring in any money.'

Food: 'I've made a steak for you.' 'Please give me a pork chop for my husband and a slice of liver for the child.' 'I'm not hungry when I'm all alone.' 'The restaurant is too expensive; I'll take a snack along with me' – said by a secretary whose husband works in a small workshop; she stays in the office for lunch or buys a cup of coffee; her husband goes to the little restaurant in the area where he works.

Decision-making: 'That guy, it's his wife who pushes him' – apparently it is not herself that she pushes. 'Pillow power.' 'Really, believe me, it is the women who dominate' – no, I do not believe you. It is amusing to observe that these remarks amount to saying not that women do the deciding (as their authors insinuate), but precisely that someone else does it. Guess who.

12 Since the 1960s, there has been a steady increase in the number of works which tend to *seek*, and thus to *attribute*, a genetic reason for the condition of being dominated in social relationships. This is equally true in the United States, the Soviet Union, and the European countries which, being a little less wealthy, do not produce such huge masses of papers. These studies, directed mainly toward colonized groups, national minorities like Afro-Americans, or toward sexual characteristics, have recently pushed into domains which until now had been considered areas of social or political concern, such as delinquency, political protest, drug and alcohol abuse, prostitution, etc.

13 According to remarks made in the autumn preceding the 1977 elections, remarks which recommended: (1) an increase in the birth rate; (2) the family vote (proportional to the number of children); and (3) the strengthening of the family – a perfectly coherent politics for the maintenance of sexage!

14 In so far as divorce can be the sanction resulting from the non-satisfaction of a husband who considers the tool unfit to carry out the tasks for which he acquired it. Cf. Christine Delphy, 'Le mariage et le travail non-rémunéré', *Le Monde diplomatique* 286 (January 1978).

15 *Oppressed*. This is the point on which differing interpretations unanimously agree. We all feel that we are hindered and fettered in most areas of existence, that we are never in a position to be able to decide what is fitting for our class and for ourselves, that our right to expression is almost non-existent, that our opinion doesn't count, etc.

Exploited. Although we all feel this oppressive weight bearing down on us, far fewer of us clearly perceive that men get substantial material benefits from it (psychological benefits also, of course, for they go hand in hand); that a part of our existence (our work, time and strength) is appropriated to assure the class of men a better existence than they would have without this appropriation.

Appropriated. Few of us realize the extent to which the social relationship based on sex exhibits a specificity that makes it very close to the slave relationship. Social status based on 'sex' (we are sex) derives from sex class relations which are founded on material appropriation of physical individuality and not simply on monopoly of labour power, as we saw in Chapter 9.

16 As analysis of the historical development of racism in France (and doubtless in the whole western world) in the eighteenth and nineteenth centuries shows, the dominant group, although it was fascinated by other groups as

groups, spontaneously did not see ITSELF. Not seeing itself, neither does it make any judgement about its own social existence, which is taken as a matter of course. And it remains fixed on the idea that it is a group of particular individuals. Besides, it accords only to its own members the right to individuality, a right which is inconceivable for the dominated group; individuality being a human quality, it cannot be applied to natural groupings. The élitist discourse, centred on itself, proclaiming rights over the world, is *secondary* in time and logic. Gobineau only develops his hymn to the Aryans once racism has crystallized. See Colette Guillaumin, 'Caractères spécifiques de l'idéologie raciste', *Cahiers internationaux de sociologie* LIII (1972), translated as Chapter 1 of the present book.

17   See Nicole-Claude Mathieu, 'Man-Culture and Woman-Nature?', *Women's Studies International Quarterly* 1(1), 1978: 55–65; and Nicole-Claude Mathieu, 'Biological Paternity and Social Maternity', in *The Sociology of the Family*, eds C. C. Harris *et al.* (London: Sociological Review Monograph, Keele, 1979).

18   Nicole-Claude Mathieu, 'Man-Culture and Woman-Nature?', op. cit.: 60.

19   Cf. Ti-Grace Atkinson, 'The Older Woman: A Stockpile of Losses', in *Amazon Odyssey* (New York: Links Books, 1974) pp. 223–26.

20   An eloquent anecdotal example is the panic of the columnist in an evening paper at the idea that he cannot make the 'right decision' when he finds himself in the situation of arriving at a door at the same time as a woman. For, he says, if you allow the lady to go first you are a male chauvinist (as women would say), but if you go through first, you are undoubtedly a cad; so (he groans) it's hopeless. But no, Mr. Columnist, not at all. It has obviously never entered this man's head that a woman could also take the initiative herself in these areas of daily life, where the heavy burden of the male man consists mainly of preventing women from making a move or taking the slightest initiative.

21   This doubtless also explains why traditional political parties never recognize that a feminist position is a political position.

22   All science is elaborated in opposition to 'the obvious', by showing what the latter hides/exhibits. To think that which has not yet been *thought* with respect to that which is considered to be *known* (and which is considered to have no significance other than 'natural') is the object of a feminist science.

23   And that we should wax lyrical about our nature! We! This evokes that eminently civilized custom of insulting people with a smile in such a way that they interpret the plainest expression of contempt as a compliment. The insulter thus gains a double satisfaction, first of insulting, and then of seeing the insulted party being naïve and simple-minded enough not to perceive the insult and to claim as praise that which was intended as irony.

24   The exercise of violence, *always potentially present*, is at the root of this fear which is endemic in women's lives – fear that certain women now brandish *against* feminism, which they accuse of causing an increase in male violence.

25   *Le Fait féminin*, ouvrage collectif sous la direction d'Evelyne Sullerot avec la collaboration d'Odette Thibault (Paris: Fayard, 1978). See Emmanuèle de Lesseps, 'Female Reality: Biology or Society?' *Feminist Issues* 1(2), Winter 1981: 77–102.

Chapter 11

The question of difference

RECALLING TIMES GONE BY – (GONE BY?)

A while back, in the good old days, a woman's worth was determined on the basis of her animal qualities. The amount of menstrual blood (this is important: the value of a woman is measured by the litre, like that of a milk cow), the number of children she had in marriage, the age at menopause (the closer you were to 60, the more valuable you were; a hectolitre of blood up past the age of 60 was the general goal).[1]

INTRODUCTION

The notion of difference, whose success among us is now prodigious – among us, as well as elsewhere – is both a heterogeneous and ambiguous notion. The one because of the other.

It is heterogeneous because it masks on the one hand anatomico-physiological givens, and on the other socio-mental phenomenona. This permits a double-cross, conscious or not, and the use of the notion on one level or another depending upon the moment or the needs. It is ambiguous in that it is typically a manifestation of false consciousness (and politically disastrous) and *at the same time* the mask of a real *repressed* consciousness.

Its very ambiguity assures its success, for it permits the lumping together of antagonistic feminist political aims into a sort of superficial consensus. Difference appears to be gaining on all fronts.

This text seems to render these different levels of 'difference' understandable – levels which are inseparable because they are the consequences of each other, but which are none the less distinct in the analysis. I should like to show that difference is an *empirical reality*, that is to say that it manifests itself on a day-to-day basis in a material fashion; briefly, that it is something that happens in actual life. At the same time, difference is a *logical form*, that is, a certain form of reasoning, a way of understanding what happens in and around us; briefly, it is something which happens in our heads. Difference is also a *political attitude* in that it presents itself as a demand, a project; briefly, it is something which has consequences for our lives.

Finally, we cannot speak of 'difference' as if it occurred in a neutral world. In fact, since one speaks of 'woman's difference' so easily, it is because it is something which happens to women. And women are not milk cows ('females') but a defined social group ('women') whose fundamental characteristic is known to be the fact that they are appropriated. And they are appropriated as a group (and not only as individuals bound by personal ties). And it is known that this appropriation is collective: it is not limited to the private appropriation of some of us, by the father when one is a minor, by the husband (or concubine-keeper) when one is a wife. But every man (and not only fathers and husbands) has 'rights' over all women, and these rights are lessened only by the private appropriation of a woman by a particular man. And finally no woman, even if she has escaped private appropriation, has ownership of herself.

KNEEL AND YOU WILL BELIEVE

But, concretely, what is difference? These things become decidedly less clear. Today this demand for difference leans partly on classical anatomico-physiological traits which are clear and well defined. In this perspective, what do we possess that is different? Sexual organ, weight, height, reproductive physiology, speed. Difference also includes a group of feelings, habits and daily practices: attention to others, spontaneity, patience, the gift for making, or the taste for, preserves, etc.

But this notion implies, while it also hides, a certain number of facts which are more complex and removed from anatomical materiality or subjectivity: the use of space and time, longevity, clothing, wages, social and legal rights. In sum there must be as much difference between our world and the world of men as there is between Euclidean geometric space and curved space, or between classical and quantum mechanics.

Let us take several *reputedly superficial* (I am emphasizing deliberately) examples of this famous difference – practices which we had all been led to believe, quite wrongly, to be in the process of disappearing in these last years:

(a) *Skirts*, destined to maintain women in a state of permanent sexual accessibility, make accidental falls (or simply atypical physical movements) more painful to one's dignity, and ensure a deeper-seated dependency based on the insidious fear (one does not think clearly here) that women have about maintaining their equilibrium and about risking any freedom of movement. Paying attention to one's own body is guaranteed, for it is in no way protected; on the contrary, it is offered up by this artful piece of clothing, this sort of flounce around the sexual organ, fastened at the waist like a lampshade.

(b) *High-heeled shoes.* We pity the feet of Chinese women of former days, yet we wear narrow spike heels or platforms which are akin to ice skates (and not so long ago buskins several centimetres high). These various shoes hinder running, twist ankles, render moving about with parcels or children, or both, extremely difficult; and they have a particular affinity for all kinds of gratings and escalators. The limitation of bodily independence is well assured by such prostheses. I do nevertheless recognize a certain superiority over bound feet; while one cannot take off one's feet, one can remove one's shoes.

(c) *Diverse prostheses of the lace-up family.* Belts, wasp-waist cinches, suspender belts, girdles – there are no more corsets (however, it is not such an antique article; I have seen them with my own eyes) – limit their effects to hindering or reducing normal breathing. They make stretching difficult and distressing. Briefly, they do not let a woman forget her body. The veil, which has such a clear significance, is an extreme case. There is a difference of degree, but not of kind among all these instruments, whose common function is to remind women that they are not men, that they must not confuse the two, and above all that they must never, *for a moment*, forget it. (When we say 'men' here, it should be understood that we mean human beings, of course, not males.) To summarize, then, it is a question of memory aids, of concrete reminders of 'difference' which effectively wear down any tendencies a woman might have to think herself free – free as in 'a free man', or even 'one who decides for oneself', etc.

(d) *Diverse loads* (children, shopping bags, etc.) also mark difference quite effectively. Such loads accompany a good part of women's movement outside the home, including on the way to work. For when one is a woman every movement must be useful; nothing of our precious being must be lost. *Necessity alone never suffices to justify what a woman does*; she must add utility to necessity, the necessary to the necessary; do the shopping while returning home from work, drop the kid off on the way to work, knit while watching the children in the park, peel vegetables while discussing all the family business or problems with any and all members of the family, cook dinner while gobbling down her own breakfast, etc. Briefly, never one thing at a time, and as far as possible, never with her arms free-swinging at her sides, never with an unencumbered body, never with idle empty hands.

Clearly we are speaking of *a comparison with* male activities, clothes and prostheses. (The people whose men and women share common clothes and hindrances obviously would teach us nothing about difference. For however discomforting or mutilating a custom might be, if it is practised by all persons it does not indicate a relationship, a 'difference'!) In sharp outline I see long parades of men in the streets, without skirts, without high-heeled shoes, arms swinging free, who do not knit in the parks or in the underground but relax there (far from wishing to censor this, I would prefer, on the contrary, that we all did the same thing), and who return home at night not exactly fresh (everyone's tired, men too),[2] but at least not on their last legs, and, in any case, in flat-heeled shoes.

There you have a collection of signs, considered minor by many people, and which are anything but. They certainly indicate women's dependence, and we will all agree on that score. But these signs do not merely indicate dependence. They are also and above all the *technical means* for maintaining perpetual domination of the bodies, and thus of the minds, of those who are so dominated – the means for not allowing women to forget what they are. *More*, they are the means for providing women with minute-to-minute practical exercises in the maintenance of a state of dependency. Pascal was not an innovator when he stated: 'Make no mistake, we are as much automatons as we are mind . . . Custom . . . influences the automaton, which in turn influences the mind without its ever thinking about it' (Fragment 470 of Pascal's *Pensées*). Wearing a full, short or slit skirt, very high-heeled and pointed shoes, and carrying a full grocery bag are infallible means, among others, for teaching us over and over again our difference, what we are and what we must be. This is not done on a conscious level, but, as Pascal saw, through *ingrained bodily comportment*: identity in the process of being born. And thus a dependent identity is re-formed at every single moment.

This reminder in our dress, our movements creates a very unique habit of carrying ourselves, one to which we have, perhaps, not paid all the attention it merits.

(e) *The smile*, always hanging on our lips, the characteristic of an automaton, which we exhibit with the least word – and even when we are silent. Of course, not always, and not all of us (the same is true with high-heeled shoes and skirts), but only we women, do this. The smile, the traditional accompaniment of submission, obligatory and almost part of the contract in the professions of stewardess or saleswoman, is also demanded of female children and domestics. Required of wives performing their 'social duties' and in a general way of all subordinates of the female sex (which is a tautology), the smile has become a *reflex*. It is a reflexive act which at every instant reminds us that we must yield and acquiesce whatever the circumstances, and reminds men that we are available and 'happy' to show our availability.

And with the smile comes that zone of evanescence, that halo where tenderness, spontaneity, warmth, graciousness, help, etc., create a mixed image of geisha and Virgin Mary, purported to be the quintessence of virtues for a woman (*Woman*). The virtues demanded of us today are no longer those of a Rachel, the strong woman whose solid virtues guarantee the ease and luxury of her master; they are other virtues, but still 'different'. In this realm, that of the smile, of concocting potions, even of less delightful things like hysteria or the gift for poetry, there now arises the demand for 'difference', for the right to be different, for the minority culture and its respectability – woman's language, poetic or medical secrets, ravaging passions, table or bed manners, 'feminine culture'.

HEY! ME, I WANT . . . HEY! ME, I WANT . . .

We find ourselves in the strange situation of already possessing something (difference) and of demanding with hue and cry the possession of this very same thing. This could make someone think either that we do not have what we have, or that someone wants to deprive us of it. Well, the most dispassionate and least biased glance at our daily lives must reveal on the contrary that they accord us, that they give us – what am I saying? – that they throw! they force! 'difference' upon us. They do it in all areas and by all available means. So? What's going on? How is it that certain oppressed groups (and not only women) have at certain moments (and not just today) demanded 'difference'? At least something that we can today call 'difference'.

The expression 'the right to be different' made its appearance in the 1960s, in international organizations and anti-racist movements at first, then in the media. I recall my amazement at that time. It was visibly, in the political context, a *flight* of the oppressed (a flight which was accepted extremely favourably – understandably – by those who rule): a reticence, or more exactly a refusal to analyse the shortcomings of the battles for integration which had been fought within the legal system.[3]

The legal independence of previously colonized nations, the conquest of civil rights by Afro-Americans then appeared to have been accomplished. But these formal rights began to reveal their inadequacy to produce real equality; the distance between the hopes which had sustained the struggles, and the practical consequences of those struggles revealed itself to be very great, indeed. National legal independence is not yet real independence; civil rights are not yet real rights; constitutional equality is not yet equality. For example, we have the legal right to the same wage as men, *but we do not have the same wage*.

We have also seen this flight reaction in the course of the decade of the 1970s. Briefly, anxiety and the feeling that we have been had provoked a pulling back from political analysis, from the analysis of the *relationship* between the dominant and the dominated, and of the nature of that relationship. So much so that a sweet song arose from our ranks, and certain ones began to whisper the word 'difference'. This pleasing whisper really started something; one would have thought that it had been carried over loudspeakers. Suddenly we found ourselves surrounded with kindness, and even attention, and it became a race between which ones – the dominated or the dominators – would scream 'difference' the loudest.

The great unfolding of the idea of minority 'cultures' postulates that reggae or preserves, soul music or maternal tenderness are in and of themselves the justifications for our existence. And even more, that they are the virtues, the eternal, isolated virtues of those who produced them. We persist in considering them isolated from that which brought them into life, and from that which maintains them materially in their daily existence. For there is no maternal tenderness without the raising of children, without their being taken care of materially; there are no preserves without domestic relationships, no reggae or soul music without unemployment.

It is striking that the 'demand for a culture' – whether it is 'blackism'[4] or the mystique of the witches, or any other of the many literary revivals – associates the tolerance of the dominant with the powerlessness of the dominated. Calypso or creativity most often only encounter amused, more or less condescending (and on the whole not very repressive) interest on the part of the dominant group. Let's dance in the moonlight, invoke the goddesses, glorify our ancestors, admire our beauty, jealously guard the secrets of our potions. What is there that is sometimes so consonant with the interests of the dominant group that they do not get all unnerved by certain cries? He who holds in his hands the material means to control the situation easily allows (although with sometimes abrupt fits and starts) these more or less visionary messianisms, which in any event do not have the perspective for winning the concrete means of independence.

What happens that seems so dangerous to the eyes of the dominant group that the paternalistic permissions and the interested (or amused) smiles change into threats and then into an exercise of force? The quest for and the acquisition of practical and concrete *means* for independence – wouldn't that create the dividing line? The harshness of conflicts in this area, whether they are collective or individual (as in divorce, for example) clearly show that what the dominant group fears above all is the *concrete autonomy* of the dominated, and even just its possible eventuality.

A WORLD IN ORDER

In the word *difference* all our 'specific' characteristics are pell-mell engulfed in a tidal wave. In this way difference joins up with the classical folk ideologies which, from 'noirisme' to femininity, have always claimed that they – the dominated – possess something particular, that everything about them is particular. (The others, the dominant group, are no doubt content to be general rather than particular.)

One can have a psychological appreciation of the demand to be different and discern there the desire for specificity, for particularity. This is not wrong, for we do say: we are not 'like something', we are 'ourselves'. And what could be more true or more deceptive? This kind of breathless chase after a fleeting identity, this hopeless desire for reunion with ourselves – this is no doubt what we call 'difference' and what we demand.

We experience the greatest difficulty in trying to unite ourselves into a single self. How not to be crushed by the multiple uses made of us? These uses do not succeed in connecting with each other organically inside us, and for good reason! Much has been said about assembly lines in industry and their fragmented tasks. But it seems that no one has deigned to devote an analysis, from this perspective, to that which, moreover, had not even been considered work until recently: work in the area of domestic relations (I am speaking here of 'housework'). Factory work, as fragmented as it is, is characteristically carried out in one place and concretized by a wage. But, more importantly, it is done in the framework of a transfer of labour power, that is, by the individuals who, *themselves*, sell something of themselves, but not their own bodies. This is not the case with domestic work where *all* of one's individuality is alienated (yielded). In this case there is no *place* where the *I* articulates itself socially – the *I* signifying one's own unity and determination (for men the body is this place). For a woman the only unifying factor of her experience is in the person of the owner of the things and the people to which her activity is applied. Apartment, nourishment, fields, animals, children, business, store, etc. belong to the one who possesses her as well. This is not to say that the only factor of unity is that same one which transforms the woman (female, companion, wife, mother – 'woman' means *all* of these and *nothing but* them) into an object. That which for the class of men may be divided into 'private' or 'public' based on their possession of themselves, cannot be so for us; in a certain way *everything is exterior to us, including ourselves*. For us nothing is separated, it is we who are dispersed and in pieces; there is no unity in us with which to be able to determine a private or a public, an interior or an exterior.

The mystique of 'love' (which today tends to transform itself into a mystique of sex: desire, sexual pleasure, climax, etc.) is an attempt to escape into some minimal unity – sensation or feeling. It is an attempt to become a subject (I) through the experiences of one's own body. But we do not succeed for all that, *because socially we do not have possession of our own bodies*. Therefore there is no place in which to reunite and repossess our various practical activities. From this comes the extreme fragmentation of our acts, which have a reality not as much in connection with us who perform them as in connection with a relationship within which we perform them. This relationship imposes upon us an indefinite accumulation of acts applied to objects and ends of which we are not the common denominator even if we mentally strain for it. For the taking back of individual homogeneity is only possible when one is in a position of subjectivity, *which sexage[5] deprives us of.* We are 'used'.

In reality we are aiming at *originality*, not difference. The thirst to be recognized as unique and, no doubt more deeply, as irreplaceable, seems to be a powerful and tragic common feeling. But we women experience this feeling with more intensity than many, to the very degree that existence is systematically and institutionally refused and denied to members of our class, refused and denied to female individuals. I have always been struck at seeing in people of dominated classes, women and men alike, the desperate desire to be recognized as unique manifest itself in the form of the 'rare malady'. Let the doctor see in you a beautiful specimen, or a rare or exceptional form of illness, and this seems to be a powerful consolation in a life that is not exactly bursting with them; it seems to be the sign of an originality that augments existence and awakens in one a unique and individual identity. In our 'difference' there is a little of that, and it is one of the effects of domination.

Because the search for a personal originality is particularly strong in oppressed persons, it takes quasi-desperate, paradoxical forms in contrast to the dominant originality which goes without saying, like a gift of life conferred by birth. In the oppressed the desire to be recognized is a rarely stated thirst; they thus experience it much more painfully than the individuals of the dominant classes. In our cry for difference there is the passionate rage to signal to the dominators that we are not them, but that we are definitely us. The psychological impact of this 'demand' is thus considerable.

But the idea of characteristics 'appropriate' to a group relies heavily upon a completely mythic belief in the *independence* of the opposing groups, in their existence *per se* – an existence which would owe nothing to the other groups, to the other group. As if the groups of *men* and *women* could exist in themselves and show a permanence which would allow them to be defined outside of their relationship to each other. *It is an imaginary way* of affirming the independence of the dominated group, of guaranteeing its existence forever: to the extent that we ourselves will never be in danger since we exist absolutely, nothing really threatens us. This is a proposition which is very useful to the dominant group, because by affirming that we exist eternally in ourselves, in our essence, the fundamental questions are evaded. This proposition hinders us from seeing how we are concretely fabricated, how transitory we are, and how rooted in material facts and real power relationships. (Not imaginary, not symbolic, not eternal. And not to our advantage.) From this comes men's inevitable complicity, inevitable because it strengthens them in what is their *practice*: to make us into separate beings designated for all eternity to be tools.

In summary, somewhere behind all that there lurks a conception of the sexes in terms of BEING. 'Femininity' is a sort of being-all-alone, which occurs outside of social relationships. And even outside of supposed 'natural' relationships, because if the human species is anatomico-physiologically a sexed species, this implies precisely that there can be no women *per se*, any more than there can be men *per se* (but this latter error curiously does not get anyone excited; absolutely nothing at all is made of 'male reality').[6] The sexing of the human species, the fact that it concerns a species whose reproduction is sexual, implies by definition that the species is *one*, and that there do not exist two kinds of human beings.

But let us leave aside the 'natural', which is a socio-ideological

category, and stick with the fact that human societies consider themselves to be divided into men and women. In this they are not wrong,
without, however, being right, about the mode of existence of the two
groups. For there do exist in fact two groups in the heart of the society
in which we live, two classes which are born of a social relationship, and
whose social existence is *masked* by anatomico-sexual division.

One thus makes short shrift of the analysis, and, in the short term, of
the struggle as well. We believe that we will get away with a certificate
of recognition of our originality, in good and due form, from our boss.
This certificate will be obtained with reciprocal amenity and gentility,
and at the moment of the exchange will give rise to a few discreet laughs
and a complicity all in good taste. Just the kind of pleasant laughs and
complicity which accompany – I have always noticed this with great
surprise – theoretical exchanges between men and women on subjects as
distinguished, pleasing and amusing as those of battered women, the
abandonment and infanticide of girl children, the exceptionally high
mortality rate of females, the double work day, etc. I note in passing that
I have never met (I repeat, never) or heard even a hint of such laughter
in mixed groups discussing men dying in war, in work-related accidents
on construction sites or in heavy industry, or discussing executives'
heart attacks, etc.

Here is the source of our hypocritical reasoning: We will not have to
face the real problems. We will get away with symbolic considerations
– the symbolic being a guarantee of a world in order where each one of
us knows her place. We thus give ourselves the means to avoid confrontation – confrontation which frightens us even more in our heads than in
our bodies. We have this insane hope that men will decide to stop
dominating and using us, that they will make this altruistic decision
themselves, that they will 'recognize' us, that they will *give* us permission to liberate ourselves, that they will give us freedom and, for
good measure, that they will give us love. And they will do that, we
believe, because if we are not 'like them' but 'different' they will have
nothing to fear, but nothing, about what we are going to do or what we
can do. When we think difference, *we* think: 'We'll not harm you, so
spare us'. When *they* think difference, they think: 'They'll stay in their
place'.

The demand for 'difference' is the expression of the fact that we are
defenceless, and, furthermore, that we do not wish to defend ourselves,
or to acquire the means to do so, but that we ask for esteem and love. In
fact, it comes down to a demand for weakness. But can the demand for
dependency and weakness eliminate dependence and weakness?

FALSE CONSCIOUSNESS?

But we can also discern a political, or at least a proto-political, protest in this demand for difference. For if it is a tactical error in judgement in that it serves to distinguish our interests, if it is a manifestation of false consciousness, it is also something else in its ambiguity. There is a great probability that a 'misunderstanding' explains the success of 'difference'. For, a veritable stroke of good luck for the dominant class on the one hand, it is at the same time a *compromise* for a great number of us. A compromise between the emergence of a political consciousness of what we really are as a class, and the repression of this emergence. A political consciousness repressed at the same time that it is expressed by the idea of difference. The latter is therefore – also – the beginning of a true consciousness, our consciousness, the one before which we hesitate because its development scares us. It may make us discover our existence as a class. For we are in fact different. *But* we are not different FROM men (as false consciousness claims) *as we are different FROM THAT WHICH men claim that we are.*

This co-occurrence of two meanings (that we are different from you AND that we are different from that which we are supposed to be) comes from the fact that *we cannot not know somewhere*, even if it is hidden in our deepest recesses, that a *use* is being made of us, from which comes the violence which surrounds us, and the contempt which encircles us. I say violence and I say contempt, this contempt which we cannot really endure because it signifies to us that we are . . . No! We are something else, we are different, we are not that! I am not even speaking of intense hatred; for if hatred is physically destructive, contempt is psychologically destructive. It deprives us of self-esteem (which we know), but it also deprives us of our intellectual and political strength by attempting to force us into accepting and interiorizing the status of an appropriated object.

So we censor, we cover up, we say something else, we say we love children and peace, we say that we do not give a damn about power – without specifying what we mean by 'power', as if it were an object one could take or leave, as if it were a thing in itself – *as if it were not a relationship*. In fact it is not obvious that we so easily accept not being paid, doing the nasty jobs, being beaten or sexually harassed, etc., that we accept being without any means of real response.

No, we remain vague, defining neither 'power' nor 'difference'. What is the goal of this demand, unformulated as to its objective and its modalities? On the one hand there is the feminine mystique or neofemininity; on the other, the refusal of 'power' (but was it really ever offered to us?) and the horror of violence and contempt.

DIF-FERENCE

So let us talk about the right to be different, about the fact that we believe that it would be doing us wrong not to recognize this difference that we experience so strongly and which appears to us to be our own territory, our freedom in the face of permanent encroachment.

A short etymological but not useless comment at the beginning (those who say that words do not mean anything are either hypocrites or they are desperate), for no word is ever chosen at random. We know very well what words mean, something psychoanalysis and the fierce harshness of verbal relationships jointly teach us. *Difference* comes from a Latin verb (*fero*) which means 'to carry', 'to orient'. Dif-ference adds the idea of dispersion (di) to this orientation; we say 'to differ *from*'. What is important is this little *from*. We can certainly speak of difference *between* one thing and another, each term in this case being the point of reference for the other. But this is a rare usage. The kernel of the meaning is the distance from a centre, the distance from a referent (still *fero*). In practice one perhaps claims to mean: 'X and Y and different from each other'; but in reality one says 'X is different *from* Y'. Y is put in the position of the referent. If language offers the possibility of an egalitarian articulation (between), none the less it is hierarchy (from) which is the rule.

In short, difference is thought of (a) in a relationship, but (b) in a relationship of a particular type where there is a fixed point, a centre which orders everything around it, and by which all things are measured, in a word, a REFERENT. This is in fact the hidden reality of difference.

The ideological significance of difference is the distance from the referent. To speak of 'difference' is to articulate a rule, a law, a norm – briefly, an absolute which would be the measure, the origin, the fixed point of a relationship, by which the 'rest' would be defined. This is to suppose an immobile entity somewhere out there. And it is tantamount to acknowledging that there is no reciprocal action. It is quite simply the statement of the *effects* of a power relationship. There is a great realism hidden in the word 'difference': the knowledge that there exists a source of evaluation, a point of reference, an *origin of the definition*. And if there is an origin of the definition, it means precisely that this definition is not 'free'. The definition is seen for what it is: a fact of dependence and a fact of domination. From this comes logically the idea of a 'right' to be different.

THE RIGHT TO, THE RIGHT TO . . .

A right, whether in fact or in law, is something which is defined *in relation to* – in relation to a rule, a norm, a tradition. And therefore, by definition, a right refers to a request for power. To have the right is to be in a position decentred from the decision-making authority. A right *is obtained*, thus it is situated in a perspective of dependence, of a concession – not of negotiation or of exchange.

A member of the dominant group would obviously not claim the 'right to be different'; first of all because his practices and his ideal of existence are effectively the norm of society – what the dominator does goes without saying; then, because he considers himself, in as much as he is an individual in the bosom of his group, as exquisitely specific and distinguished; and because he exercises this distinction by right without having asked for, without ever having to ask for, anyone's authorization, individuality being a practical effect of the position of the dominator. On the contrary, the 'right' to be different is a recourse to authorization. Please give us the right to be otherwise than you are. Or even more clearly: You are the centre of the world. The proposition is tantamount to saying: 'You are the Law'. This drags us into the problematic of established orders, that is, of disorders guaranteed by power.

For the 'right to be different' occurs in a not at all undifferentiated, and in a not in the least bit neutral, relationship. In fact, in what circumstance do we speak of the 'right to be different'? We noted above: in the relationships between the 'developed' world and the exploited world, in the relationship which one can call that 'of race' and in the one which one can call that 'of sex'. It thus concerns determined human groups which have precise relationships between them, relationships precisely of domination and dependence. It concerns groups which are born of a relationship such that the existence of one draws its substance from the other, and where the existence of the other is at the mercy of the power of the one. To speak of a 'right to' is thus in some way or in some place to accept the status quo of the power relationships to which we are subject, to accept these relationships themselves. This is quite different from being aware of them. For want of being aware of them, in fact, we accept them. This puts us in a very bad position to combat and destroy them.

Contrary to what we are often told, there is no question of an alternative. 'Different/Same', there is no choice since we are in a determined place, that of difference. Zero options. The visible dichotomy hides from us a relationship which makes us, women, tools, instruments of survival or of luxury for the dominant class, men. In this relationship there is no choice. When they try to make us believe that there is a choice, they treat us like a child whose anger or bitterness one tries to divert by directing it (often very materially) toward a trap (Oh! the pretty flower), so that absorbed by another object than its own pain, the child ceases to see it, stops thinking about it, and in this way the object finally disappears from perception.

Thus there is no alternative 'Different/Same' with which we might be confronted. The one and the other are the two faces of a power relationship. Unless we adopt a mystical point of view and rally around the famous moral which claims that freedom is choosing what is imposed on you (the freedom of the slave is thus assured), the point of view of choice is absurd.

In addition to that, the fact of its having been presented as a real alternative (although there is only one place and no choice) hinders us from analysing the power relationship itself by turning our attention away from it. This also prevents us from thinking about *what is destroyed* by this power relationship, which probably includes diversity, the infinity of possibilities, etc. For we are deprived of those concrete elements which, in a determined society, are the *conditions* – material and therefore mental – of creation, of invention, of personal determination. Inside practical relationships, such as nutrition, space, relaxation, autonomy, etc., it is easy to see what that means.

THE PRICE OF BREAD

Let us look at the *material means of existence*, and let us see how 'difference' is a concrete relationship: the hierarchy of wages.

We know, for example, that the pressure to marry (that is, the passage from collective appropriation to private appropriation – or from one private appropriation to another) is transmitted through the hierarchy of wages. We know very well that this relationship (between a woman's wage and that of the head of the family) not only pressures women to marry and allows each man to acquire a unit of physical and affective material servicing of his person, but also leads women (statistically) to accept men older than themselves.[7] The hierarchy which gives the best wages to men who are settled down, and the worst to women as a whole (whatever their age) is a homogeneous mechanism which puts the private use of young women at the disposition of mature men (without however depriving the men of general usage of young women).[8] As a result there are not two distinct hierarchies, which would be that of sex and age, but one continuous hierarchy which is only visible when we put the two sex classes at the centre of the picture.

(1) This hierarchy results from, and guarantees, the physical material maintenance of one class, that of men (and the children of men), by another class, that of women. This means, as we are coming to know better and better, all material maintenance: from shopping to cleaning, from cooking to the moral and physical supervision of children, from maintaining social ties – whether they are familial, professional, worldly or quite simply friendly – to being obliged to serve as the ornament of man in society.

(2) *And*, as a result, it also deprives women of the material means of existence in their middle years and *in their old age*. Abandoned, divorced, they are excluded from social rights (health insurance, pension) once they are no longer private property. Forced into unemployment or reduced then to the National Allocation of Funds, which may ('may', but not necessarily does) allow her to obtain as much as 1,000 francs a month (in 1978). Women are deprived of the means of existence in the most material and immediate sense of that word *when* they return solely to the status of *collective ownership*. They are then reduced to being beggars in the literal sense of the term: they no longer have the right to anything which had been assured them by the fact of being possessed by a particular man. Not only do they lose what that man's money can pay for, but also the very rights which are (in theory) guaranteed by the community to each of its members are taken away from them. It could not be established more clearly that a woman is not a member of the community, that she is only the property of her husband or of her companion. A woman, in so far as she is a woman, that is, without her own income, has no individual rights, no existence as a social subject.

From this there flows a number of 'womanly qualities' which may be considered unique and precious, likeable or fascinating – 'feminine characteristics' which come to be ensconced in the famous 'difference': ties between human beings, inspiration in daily material life, attention to others (just between ourselves, we would prefer that this attention to others, for example, were a bit more shared out). Praised as such, these characteristics are the consequences – happy, value-laden, inestimable (all that one could wish for), but consequences all the same – of a material relationship, of a certain place in a classical relationship of exploitation.

This is true, unless one believes – a very convenient and very reassuring belief for all (dominant and dominated) – that 'whims', tenderness and preserves are directly inscribed in the genetic code of women, which in this way – an interesting novelty – reveals itself as distinct from that of men; and that in some way it is a question of our nature. In this case we would be right to defend it fiercely against the assaults of those who would want to traffic in 'our' genetic message and to make us against our will into men.

Into 'men'? There are two important things here:

(1) We have just surreptitiously changed terrain by ideological slippage in a vocabulary laced with traps. We are talking about females and males, not about women and men. This is not at all the same thing even though they constantly try to make us believe it. For in one case we are talking about *physical characteristics appropriate to sexed reproduction*: all organized beings who reproduce by cross-fertilization comprise a female and a male sex. In this regard human beings are not in any way particular; they possess both female and male. When we speak of women and men, we are speaking of *social groups which maintain a determined relationship*, and which are constituted in the very heart of this relationship by specific practices. These practices affect the entire life of each of the individuals concerned and rule her/his existence, from work to the laws which govern her/him, from clothes to the mode of possession of the material means of survival, etc.

(2) However – and this should not escape us – we do not have to defend ourselves against any aggression which aims at taking our youngest children away from us,[9] against tenderness, against whims or against the detergent which washes gently. On that front, we can even affirm that everything works together to guarantee us precisely these privileges and the *material means to cultivate* these exquisite characteristics. On that front, there is not the slightest danger on the horizon. No, they will not deprive us of our children, nor of the aged, nor of family relations, nor of laundry, housework, preparation of meals, and listening to men's personal, professional, political and amorous problems. Thus they will not take away from us those things which also make possible the 'bad characteristics' based on difference – hysteria, mythomania, anger, fatigue, despair, insanity. No, they will not deprive us of the control constantly exercised over us at home and in the street, of the harassment and self-conceit which surround us, of the unfathomable self-centredness of the class of men. They will not deprive us of the state of uncertainty in which the majority of us are institutionally kept: He

will come home, he won't come home. He will be drunk, he won't be
drunk. He will stay, he won't stay. He will give me money, he won't
give me money. They will not deprive us of silence and decisions made
elsewhere without us. Decidedly not. Let us not get agitated by an
imaginary fear; they will not take away from us that which makes us
different. Let us not waste our time asking for what we already have.

DIGNITY

This 'difference' which is being demanded is supposed to be an effort to
take back a little dignity for those who do not have any socially.
Unfortunately, dignity is not fabricated only in one's head; it is first of
all created in the reality of facts. Thus to believe that a request for esteem
and consideration will be able to assure us this esteem and consideration
is day-dreaming. Don't you remember Mother's Day and the campaign
for the 'rehabilitation' of manual labour? Let us talk about this campaign, where 'manual labour', photographed in huge posters on city
walls, was incarnated in miners' hats, mechanics' hammers, builders'
frames, cranes and men's faces. Manual labour is not bringing food to X
number of persons, doing the wash, changing and bathing an infant,
cleaning the family dwelling. No, that is not manual labour; that is
women's mission – a fine distinction. But neither is it visibly assembling
the pieces of an article of clothing, soldering an electric circuit, book-
binding, or fruit-picking, and so not a single woman's face appeared.
Only men work with their hands. Moreover, what did this publicity
campaign resemble if not at best the atrocious length-of-service badges
and the touching speeches about the good and faithful service of those
loved in their place and, above all, nowhere else. Our place is 'difference'. They do not refuse it to us, and they even want to praise us for it
at some festival celebrating procreative work. And even when we have
passed beyond this kind of work, we can have a place almost right up to
the end: when we are old, we are still useful for the 'little' chores where
we are irreplaceable as grandmothers, cleaning women, or servants who
form part of the family (not always part of the family, though, although
old and servants just the same). It is truly when we no longer 'take care
of' anybody but ourselves that we are ejected from the system to become
a part of the oldsters (in fact, old hags) who in their absolute powerlessness none the less weigh down a society which does not stop
moaning about what a burden they are and the threat that they pose to the
national budget.

MYSTIQUE – OF DIFFERENCE (OR OF POWERLESSNESS?)

Mystique has very little to do with relationships of power. This is shown very clearly by the messianisms which, in the 'Third World' more than anywhere else, delude those groups most distanced from independence, from power and even from possible negotiations with their oppressors. And the dominant groups always have a tendency to see history as immobile, and eternity at the end of the road. One wonders how they would even be able to imagine that this could be otherwise, and even that it could have been different. The place of the dominant gives us an incomparably elevated view, where parasitic visions certainly do not trouble the luminosity of the perspective.

So to scream for wonderful difference is to accept the perennial existence of relationships of exploitation. It means, for us, thinking in terms of eternity. And perhaps more seriously, it means not seeing that we are in such a relationship, when we accept the spontaneous ideology according to which nature is nature. Or else it means being so desperate that we act 'as if'. And this must well be the kind of behaviour we have acquired during long experience: Do not make too many waves because in the long run we could lose something. Play the madwoman, the child; caprice goes over better than a bill of reckoning. Or play the hunchback, the idiot, the modest woman, the eternal one. Or, even better, play the diplomat, the sensible one, the one who will not go too far, who will not offend the exquisite sensitivity of the so, so fragile master.

But the history of humans is not immobile. The struggle to establish relationships which, by definition, *will not be able to be* the same as those which exist today (since it is these relations which we are in the process of destroying) gives us, moreover, the possibility of starting from scratch.

CONCLUSION

If domination divides us against ourselves because of the joint effects of the use that is made of us and internalization of our 'difference', it also brings with it the birth of our consciousness. The practices of the dominant class which fragment us oblige us to consider ourselves comprised of heterogeneous pieces. In a sort of patchwork of existences we are forced to live things as distinct and cut off from one another, to behave in a fragmented way. But our own existence, hidden beneath this fragmentation, is constantly being reborn in our coporeal unity and in our consciousness of that unity. Our resistance to the use that is made of us (resistance which grows when we analyse it) restores homogeneity to our existence.

Even if it is – and perhaps *because it is* – criss-crossed with *conflicts which are created in us by the very use that is made of us* at every moment of our daily lives, consciousness is the very expression of these conflicts. If we are torn and if we protest, it is because in us somewhere *the subject is discovering that it has been used as an object.* Permanent anxiety, so constant among us that it has become a tiresome banality, is the expression of being torn like this: it is to know that we (I), who are conscious subjects in our experience, are negated as subjects in the use that is made of us socially.

This conflict between the subject (that is, the experience of one's own acts) and the object (that is, the appropriation which splits us up) produces our consciousness. Today this consciousness is still often *individual*; it is that of particular experience, and not yet our class consciousness. In other words, it is our consciousness of ourselves as individuals, but not yet the knowledge that the relationship in which we are defined is a social relationship, that it is not an unfortunate accident or personal bad luck which has placed our person in this unliveable dilemma.

It is time for us to know ourselves for what we are: *ideologically split because employed for fragmented concrete uses.*

But we are unique and homogeneous as an appropriated class, as women conscious of being split by a power relationship, a class relationship which disperses us, distances us, *differentiates* us. With this consciousness we fight for our own class, our own life, a life not divisible.

NOTES

General note: This text does not have bibliographical notes. It is necessary, however, to indicate that it comes directly from an analysis of the 'three moments' of the feminist battle written by Nicole-Claude Mathieu in the editorial by the editors of *Questions féministes*, entitled 'Variations on Some Common Themes' and published in *Feminist Issues* 1(1): 14–19. It also owes much to the article by Monique Plaza, '"Phallomorphic" Power and the Psychology of "Woman"' in the same issue (pp. 71–102).

1 I speak here of the popular culture (the only one which I know in this area of inquiry), that culture where a certain amount of admiring commiseration always accompanies commentary on excess, excessive quantity, excessive violence, etc.; that culture which is fascinated by the stud, the bossy woman, the bigmouth, the 'gorgeous guy' (180 pounds, 6 feet tall), stomping and slapping around, the moonlighters (doing two paid jobs, not like our double day), etc.

2 A thinly veiled allusion to a delightful French Communist Party poster (which disappeared very quickly, no doubt when the enormity of the gaffe became obvious to somebody): *We can all be happy, women too.* Not having taken notes at that time, I am not absolutely certain of the first part of the proposition, but I am completely certain of the 'women too'.

3 These stages of formal integration were necessary from several points of view: (a) as a consciousness-raiser of the political character of the situation of the dominated; (b) as a demonstration to the dominant of the existence of the dominated; and finally (c) for the *real practical benefits* gained through application of what had been obtained and for the possibilities for later struggles which these stages implied.

4 The terms *blackism* and *noirisme* designate a political and cultural attitude comparable to that previously designated by the term *négritude* in French colonized countries. *Blackism* is used in the English Caribbean area, and *noirisme* in Haiti.

5 T.n.: The author coins a word, *sexage*, on the model of *esclavage* (slavery) and *servage* (serfdom), and uses it to refer to a system of generalized appropriation of women, as in Chapters 9 and 10.

6 Another thinly veiled allusion, this time to a recent book which discourses upon a supposed 'female reality'. We have left behind the 'female condition' but we have not got far beyond it. See Emmanuèle de Lesseps, 'Female Reality: Biology or Society?' *Feminist Issues* 1(2), Winter 1981: 77–102.

7 'You're not going to marry him as long as he has no job (or position or skill)', and the man who will have the job will be two or four or ten years older than you. Inversely: 'Women age earlier than men'. This permits the recommendation of this age difference, which will then reinforce even more men's authority (as if there were any need to do so!). As to the psychology of the chase: between the man who 'courts' a woman with nice things, with fancy presents, with flowers, with vacation trips – as well as the irreplaceable seriousness presented by his expanding midriff – and the man who does not yet have the means to pay court, if a woman is supernormal she will think the first suitor better, more 'in love', more serious; if she is cynical and realistic, she will simply find that he has more money.

8 But the hierarchy of wages is not the sole factor to intervene in 'inciting' women to marry. Another considerable means of pressure is sexuality; it is one of the key points of the relationship, and crucial to it. Heterosexual sexuality *cannot be separated* by a simple mental operation from the domination and exploitation of women by men. Sexuality is women's problem. Men want to keep women in order to have a companion. Women do not only want a man because he is the main means of subsistence (something which is not always clearly conscious) and the guarantor of access to a recognized social existence, but also because he is the sole certain provider of sex. There is for women no socially guaranteed sexual exchange outside of companionship, *even a fleeting one*. This is not the case for men, who have shared women, whether in the framework of a monetary service, or in the framework of seizure and the use of force, either physical or persuasive.

9 T.n.: In the United States, men are, in fact, trying more and more to take their children away from women upon divorce.

Chapter 12

Herrings and tigers
Animal behaviour and human society

During the 1960s the field of animal behaviour studies took over the place of psychoanalysis as the fashionable field in the social sciences. At first seen only in the domain and field of influence of traditional psychology, this vogue later reached the general public, first in the English-speaking countries and then in the French-speaking ones. This boom took various forms. In the style of literature, adventure story or journalistic exposé, books appeared about our simian ancestors. Desmond Morris produced some noted best sellers; Lionel Tiger and Robert Ardrey won some enthusiastic partisans. A certain number of more recent works are written from the perspective of a general theory of human socialization; in France, Serge Moscovici and Edgar Morin have taken up this theme. Finally, the classical image of ethology (the study of animal behaviour), more interested in animals in general than just in simians, is dominated by the figure of Konrad Lorenz, who combines the traits of the 'old sage' and the scholarly observer.

This all took place on a grand scale, with books in huge editions, advertising and promotion in big newspapers, on the airwaves and television, in scientific and popular journals, and with publicly and privately financed research projects. And gradually there came to be a growing reference to animal behavioural models. This calling on animals to represent humans is certainly a very old tradition, but today it is given respectability by a 'scientific' guarantee – these are no longer the fables of La Fontaine. And if the saying 'man is a wolf to man' is not specifically twentieth century (it is really rather strongly retrograde), this wise old adage has been supplanted by a proposition which is supposed to account for the inter-species identity of living creatures. Now, choosing the field of ethology in order ultimately to analyse human societies or furnish a model of them is not at all a neutral choice. It implies a very particular vision of the world.[1]

It is not that animal societies should not be studied. Why should they be left in the dark of ignorance? It is not that observations made about them are not full of interest. But it is a question of understanding *those* animal societies and not of speaking about something else through them. For the presupposition in these works, sometimes explicit but more often hidden or even unconscious, is the reducibility of human society to a homogeneous 'animal' sociality. Or, more precisely, it is its regular reducibility to *each* of the animal societies studied, however diverse they may be, or even however opposite. If the search for a common denominator is sometimes necessary in order to establish new comparisons and thus to discover new relationships between data, it is only a stage in research and can be nothing but that. For, after all, such an approach will be rewarded by the abolition of its object, as is shown in this example drawn from linguistics:

> Certain points of resemblance have already been established between Indo-European and Finno-Ugrian. In the Semitic field, where the comparative work is well-advanced, we find some characteristic features bearing a strange resemblance to Indo-European . . . Thus both may turn out in the end to be representatives of a single linguistic group; French, reduced to its last terms, would then be the same language as Arabic or Ethiopian, just as it has been proven to be the same as Russian, Persian, and Irish.[2]

But there is not such great frankness in the study of animal behaviour. The idea that 'man, reduced to his last terms, would then be the same animal as the tiger, just as he has been proven to be the same animal as the baboon' is not written even though it is strongly believed. And as it is in fact postulated that white rats and humans are social animals (or occasionally 'mammals'), this is 'identical', one ends up with the explanation based on one isolated trait which on principle ignores the specificities of each of the groups: the one which is openly on the table (the animal group) and the one which is hidden under it (the human group). And this is done to further the idea of a supposed homogeneity of the sociality of all living creatures. The correctives of a more sociological hue which are sometimes brought to bear on reductive interpretations do not resolve the question because they ignore the fact that every element present in a configuration implies a totality which shapes this element itself just as it is shaped by it. The sociality of baboons and the sociality of termites cannot be superimposed on each other. The forms of their relationship to their environment are not the same since their equipment is not analogous; the relations between individuals of these groups thus cannot be identical. Everyone is in agreement on that as long as one is speaking of baboons and termites, despite the fact that they are both living creatures. This all gets complicated when one makes this claim about the sociality of humans as compared to that of Scotch grouse. It is strongly frowned upon to say that each of these is specific.

It is indeed strange that, although a common animal nature allows man to be made (by turns and according to the needs of the moment) into a chimpanzee, a wolf or a Scotch grouse, no one makes any attempt to explain the wolf by the grouse or the chimpanzee by the wolf. This unidirectionality hides at least one thing: ethology *describes* animals but *explains* man; the referent is man and not socio-animal behaviour as such;[3] the animal is the mask which conceals (rather poorly, it must be said) the scheme of verifying man (in the sense of verifying one's identity or one's address). Decked out in his unique animality, man's nobly modest figure is the sole object of these long incursions, regarding the most diverse species, into territoriality, aggression, hierarchy, etc. There at least, pathetically, if man is an animal, he is the only one to be really one. A paradoxical suggestion? Not really, as we shall see. We can see there the reflection of the fluctuations which change the conception of 'Man' and his 'place'. Demiurgic, sacred or tiny, this place is central in any case, since all paths lead there without ever meeting.

In practice what are the interests of the ethologists? What are the questions that they indirectly pose about man through animals? And what animals do they choose to explain these phenomena? Many works are about monkeys and apes (it is certainly these which most fascinate the popularizers and the reading public) and about land mammals (dogs, wolves, cats, rats, etc.); there are not many about fish. Aquatic mammals play a role that is important but more complex than that of the simple analogy which usually governs these commentaries. These somewhat dubious mammals, such as the dolphin and the whale, seem to inspire an altogether conscious projection; 'human' feelings are attributed to them in a sort of feeling of tender solidarity; besides, they are placed on the fringes of the general field of ethology. There are still fewer studies of frogs and reptiles. If the wolf is supposed to explain human behaviour by acting as a noble foil for it or as a pessimistic comparison, the crocodile has not found out how to use its tears to obtain the status of an animal referent. Beyond these, one finds anthropomorphic meanings given to insects and even to unicellular organisms. Ants and bees – insects – were the pioneers in the study of animal behaviour; the fame accorded them at the beginning of the century by Maurice Maeterlinck carried on the interest that Darwin took in them from the middle of the nineteenth century.

It is at this level that one sees a certain number of interests become the exclusive ones in the research – those which relate to number and to food. The *small-sized animals* seem appropriate for inspiring reflection about the *great number* of individuals. The phenomena of demographic expansion, reproduction control, excess population and exploding birthrate are more and more exclusively studied as the individuals who compose these classes become less considerable in size. These problems are not studied so much among the great apes, although the concern is not absent. They are very much studied among birds and almost exclusively among mealworms.

But it is the phenomena of territoriality, hierarchical behaviour and domination which are the favourite object of study among ethologists. These are the phenomena which were the starting point of the new wave in the study of animal behaviour. If domination, territoriality and birthrate are at the heart of animalist thinking, these terms (whatever may be the double meanings that they conceal) can nevertheless be usable to the extent that they designate (badly without doubt, but in a transmittable fashion) a certain number of *facts*. It is not the same thing, however, when one drifts into metaphors which sometimes go as far as 'faithfulness', 'altruism' or 'responsibility', and even 'honour' (and why not manly honour!) which is higher among wolves. In short, the phenomena sometimes studied and the ideas employed are so obviously set up according to an anthropomorphic perspective with a moralizing blueprint that it is difficult to find them a conceptual base that is neutral and free of reference to 'values'. As a result, it is difficult to see what facts could be lodged beneath such ideas without being visibly distorted.

And it is at this point that the ambiguity of the approach used by the ethologists is revealed. Our inability to disregard the forms characteristic of our sociality, of its specific characteristics – for example, 'values' – in apprehending and describing other forms of sociality becomes obvious in this approach. Despite appearances, we are not so far from the universe of La Fontaine and Aesop, incapable of not projecting our 'passions', of not peopling the world with the constructs which our relations among ourselves generate.

Moreover, it is not that certain people, themselves ethologists or sociologists, are not sensitive to this fact and are not vexed by it. Pierre Paul Grassé, in an interview on *France Culture* in 1974, commented on this practice and protested against the tendency to assimilate empirical observations collected in animal societies to human behaviour. This tendency might seem to prevail solely among the reading public. In fact, it is threaded through all the studies of animal behaviour, through the works of popularization, as well as through a large part of the texts regarded as scientific, in which it is explicitly stated that there is continuity in the animal data. Max Gluckman, in an article in which he particularly cites Tiger, analysed the implicit teleology of these comparisons.[4]

The wisdom of animals, their maternal sense, their respect for hierarchy, their genetic guarantee, etc. leave certain readers with a taste of bitterness or black irony, for it does not escape them that the subject is broader than the care of progeny among starlings. There is no doubt that in the study of animal behaviour there is being expressed something which oppressed and dependent groups know only too well: the veiled affirmation of their animality. It is, in a certain way, the other side of the process, the reverse of anthropomorphism. For if the wolf is a mask for the human in this discourse (whether it is the discourse of fables or of ethology), in certain actual social relationships the human is treated as an animal and disappears behind the cow, the ant or the monkey. It is an animality foreign to the world which proclaims itself human, the animality of those who provide the upkeep, which is the guarantee of the humanity of those in the dominant position – the animality of the former guarantees their submission and their dependence on the eminently human world of the latter. It is shown by the wordplay, the jokes, the clothes, the advertisements which turn female human beings into animals on a lead. Moreover a constant assimilation between animals and women runs through daily life: 'My wife and my dog' turns female human beings, human females, into animals. Or in a perfectly clear symbolic behaviour, dogs and women are whistled at in the exact same way. And this is scarcely concealed, for a remark about the class position of women frequently brings a response of 'amused' irritation and some remark in the vein of common sense: 'And why not be interested also in cats (or dogs or baby seals, etc.) while one's about it?'[5] And it is precisely dogs and cats, those domestic 'companions' wearing collars and name-tags, living objects 'belonging to' somebody, which are the most often connected with or assimilated to us – it would be more correct to say that we are assimilated to. The time when one used to speak of a woman as a well-built or beautiful mare – actually not so long ago – now seems dated and cynically naïve. Moreover, mares are useful and necessary, and it was a solid comparison which assimilated the bearers of burdens and pullers of ploughs with the animal which did the same. The comparison was simple and not malicious, free of hate as well as of a bad conscience.

But what do we have to learn from being compared to mares, cats and dogs? The process has a double disadvantage. The first is that it reminds us that a woman and a domestic animal are equivalent, that they have the same status in some way, that, in short, they become identical. The second advantage is that it says to us that the lot of these animals should not make anybody cry, that human cats and dogs should have the decency to shut up, and that they can only be allowed to share with humans by recognizing themselves as animals. The everyday, habitual order to shut up is laid on us under an ironic threat: all protest has limits, the limits of animality, which is the status of the oppressed, who have to return to their place of an animal belonging to, and submissive to, the dominant ones. So there we are – turned over to the protection of the RSPCA.

In fact, ethology, which is the model for the articulation between genetic inscription and socio-human relations, is the linchpin of the natural guarantee which is supposed to assign their place to the oppressed. We are animals to such an extent only in order to make more clear the distinction between the dominant ones and the subordinate ones. All those hierarchies inscribed in the genetic code, all those territories conquered by the élites of strength or astuteness, that inner nature which produces submission, obedience and absorption in the tasks of maintenance, reproduction of the species, and incessantly re-begun materiality, are woven into that 'wonderful' order which Darwin already, in *The Origin of Species*, looked at with a look free of any bitterness. And that which among ants allowed him to praise the 'wonderful' 'slave-making instinct' would not evoke the same enthusiasm among human beings who found themselves actually enslaved. But Darwin was certainly in a better position in this regard; no parasitic phenomenon troubled his evaluation of an order guaranteeing that relations between humans are only the result of instinctive laws, beyond the reach of human hitches.

During the second half of the nineteenth century there was a greater sensitivity to what was being implied here. Zola, in *Germinal*, put into the mouth of one of his heroes, an intellectual and worker, a remark showing his disillusionment with Darwinism and its élitist outlook. Engels, in *The Anti-Dühring*, regarded that aspect of Darwin's work as the expression characteristic of the dominant class. The study of slavery can be done in various ways; it is not the *study* of the phenomenon that is at issue. On the contrary, because his analysis is outstanding. It is rather the perspective through which it is viewed that is questionable. Choosing that angle of attack, Darwin brought to the social relationship of 'slave-making' (which in the final analysis provided him with the economic support that enabled him to write) a form of interest that was logical in that it suppressed any *questions* about the slave-making *process*. In that period people at least were not hypocritical, and when they found slave-making wonderful, they said so, and when they thought that this was class language, they did not hide it. Nowadays they are on their guard (only a bit, in fact) and they describe (without too openly singing its praises) that which they project onto animal societies. A certain cool cynicism today tempers the romantic voices. How do wolves hunt? And how do birds sing? According to their inscribed or potential instinct, they tell us, and this by apposition teaches us how the comparable social animal-man demonstrates by his social behaviour the genetic programmes which rule him. A heterogeneous and expanding body of studies, ethology, by placing its discourse in between social phenomenon and instinct, presents itself as the empirical voice of biological determinism. And so, in the phantasms of domination and order, of over-population and population explosion, of the irrepressible force of the instincts, the pessimistic song of romantic lyricism finds a new voice. Also, and conversely, according to the Lorenzian variant, if man is unfaithful or deaf to his instincts, he is precipitated into a still darker world which leads him inevitably to catastrophe. This is the result of not having recognized in himself the animality which is the guarantor of order.

And it is precisely this which the animal metaphor expresses when it is used by dominated groups to protest against certain power relationships: being treated like beasts of burden, like dogs. 'They are not going to throw us out into the street like a dog', said someone expelled from an urban renewal project, 'we are not animals'. The vague knowledge of the meaning of animality extends to actual human relationships and not only the symbolic, as is unthinkingly believed.[6] In relationships between sex-classes, between classes, between peoples, between 'races', the frequent reduction of the dominated ones to animality is a social form. And for the social sciences it is desirable to recognize animalism as a social fact.

The remark of a radio journalist in 1974 – just a marginal, offhand remark – is suggestive of this type of thinking: 'Three million years ago man walked upright and was already no longer a monkey'. This is very close to the famous cliché: 'When man came down from the trees'. Thus in the past *we* walked on four feet (or otherwise, but in any case not on two feet), and *we* were monkeys. If one stops there, one sees the species from a fascinating perspective. The homogeneity of the animal world is thought of as an *intraspecies* solidarity and not trans-species – not *between* different animal species but *within* a single species: the animal one. It is a paradox to see affirmed and regarded as an *established fact at the animal level* that which is stubbornly *denied at the human level itself*: the existence of one unique species, the animal, is affirmed as such at the same time as is the presence of several races or sexes in the human group, uncertain categories on the borders of the concept of 'species'. In this perspective, 'man' is then only a general equivalent of 'animal' and not all *one* specific animal.

And the vague belief in the homogeneity of the animal category is also evident in the sense of the man-animal, just as it is in the reduction of man to the other animal species, since one can also speak of 'humanization' by animals. In an article in a French newspaper in 1973, for example, the hamster was endowed with the quality of *humanizing* the quarters where it lived, and André Lwoff himself attributed to horses the ability 'to humanize, like all animals', the laboratories where they are used.[7] These are images of course, but not chance images. (And are there others besides?) They are evidence of a system of thought, the system of thought of our society. For, I repeat, this amalgamating method places the human in the animal world, or vice versa, but does not do the same to the other animal species *vis-à-vis* each other. If 'man is a wolf to man', the herring is not 'a tiger to the herring'.

Darwin said that if man had not been his own classifier, he would never have dreamed of establishing a separate order to place himself in. Quite so. But it is equally noteworthy that he is a classifier, and that, like his skeleton and his habitat, this *fact* specifies him and defines him. And whatever Darwin thinks of it, the discourse based on animality is not the inversion of a naïve megalomania; it is a sophisticated form of it. For this consequence of false modesty or admitted hypocrisy permits not the elimination of the 'cutoff point', but the placing of it elsewhere: one human group, well placed, 'escapes' animality in a certain way, leaving behind the 'remnants' of the human species. And, above all, this group gets rid of its human animal specificity by discarding one of its characteristics – the practice of making classifications – in favour of traits characteristic of other animal species, which are afterwards raised to the dignity of general characteristics of animality.

One can go a bit further with a remark made by Claude Lévi-Strauss in an interview.[8] He said that a study made of sexual avoidances in an animal society (simian in the present case) curiously reproduced in fact the prohibitions of the society to which the observers belonged. Since the study was made by scholars from Japan, where the rules of kinship, says Lévi-Strauss, are quite particular, the displacement made one aware of the similarity between the characteristics of the observing society and the observed society. Here we have to do with the meaning of ethology in the societies that produce science. The least that can be said is that there are relations between the interpretations that guide the study of animal societies and the *practices* of the society that produces these studies. In the first place, the choice of the data described, their arrangement, their implications (explicit or not) are not neutral and, above all, are not independent of the specific social relationships which regulate the society of the observers. In the remark made by Lévi-Strauss, the kinship relations, the concept of incest which is their correlative, arouse little emotion, so the influence that they can have on the observation is recognized without too much dispute. It is not the same thing when the *power relations* of a society are projected onto (and justified through) animal societies, as is the case with observations on 'territoriality', 'hierarchy', 'sexuality', etc. It becomes more difficult – and at any rate, openly disputable – explicitly to posit a relationship between animal descriptions and human social structure.

When a famous anthropologist considers that the risks of conflict between human groups stem from too great physical proximity (as a consequence of the demographic explosion), the poisoning by meal worms of each other, when their number grows, seems to him a good comparison, explaining the nature of the conflict. It is paradoxical that historians are so cautious about the feasibility of comparing human societies to each other, that anthropologists refuse to do it, and that nevertheless it is easily accepted that the behaviour of human groups should be commented on in the light of another animal group, whether they be rats or sea urchins. Historians – and anthropologists and sociologists – know that the multiplicity of factors involved in socio-human phenomena imply the impossibility of the same situation's being produced twice. Is this not only because of two reasons specific to human sociality: continuous technological changes, and the fact that human behaviour is historical, that it involves consciousness as well as reflexive memory? These two characteristics distinguish human sociality from that of other animal societies subject solely to variations in resources and to the heterogeneity of the environment. Technological variations and historical-reflexive consciousness are indeed integral parts of human society – human animal society, if you prefer – and their significance cannot be regarded as a simple 'addition' onto the group of data which constitute the animal socius, but as factors whose presence modifies social organization itself.[9]

Is it that certain contemporary scholars, secret metaphysicians, believe that technology, consciousness and history are divine gifts? And that to regard them as elements constituting human sociality would be to depart from an animal conception of man? A remnant of theological reverence crops up in this throwback to analysing the society of humans like any other animal society (and nothing more) by integrating their specific characteristics. In order to prove that herrings are animals, it does not seem that one must absolutely define them as amoeba. Yet that is what they do with human beings, who do not deserve such treatment.

In fact, it seems that it is not so much a question of integrating human beings into the animal class as of showing human beings in a 'natural' light. And what is more natural than the animal, what is better suited for giving human beings the desired image? This is particularly discernible in the place that human beings are given within the ethological field – that of referent, explicit or implicit. The construction of the model is guided by this *discriminating* referent. On one side there is the object of our interest, either friendly or hateful – man (human society). On the other side there is the totality of animal societies, which are the image of, and accountable for, human beings in their specific characteristics as much as in their totality. They mirror each of the aspects of the sociality of human beings: simians for raising of the young and for nurturing, grouse (or starlings) for territoriality, wolves for honour and aggressiveness, fowl for hierarchy, starlings and mealworms for reproduction, and other species for other purposes.

For, in fact, not *all* the aspects of a given animal society are going to be used in their totality to 'explain' human sociality, but only the atomized aspects of human society which are best suited to confirm the preconceived idea about the dominant characteristics of human sociality. The fundamental hypotheses of the researchers about the nature of human processes guide the choices made. The animal societies most suited to furnish an image both suggestive and powerful of the ideas that one has developed about human society come to the fore, whether one supposes that human society functions in the same way as certain animal societies, or whether in another way one seeks in the latter a model of *what* the relationships among humans *should be*. Some ethologists assimilate chosen animal behaviour to wisdom, to nobility, and to a certain number of other 'values' which are quite personal to them, or at least which are perfectly clearly the values of the dominant group – values of hierarchy, of order, of ownership. If we were more faithful to our internal wolf, eagle, cow or ant, we would 'preserve' the species, and we would firmly avoid changing the equilibrium of forces in human societies.

For this famous equilibrium is always on the point of breaking down, they think (although it is always very present).

From the ethological perspective, human society, being an animal society, in the final analysis is ruled by instinct like other animal societies. The non-human animal societies are thus the direct reflection of human societies. And instinct can be chosen in a manner most appropriate to our tastes and interests from the extraordinary array of possibilities for metaphor. Suppose, for example, that we are particularly sensitive to 'over-population' and that we believe we see in this the end of Humanity. (if we were being perfectly candid, we would say 'our' humanity, because in fact it is that which prompts our anxiety, although it is not especially proliferating; but we are hypocrites.) In short, if we see a risk (for us) in over-population (of others), we are going to choose, according to the mechanism described above, an example of the destruction of the species as our 'answer' to over-population. Obviously we would not choose, in a different species, an optimistic mechanism of adaptation, for that would not only not help our explanation, but it would also reduce to nothing our expressed concern.

Or else if the object is to keep women in the kitchen and to reserve entirely to them the joy of children (talk about the happiness of every instant with the dear little ones, and there you have an altruistic progamme), you will not fail to find baboons or cows who through their solitary female parenting will come to back up the most strongly held views on the natural specialization of women and their biogenetic specificity for hearing crying and for remaining attached night and day – without pay – to the needs and the presence of their particular and personal offspring. The animal species in which males and females indiscriminately pour their pain, time and sweat into the upbringing of the young are discreetly glossed over. And those species in which the dear little ones set up their own living arrangements or where the paternal sense alone takes care of the preservation of the species are even more buried in obscurity. Moreover, 'Nature' would never be seen defending the paternal instinct or collectivism. 'Nature' prefers the maternal sense and 'free enterprise', and everybody knows very well that it is into the paws (arms) of mothers (and of them alone) that Nature throws the little ones.

The pecking order of fowl, which has so fascinated the social sciences, appears as the guarantor of a hierarchical order written on the tablets of Nature.

So, if one leans toward the good old model of the sexual relationship as a natural power relationship, one sees flooding from it examples designed to show women that it is 'natural' that they should be re-strained and/or beaten, and that it is natural that they find this normal, or even pleasant. And if such is not their opinion, it is because they are unnatural and even against nature. To prove this, there will be a series of crabs, monkeys, assorted mammals, and more or less probable saurians. Those who have read the learned interpretations of sexual presentation (of the female type, of course) as the universal image of submission remain divided between laughter and anger. The observations of the simulating rituals of monkeys contain a hefty dose of consensus about the eternal characteristics of (human) femaleness. But certainly there do not appear in this tableau the species which function without having read de Sade, or which at least cannot be reduced (through whatever anthro-pomorphism is used) to the self-satisfied fantasies of our experts, who are also, by the way, well-armed with ideas on the perfidy of females.

Child-rearing and sexuality, along with power relationships, cer-tainly are the preferred locus of these phantasms.

Animal societies offer such a vast range of data, interpretable in fundamentally different ways, that it would not be possible seriously to defend the idea of a universal, immutable natural order, peculiar to the sociality of all animal forms, and still less the idea of a uniform structure of relations between individualized elements of the living kingdom. But this is not done explicitly. They only make a series of point-by-point comparisons, which are more like imagery than 'proof'. Pushed into a corner, the ethologists would very likely not maintain that human society and the society of partridges are analogous, and thus comparable. It is even more certain that they would not say that the society of termites and that of orangutans are governed by the same relationships. They might, however, maintain that there exists between monkeys and humans a resemblance that can be pushed to the point of analogy and that the former effectively explain human society. In any case, this is the area in which the statements are the clearest. However, most often these etholo-gists remain in a state of artistic fuzziness, which allows them to raise the cry of intentions at the least allusion to the anthropic-normative character of the animal description and its human meaning.

Moreover, can we be absolutely sure that a simple metaphor – if there is such a thing as a simple metaphor – is as innocent as we were once led to believe? For, if in the case of dispute one falls back on the excuse of metaphor (the comparison with animals would be a simple figure of speech which would not at all involve the presuppositions of the author), when this same metaphor is explicitly used as the research model and preferred form, when it is not solely the vehicle for exposition but actually the foundation stone of the analysis, the margin is narrow between metaphor and *analogy*, the mode of approach that constantly supports the idea of 'order' through its refusal to analyse the process of change. One has to be a very shrewd detective to make a firm distinction between the 'picturesque' form of metaphor and the 'explanatory' form of analogy.

Using animals as the referent is the dominant model these days in the approach to social relationships. The mixture of the emotional power produced by the evocation of animals and the simplicity of ethological models encourages this semi-metaphorical treatment in the explanation of human phenomena. Animalism, whether it is classical ethology or animal comparison in the more extended field of naturalism, expresses a certain *suppression* of reality. This scientific choice *removes from its field* a particular body of phenomena. This body is called by different names according to various schools and without covering exactly the same data, but it nevertheless comes down to a central core which can loosely be referred to as *the distance that human societies maintain in relation to themselves*. 'Superstructure' some will say; 'the symbolic' others will call it; 'philosophy', 'language', 'history', etc. – in short, everything that relates to mediation in the relationships that humans maintain with concrete reality and among themselves.

Animalism postulates more or less explicitly that the relationships between humans and their relationship to the material world are immediate, spontaneously genetic, and (even if sensitive to the environment and likely to be adaptive) defined in the final analysis by the organism itself and its reactions. Comprehension of reality is handled through the consideration of organic sets conceived as autonomous, and the process can only take the shape, at best, of interactions between organisms. Therefore, the transformation of the world (work) has no place in such a perspective. The invention of techniques (investigation of physical 'laws') falls into a sort of no man's land and then can only appear as the fruit of a spontaneous genetic burst. This is the way, for example, that C. D. Darlington interprets the appearance of agriculture. In this perspective the individual of genius provides the necessary substratum for the miraculous incarnation.[10]

Naturalism expresses the mutation of matter into symbol *without the intervention of a process*. It eliminates production and does away with a major characteristic of the relationship between humans and their world – transformation. In the end it amounts to syncretism. It lumps together a group of human or animal phenomena, not as related or dependent upon each other, but rather as homogeneous, not distinguishable, and all reducible to each other. From this comes the close affinity of naturalist thinking with magic. Pronouncements of healing or death are not distinguishable from death or healing. Thus intelligence is not distinguishable from the brain, talent from power, or power from skin colour. Moreover, it is very necessary to do this, for naturalism is the only mode of thought that allows the binding together in an intangible way of characteristics which if analysed – that is, forcefully dissociated – would as a matter of fact cause *their relationship* to become obvious. In other words, the fact would become obvious that they have a history, that they are born of specific relationships, of the links which exist between mental activities and material activities; between slavery (a material practice) and skin colour (a mental practice), between domestic exploitation (a material practice) and sex (a mental practice). From the moment that the mechanisms which *create* the one (mental practices) *from* the other are made visible, these revealed links make obvious the syncretism which merges the relationships into the deeds and shatters the affirmation that the deed and the discourse on it are one and the same thing.

In the naturalist exposition this consubstantiality is asserted with force, and sometimes with violence – in the fascisms which feed ideologically on the 'natural order' of relationships among human beings. Affirming like Darwin that slave-making is an *instinct* is to make it impossible – because *unthinkable* – *to analyse the relationships of slavery*. Conversely, analysing the characteristics and transformations of the relationships of slavery is to shatter the notion of instinct and to break apart the syncretism of body/slavery/property, the syncretism whose name is 'black'.[11] In the same way, analysing non-paid work shatters the idea of body/domestic work/property, the syncretism whose name is 'women'.[12] In the same way, analysing childbirth and finding there engendering and maternity shatters the idea of body/engendering/property, the syncretism whose name is 'women'.[13]

Syncretism is in fact the only adequate attitude that an established order could adopt, at least within the social relationships that we know today. A spontaneous feeling, it floats in the universe of appearances, it drips with the naturalness of the easy approach to life. And introducing the wedge of doubt into this tight block of 'law immemorial' is no small matter.

NOTES

1   This analysis made its début only recently. It was crystallized in 1975 in the US around sociobiology, well after the beginning of the vogue for ethology.

Concerning Lorenz in particular and the world vision that he incarnates rather well, the following works can be consulted: Ashley Montagu, *The Nature of Human Aggression* (New York: Oxford University Press, 1976) and Elizabeth Lage, 'Le péché capital de l'éthologie', in *Discours biologique et ordre social*, eds Pierre Achard *et al.* (Paris: Le Seuil, 1977).

2 Joseph Vendryes, *Language: a Linguistic Introduction to History* (New York: Knopf, 1925), p. 303.

3 Slips by authors are very revealing. Consider the following example by Edgar Morin in *Le Paradigme perdu* (Paris: Le Seuil, 1973), p. 40. In a description of 'various societies (*baboons, Rhesus monkeys, chimpanzees*)', using the works of a number of ethologists, the author reports to us that 'thus the males protect . . . lead . . . guide . . . The females are solely devoted to . . . The young play on the fringes . . . The *women* constitute the nucleus' etc. (emphasis added). We are delighted to learn that in reality he is speaking to us about human society, since there are WOMEN there. If there is an error (unless female baboons, Rhesus monkeys and chimpanzees are women), neither the author, nor the typist, nor the editor, nor the proofreader noticed the error, any more than the author himself – later – when reading the galley proofs or the page proofs. One sees that the penchant is 'natural', being so widely shared.

4 Max Gluckman, 'Changement, conflict et règlement: dimensions nouvelles', *Revue internationale des sciences sociales* 33(4), 1971.

5 Refer again to the perfect example cited in Note 3 from Morin, *Le Paradigme perdu*, p. 40. If the slip conveys (1) that the subject really is the human species since the author speaks of 'women', then he specifies to us *at the same time* (2) that it is women who in reality, in the human species, are the animals (monkeys and baboons).

6 Noëlle Bisseret notes the importance of the animal referent in the language of dominated classes: 'Language and Class Identity: the Mark of Dominant Ideology', in *Education, Language and Ideology* (London: Routledge and Kegan Paul, 1979). (Original publication in French in 1975.)

7 *Le Monde*, 29/30 April 1973.

8 *France Culture*, 7 May 1972.

9 Serge Moscovici advocates this neo-Engelsian point of view in *La Société contre nature* (Paris: Union Générale d'Editions, 1972).

10 C. D. Darlington, 'Race, Class and Culture' in *Biology and the Human Sciences*, ed. J. W. S. Pringle (Oxford: Clarendon Press, 1972).

11 See, for example: Eric Williams, *Capitalism and Slavery* (New York: Russell and Russell, 1961 [first edition, 1944]); and Chapter 6 of the present book, previously translated in *Feminist Issues* 8(2), 1988, and originally published in French as 'Race et Nature, système des marques, idée de groupe naturel et rapports sociaux', *Pluriel-Débats* 11, 1977.

12 Christine Delphy, 'The Main Enemy', *Feminist Issues* 1(1), 1980: 23–40. (Original publication in French in 1970.)

13 Nicole-Claude Mathieu, 'Biological Paternity, Social Maternity: On Abortion and Infanticide as Unrecognized Indicators of the Cultural Character of Maternity', *Feminist Issues* 4(1), Spring 1984. (Original publication in French in 1977.)

Chapter 13

Nature, history and 'materialism'

The battle between history and nature is not so new as people nowadays (in 1979) so often like to suggest. But that in no way means that time has dulled the virulence of the debate. The insistence and violence with which it is now reappearing, the powerful emotions which it generates, and a blind refusal to remember the lessons of the past show that the question is far from being settled. On the one side are those who believe in the iron fist of an immovable order – an order which, paradoxically, constantly needs to be restored! – and on the other, those who think that there is no pre-existing order, and that human history is constantly being made. Are things that simple? Yes, perhaps they are. For we should be in no doubt, and everything we see around us confirms the fact, that in this cauldron emotive pressures far outweigh the intellectual complexity of the debate.

In fact, there is no intellectual debate as such. That is probably what many people mean when they say that these squabbles are the product of extremely short-lived and superficial fashions. This is true, but only part of the story. The verbal forms taken by current theories of order are certainly modish, but fashions have precise things to tell us about the societies which secrete them. What they tell us in this case is not very pleasant.

First, though, which debate are we talking about? The debate about how to define relations between human beings. What are these relations? How can they be studied? How can they be understood? What practices might emerge from the different ways in which they are envisaged? But also – and above all – what *de facto* practices lead us to conceive of human relations in one particular way rather than another? This last question goes to the unspoken heart of the whole debate, the deep-seated reason for its violence.

Our debate is a variant on the virulent but (in appearance at least, to the inattentive observer or one not directly involved) less politically committed battle of an earlier age, between nature and nurture, heredity and environment, etc. It does not overlap entirely with that battle. Indeed, it itself never remains the same for long; a shift in argumentative mode or a more complicated way of saying things will allow some people to claim that they are breaking fresh ground, while others feel a weight of weariness fall on their shoulders and a sense of irritation that the same underlying debate should be wrapped up in such obsessive verbal ceremony. We are doubtless also aware today that this is no mere 'academic' debate, for the social stakes are now clearly visible to all.

Nevertheless, a noticeable displacement of the traditional boundaries of the debate has taken place. Since the powerful comeback at the end of the 1960s of what might be called social-Darwinian ideas, the positions adopted on opposing sides of the debate have been generally defined as 'idealism' on the one hand and 'materialism' on the other. It is thus widely accepted and regarded as proven, as almost a common-sense truth, that the supporters of heredity and nature are 'materialists'. This leads to an implicit (and sometimes explicit) assumption that those who believe in understanding human reality in social (i.e. historical, cultural, 'environmental') terms are *a contrario* idealists. But this makes for some odd bedfellows, for among the idealists we find Marxists (orthodox and heterodox), free-thinkers, radical feminists, and the various breeds of rationalists: in short, all the intellectual heirs of the materialist thinkers of the last two centuries. Further spice is added to this situation when we realize that among present-day 'materialists' we are supposed to include believers in the depths of the Aryan (sorry, western) soul, the perenniality of the Teutonic (Celtic, Saxon, Viking, etc.) spirit, or the élitist dandyism of 'natural leadership'. All of which fills one with astonishment and a certain incredulity.

These approximations of vocabulary seem just too crude to be real. All those who advance into this arena do so preceded by the dignity of high reputation and girded with the eminent credibility of the specialist, and most of them do not actually believe that 'materialist' can be adequately defined as 'attributing importance to the materiality of things', while 'idealist' signifies no more than 'having an ideal in life'. These definitions are so obviously short of the mark that we do not believe them, and start looking behind such a minimal degree of meaning for hidden intentions of a different kind.

In fact, these inadequacies of language allow the contending forces to be grouped together on either side of a divide very different from the one with which we are familiar from earlier forms of the debate. For instance, we now find the Communist Party and certain religious fundamentalists side by side in the 'idealist' camp, while the 'materialist' opposition includes everything from élitist clubs of technocrats to practitioners of the magic arts and societies of chivalry! It is hard to make head or tail of such a situation. The insistent and incantatory appeals to Science do not make things any easier, but at least they are not new to the debate, for 'Science' has always been invoked by the supporters of the natural order, who regard it as the great goddess, or some fetish guaranteeing respectability and infallibility.

Two opposing political attitudes (in the profound sense of the term), two conflicting conceptions of existence and visions of the world, govern the 'academic' options available here. That is always the case with scientific work; it is just that the options are not usually so clearly defined, and what is at stake moment by moment, and the political implications of the question, are rarely as sharply delineated as they are today.

In the present-day debate, political realities have in a sense forced the academic world to admit that this is not just a 'formal' quarrel. The first significant scandal was probably the award of the Nobel prize to an ethologist whose past Nazi activities were just becoming widely known. This year the furore created in France by the 'New Right' – which also claims to be producing 'scientific' ideas – has brought home to a certain number of intellectuals the fact that trying to analyse the way human groups function is not just a matter of disinterested speculation.

The two ways of approaching problems have always been there in the human sciences. They condition scientific aims by determining the direction of research, the choice of subject and the empirical methods used. Even the definition of a conceptual apparatus is closely dependent on the way in which relations between things and people, and those within human groups, are understood.

These different conceptions are to be seen in the successive quarrels, whether supposedly academic or clearly political, whether led by intellectuals or not, which have shaken the social fabric. The debate centres on the origin and development of human behaviour patterns and relations between people. It is conventionally regarded as neutral, capable of being resolved in a way completely external to the investigators themselves. It is assumed that they will be able to examine the history and relevant material in a transparent way, and arrive at an answer which owes nothing to the way the question was posed, but on the contrary dispels uncertainties, rectifies incorrect assumptions, etc., etc., the question itself being merely the result of some pure scientific reflex. To put it crudely, it is generally assumed that someone investigating social relations in terms of heredity would suddenly find those relations unambiguously saying to him: 'Here you are, sir, we are heredity and we are now revealing ourselves to you'. Or: 'Now, sir, please be so kind as to move one step forward for the next revelation'.

Our explanations of the 'origin' of human behaviour are coloured by two fundamental tendencies. For some people it depends on variations in the environment – cultural or material. For others, believers in heredity or nature, it derives from a powerfully determining genetic message, which they regard as both the iron rule of human behaviour and its uncrossable boundary; as both imperative and limit.

From a historical point of view, human reality is seen as a succession of specific relations between people. These relations can never be reduced to those that went before them, or those which, in other places, coexist with them in time. In short, the historical approach emphasizes the specificity of human societies. By contrast, the naturalist point of view is to examine human reality in terms of pre-existing models. These models are reproduced more or less accurately by reality, and roughly correspond to its configurations. Facts are introduced in the final analysis only to verify a certain number of propositions which exist prior to any experience of the relations themselves. This results at best in the confirmation of laws, and at worst in the illustration of mythical models based on parables or metaphors. Hence the fascination of those who work in this way with archetypes, ancient legends, and the currently ubiquitous animal referents derived from ethology. Lorenz is certainly the perfect representative of a tendency distinguished by its basic similarity to a children's game where the players say, 'Let's rub it all out and start again': human history is an infidelity to Nature, but humanity is natural, so let's rub it all out and start again, then we'll see what we are like deep down, etc. Models based on 'hierarchy', 'territoriality', 'aggression', and so on (models which in fact come straight from ethology) are good examples of what this approach produces.

The problem of the invention of agriculture illustrates this divergence. From a naturalistic point of view it will be regarded as a mutation or genetic accident,[1] a fortunate one no doubt (but that is not the main point, and in any case opinions on such matters can vary wildly). That this is anything but a far-fetched example is shown by the fact that the hypothesis has been defended by C. D. Darlington, among others.

The historical approach is much less concerned with model-based explanations of the appearance on the scene of agriculture than with the processes of its birth. In other words, this approach is concerned with the identifiable moment (certain or uncertain) of its appearance and the place or places at which it emerged, together with those concomitant social, organizational, architectural, even religious effects which it is actually possible to discover. In fact, the historical approach is interested in what is known about the origins of agriculture as a human activity, as a form of work, in short, as a fully articulated transformational activity.

In a naturalistic perspective, the whole phenomenon is regarded as a spontaneous property of matter. Incidentally, it is astonishing, in fact incomprehensible, that while the majority of the explanations put forward by naturalists are actually based on the postulate of the spontaneous properties of matter, and as such are clearly metaphysical, they should so often be presented as materialistic.[2] Many people apparently regard the belief that (substantified) matter is itself a cause as a sign of a materialistic attitude. Which is just one more paradox in an argument which already has its fair share of paradoxes.

We are accustomed to laughing, without further thought, at 'dormitive virtues', 'morbific faculties', and so on. But in fact we have not moved on very far from that way of looking at things. When Darlington considers the invention of agriculture to be the direct expression of a gene, where does that leave us? We find some very odd ideas about relations between the elements involved in this confused zone. If the existence of a tree is fundamental to the manufacture of a table (made from the tree's matter, its wood), that self-evidently does not mean that the wood is the table. Nor even, and this is an important point, that the wood can only become a table. The table is only one tiny part of the wood's potential, in the same way that it cannot be reduced to the wood, since it could equally well be made out of something else (stone, plastic, papier mâché, etc.). In any case, the definition of the word 'table' does not imply any connection whatsoever with wood as such. And if the two things do intersect empirically – in the wooden table – the essentialist approach can regard them as homogeneous, or equivalent to each other (table = wood, wood = table), with the concrete 'proof' of the wooden table, without it in any way following that wood and table are analogous. Neglect of the process, the history, of the transformation of wood into table, or of the absorption by the concept 'table' of a particular material suitable for its realization, in short, the failure to pay attention to the trajectory from one thing to another, leads here to a syncretic confusion between the various elements.

When Catholics say that God is contained in the bread, they have the wit to call it a mystery. But when certain people claim that Intelligence is contained in the genes, they not only believe they can convince others by proving it,[3] they frequently even invite us to regard them as materialists. It seems to me that we do not regard Catholics as materialists. Nor do we seem to regard the idea of intelligence being contained in the genes as a mystery, which is far more peculiar! Is it really because 'mystery' and 'materialism' are both categories refractory to reason, or at least to analysis? I note here that if 'mystery' is often seen as a form of (fairly dishonourable) escape into the domain of the sacred, 'materialism' is a select insult in the mouths of the elegant and the well fed. That is probably why the so-called 'materialist'(?) 'New' Right is reputed to be so cynical.

In fact, we are now in the middle of a neo-naturalistic period: in every field, from science to politics, Nature is the ultimate reference. As the supposed point of resolution of all questions, it is presented as the unshakeable rock on which the whole edifice rests. But what is this 'Nature'?

First, it is the set of material data which the world makes available to us, data which can be either things or phenomena. Since the eighteenth century the whole of the perceivable world has been called 'nature'. To this definition must undoubtedly be added those inter- or intra-material processes which, for want of a better term, we name laws. Our present-day scientific knowledge, which began at the time of the birth of physics, i.e. before thought had yet freed itself from theological attitudes, still has the shadow of theology hanging over it. And more than just the shadow; a nostalgic longing for the infallible word.

So we see that there are two types of materialism, each with a different and, of course, unspoken relation to the theological, which makes one a substantialism, the other an attempted materialism.

As a mode of reasoning which tries to avoid putting forward any abstract origin for a given phenomenon, and to understand it instead in economic terms, materialism keeps the concrete to the fore in its reasoning and analysis. Did Freud mean any different when he warned Jung that if he did not keep firmly to the domain of sexuality in his analyses, he would slide into 'the filthy domain of the occult'? In this sense, materialism is a choice based on reason, whereas substantialism is one based on faith.

The vitality of substantialism is such that it has managed to make a strong comeback in the various racist movements which have re-formed since the 1960s.[4] When we refer to 'Nature' (rather then just 'nature'), we mean substantialism. Nature in this sense is not exactly, or at least not only, the material world as a whole (which would be just 'nature'), but a quasi-personified entity, an organizational and a life principle. It is in some ways prior to itself; not just a set of mechanisms, but a vague intentionality and an all-powerful force.

How is it that substantialism can pass itself off and be regarded as a type of materialism? And by a broad consensus of opinion at that? Whether a materialism be mechanistic, or historical, or dialectical or anything else, the common denominator is that it will be concerned with processes, i.e. the ways in which two facts are linked with change over time, in short, with the relations between elements.

Whereas the type of 'materialism' we have here, one which hypo-stasizes 'Nature', is clearly interested not in processes, but in the properties of elements. Well, unless I am much mistaken, a school of thought based on the postulate of 'properties' is a classically metaphysical one. The ambiguity (which need not be one, of course) lies in the fact that this form of 'materialism' regards 'matter' as the locus of its properties. These properties can be aggression, hierarchy, intelligence, territoriality . . . or agriculture, etc. They are supposed to well up spontaneously from within matter, each in its complete, perfect essence. This completeness and perfection are seen from the fact that a property will extend itself all the more effectively if there is nothing in its way, if its expansion meets with no opposition other than its own mechanical limits, in short, if it is simply able to carry on being its own essence, like oil in vinegar, or water behind a dam. In any case, the purity of its nature shines through untainted. As with humans, properties cannot and must not interbreed. If they do, the result is a catastrophe.

It is perhaps this intellectual tendency that demonstrates most clearly why it is that thoughts such as this go hand in hand with strong-arm approaches on a practical level, whose aim is to put back in their place (back 'where they belong') all those who look as if they are about to escape from, slip out of, their class, their station in life. The concern to keep the garden clean and tidy, to chop off anything that overhangs the fence, suggests that an appropriate metaphor for this vision of reality would be troops lined up on parade. It is hardly surprising, therefore, that such theories are professed by the people who benefit most from an organized society, as well as by those who think they ought to be among their number and are trying to make a place for themselves as quickly as possible. Theory is sometimes a pretty inadequate mask to hide behind. This type of materialism undeniably reminds one of Tartuffe talking about religion while reaching out towards the object of his lust. In this case the talk is about Science and Nature, rather than God; the world is full of alibis, and why should Science and Nature be worse than anything else? Particularly since, like God, they have the advantage of being impossible to question. Better – or worse – still, they are supposed to be the Truth. Here we are back in the realm of metaphysics . . .

The reason for this is that what we call Nature is a historical phenomenon. Not some single material object slowly stripped of the obscure layers of ignorance of a theological age by the patient, co-ordinated and progressive efforts of scholars with intimations of its existence. But a particular sub-set of our knowledge, and as such, highly subject to boundary hesitations and theoretical uncertainties. We are now discovering (or rediscovering) the fact that Linnaeus's botanical classifications can perfectly well be turned upside down, and new ones invented.[5] Nature conceived of in this way is a pure convention: beyond the uncertainties of our analysis and comprehension, it stands as the figure of an ultimate reality, Being. It is here that the idea of Nature becomes superimposed in such a worrying way upon the idea of God. That which is irreducible, complete, in the realm beyond man, the Ultimate, existence both above and below him on the scale, encapsulating and guiding him . . . Nature seems like a single whole, coherent and homogeneous. A syncretic construct, it stands as a kind of grand origin, a fantasy Mother. It is of course no accident that we speak of Mother Nature.

But this intellectual and emotive construct presents itself precisely as non-constructed, as a substantial reality outside human reasoning and prior to it. In fact, we could re-use almost word for word the definition of God given in religious teaching, simply replacing God by Nature. The two are actually very close: both eternal, infinitely perfect, infinitely great, etc.

The current popularity enjoyed by 'sociobiology', to which incidentally we owe the revelation that 'scientific' does not mean neutral, shows that the notion of specificity remains central here. It was this same point that sparked off the polemic around Darwinism. But the question of the specificity of human beings in my view hides something different. It is much less a matter of specificity than of 'freedom' . . . or indetermination. In other words, if human societies have no laws of their own, but only the general laws of the animal kingdom – which is the position held by 'naturalists', from Darwinians to sociobiologists – then knowledge is not included among the processes of nature. And although this does not deny its existence, the most it can do is contemplate the inevitable workings of binding laws in which it has no place. On the other hand, if human societies are 'human' (i.e. specific), then they are subject to particular laws which integrate the phenomenon of action on the environment with the tool which is 'knowledge'. The position of the naturalists is in fact a paradoxical one, because in the end their aim, as can clearly be seen in Lorenz who is very characteristic of this tendency, is to drag man back within a Nature from which they see him as trying to escape. But if he is trying to escape, how can they claim that natural determination, instinct, the iron law of nature, are imperative? That is indeed a contradiction.

The 'historical' and 'naturalistic' approaches are two different 'eyes', two different ways of selecting and situating the object of study. And doubtless also, in the first place, of situating oneself, of working out one's position in the system of social relations, before even beginning to look at one's subject of study.

NOTES

1 How is it that the term 'genetic(s)' has been so completely taken over by the natural sciences? This can only be accounted for by reference to the extraordinary dominance of naturalistic modes of explanation in our society. Indeed, if we wish to speak of development (the true sense of 'genetics') in the fields of psychology or linguistics, we are obliged to specify 'genetic psychology' or 'genetic linguistics'. But there is absolutely no need to say 'genetic biology': 'genetics' on its own is sufficient. The idea of development in the absolute is thus regarded as the private property of the natural sciences, in flagrant disregard of the meaning of the word.

2 And referred to as 'cynically' materialistic, just for good measure. Seriously, though, what does 'cynical' mean here? That the intentions are 'malevolent'? Whether or not they are malevolent has absolutely no bearing on their correctness. Yet some people would have us believe that malevolence, to the extent that it takes 'courage' to be cynical (supposedly because the cynic swims against the current, which is highly debatable), is in itself a guarantee of veracity. In reality, cynicism is just an expression of modern-day snobbery, and is neither a guarantee of veracity, nor, equally obviously, a criterion of falsehood. Merely to proclaim that the emperor has no clothes clearly does not guarantee the veracity of the statement. We have moved on from that naïve time when saying the opposite meant telling the truth.

3 One form is the statistical proof, which does genuinely prove a co-occurrence between certain positions in the social system and what is called IQ. This indeed shows an undeniable link between the two things. But it does not prove that intelligence is organic. The regularity of the processes of growth or shrinkage in the phenomena under investigation, which is sometimes claimed to prove their organic nature because they can be described by the same curves as weight or height, is a mathematical phenomenon, not a natural one.

4 For some time these movements were not seen by everybody for what they really were. Ethology, and certain lines of investigation in biology, were pursuing an élitist agenda whose racist character was indeed not always

immediately apparent. That is no longer the case today. The interplay between particular scientific and political agendas has now become clear.

5 See André Baugé, '*Chenopodium album* et espèces affines', Doctorat d'État thesis, Paris.

Index